# The Hidden Lives of Viking Women

## Archaeological and Historical Perspectives

*edited by*

Michèle Hayeur Smith and Alexandra Sanmark

OXBOW | books
Oxford & Philadelphia

Published in the United Kingdom in 2025 by
OXBOW BOOKS
81 St Clements, Oxford OX4 1AW

and in the United States by
OXBOW BOOKS
1950 Lawrence Road, Havertown, PA 19083



Paperback Edition: ISBN 979-8-88857-186-6
Digital Edition: ISBN 979-8-88857-187-3

A CIP record for this book is available from the British Library

Library of Congress Control Number: 2024951463



Printed in the United Kingdom by Short Run Press
Typeset in India by DiTech Publishing Services

For a complete list of Oxbow titles, please contact:

UNITED KINGDOM
Oxbow Books
Telephone (0)1226 734350
Email: oxbow@oxbowbooks.com
www.oxbowbooks.com

UNITED STATES OF AMERICA
Oxbow Books
Telephone (610) 853-9131, Fax (610) 853-9146
Email: queries@casemateacademic.com
www.casemateacademic.com/oxbow

Oxbow Books is part of the Casemate Group

# Contents

# List of Tables

# List of Figures

# Contributors

TARA ATHANASIOU
Institute for Northern Studies, University of the Highlands and Islands

KAREN BEK-PEDERSEN
School of Communication and Culture – Scandinavian Studies,
Aarhus University

LESZEK GARDEŁA
National Museum of Denmark

MICHÈLE HAYEUR SMITH
Arctic Studies Center, National Museum of Natural History, Smithsonian Institution, Washington DC

SHANE MCLEOD
Institute for Northern Studies, University of the Highlands and Islands

UNN PEDERSEN
Department of Archaeology and Conservation, University of Oslo

ANNE IRENE RIISØY
Department of Culture, Religion and Social Studies, University of South-East Norway

ALEX SANMARK
Institute for Northern Studies, University of the Highlands and Islands/Uppsala University

KEVIN P. SMITH
Arctic Studies Center National Museum of Natural History, Smithsonian Institution, Washington DC/University of SUNY Albany NY

OLOF SUNDQVIST
Department of Ethnology, History of Religions and Gender Studies, University of Stockholm

# Acknowledgements

We would like to thank the authors of this volume for their contributions along with Oxbow who facilitated the publication of this book. The ideas presented here stem from both the editors' interests and research into the archaeology of women and gender in general.

It was also in part the authors of the sagas and Eddas as well as other medieval sources that brought the women of the Viking Age to life in our minds and provided the basis of the inspiration for this book by shedding light on an even broader range of women and their activities.

We would also like to acknowledge our predecessors Judith Jesch and Jenny Jochens who laid the groundwork for the study of women and who inspired us to think not only about the need for an archaeology of women in the Viking Age but also about women in archaeology, along with other scholars, such as Denys Kandyoti, Joan Gero, Roberta Gilchrist, Marianne Moen, Marie Louise Stig Sørensen, and others.

# Chapter 1

## The hidden lives of Viking Age women: Introduction

*Michèle Hayeur Smith, Alex Sanmark, and Kevin P. Smith*

The idea for this book developed out of the editors' conviction that a new book examining the actual lives and roles of women (Old Norse/ON: *konur*, *kvennur*, pl.; *kona*, *kvenna*, sing.) (Cleasby and Vigfusson 1984: 350) during the Viking Age (*c.* AD 750–1050) was needed, especially one that could focus on many of the roles of women that have been overlooked or not examined in detail by contemporary scholarship. Rather than producing an edited volume of conference papers, or a book examining the stages of Viking Age women's lives, we solicited papers from scholars working on the less well-known roles that women took on during the Viking Age, as currently understood through the lens of archaeological finds and textual sources.

The overarching questions we, and this volume's authors, address are: Did women contribute to society only as caregivers bound to the home, or were their lives and roles more complex with responsibilities and opportunities that at times might have complemented, and at other times, supplanted their roles as caregivers and domestic workers? By using the term 'caregiver' here we do not mean to minimise the significant undertaking that its myriad tasks entail but are referencing what many past scholars have assumed were women's main responsibilities and that they were considered secondary to other, more public, 'male' engagements. Can we find alternative and more 'masculine' public roles that women held than were assumed in view of past research? This volume challenges the tendency of much earlier research to view women as holding rather passive roles, such as 'housewives', without addressing or fully appreciating the multiple ways in which women contributed to the economic and social survival of their communities.

However, while this book addresses the roles of women in different aspects within Viking Age society, it goes well beyond this to explore women's lives outside the traditional frameworks defined by the stages of a woman's life (daughter, wife, mother, elder) (cf. Jesch 1991; Jóhanna Friðriksdóttir 2020) and their social roles within households run by men (housewife, servant, weaving woman, etc.). Throughout our sources – both documentary and archaeological – there are indications of other roles that women held and that need to be brought into the light in order to guide research towards areas of women's lives that have either been neglected or viewed in isolation as 'exceptions to the rule' (see e.g. Dommasnes 1991; Arwill-Nordbladh 1998: 73–83; Thedéen 2012: 64–65).

It is in this spirit that we have pulled this edited volume together, trying to identify where and when women in the Viking Age societies of Scandinavia and the North Atlantic appeared in ways that may be unexpected in the light of past research, holding roles in addition to, or instead of, their 'traditional' ones. This is not, therefore, a book on gender in Viking Age and Norse societies *per se*, but rather a book that views the subject of women's varied roles through the lens of feminist archaeology, feminist history, and a wider field of feminist studies (cf. Moen 2019: 20) to better understand these women and their contributions to society.

This is therefore a book about women, and while we hope that looking at women in today's political climate will not categorise us as outdated, or 'old fashioned', we feel that while acknowledging the kaleidoscope of genders, women – as one of those many culturally constructed genders – remain a valuable field of study. Women have been treated as a minority for millennia and, while they represent half of the world's population, we hope that looking at the category of 'women' can offer some insights on how to address the analysis of other gender categories. We recognise the work that researchers employing queer theory and other perspectives are making in trying to understand complexities in the engendered boundaries that defined Viking Age individuals as 'women' or 'men' and that are seeking to identify the degrees to which some individuals could move between those categories or operate in spaces between them. However, without intending to ignore or minimise the importance of that work, this book focuses explicitly on trying to understand how those who were defined legally and culturally as *women* could gain status through activities or practices that were not acceptable for men to undertake, or occupied roles that more recent scholarship has assumed were only acceptable and occupied by legally defined 'men'.

Over the course of working on this volume, it occurred to us that the authors whose chapters appear here come from, and have worked within, different regions (e.g. North America, the UK, Australia, Poland, and Scandinavia), each one of which has different scholarly traditions as well as different concepts of gender and feminism. We recognised also that the terminology used in these different places also varied. Rather than force this book into one overriding theoretical perspective, we have decided to embrace these different scholarly traditions and accept that terms such 'patriarchy' in North America are very much a part of the current vocabulary of feminist theorists while they may be less so in Europe. At the same time, each of the authors in their individual chapters may express different thoughts and viewpoints on the structure of Norse society, particularly regarding women. Here, too, we have decided to respect these differences in opinion. We feel that this kaleidoscopic view, presenting different perspectives on women, is important not only to respect the opinions and perspectives of the scholars whose work appears here but also to present a view that accurately reflects the current diversity of perspectives on women in the past and on archaeological approaches to studying their lives for the general public and especially for younger generations of women and men for whom some of this may resonate.

The reader will also note that several of the chapters in this volume focus on ritual practice. This was not a deliberate choice, but rather a theme that emerged from the interests and current research of the scholars whose work appears here, reflecting the state of current research on Viking Age women. Following the work of Neil Price (2002) and others, the importance of magic, religion, and ritual practice in Viking society has been at the forefront of recent Viking studies; therefore, this focus derives from ongoing research rather than a suggestion that women's work was inevitably 'magical'.

This volume is, of course, not the first effort to consider women's lives in the Viking Age, nor do we expect that it will be the last. One of the best-known pioneering works of this kind was Judith Jesch's *Women in the Viking Age* (1991), which was important as the first book not only to focus on Viking Age women but also to argue explicitly for integrating archaeological data from the Viking Age with detailed studies of Old Norse texts. While the overall themes in *Women in the Viking Age* are intriguing and remain foundational, addressing topics such as life and death from archaeological evidence and runic texts, it was largely an enumeration of the types of evidence through which women could be observed and supports most discussions with examples taken from the saga literature. This means that there is little in terms of interpretation of women's everyday life and tasks. It is this gap that we would like to address in this book. Jenny Jochens' *Women in Old Norse Society* (1995) and *Old Norse Images of Women* (1996) provided additional views on Viking Age and Norse women but almost exclusively used literary sources, notably the *Poetic Edda*, *Prose Edda*, Icelandic sagas, and medieval law codes from Iceland and Scandinavia, with little attention given to archaeological evidence. More recently, Jóhanna Katrín Friðriksdóttir published *Valkyrie, the Women of the Viking World* (2020), which offered a wider and more updated vision of Viking Age women, but it still lacks detailed analyses of the archaeological evidence and, consequently, important areas of women's lives remain unexamined.

A prevailing issue in many past publications about Viking Age society is that women and men tend to be treated as two internally homogeneous but separate groups. The wording is subtle at times but is, on other occasions, explicitly spelled out through statements such as: 'the world of women was normally very different from that of men' (Roesdahl 1998: 59). In line with this, and as suggested above, women have frequently been placed in 'passive', 'private', and 'domestic' spheres, while men are said to belong to a sphere that is 'active', 'public', and 'external' (Hastrup 1985; Clover 1993: 363–387; see also Ney 2002: 26; Moen 2020: 622 and 625). This division is at least partly due to a tendency to revert to ideas about 'essential qualities' of women and men. Sociobiological perspectives such as these label women as inactive, maternal, and tender, while men are seen to be dynamic, dominant, and violent (Arwill-Nordbladh 1998: 13–16, 53–83; Gilchrist 1999: 35, 37, 64; Raffield *et al.* 2017a). As will become apparent in the chapters of this book, recent research shows that the social lives of women and men were both more nuanced and more complex than this and that women held far more varied roles within society than previous research would suggest (Moen 2019; Sanmark and Athanasiou this volume).

What has been lacking in Viking Studies, despite recent work looking at gender fluidity, queer theory, and women warriors – the latter popularised in numerous television shows, such as *The Vikings*, and social media – is a book on women studying, in detail, the roles they held, especially new and perhaps unexpected ones, through fresh examinations of existing evidence. A long history of documentary research on Viking Age societies has noted the presence of 'exceptional' women who refused to follow prescriptive norms and who negotiated, adapted, and outdid themselves as individuals (Dommasnes 1991; Arwill-Nordbladh 1998: 25–27; Thedéen 2012: 64–65). Recently, as will be shown below, archaeological research has also started to highlight the burials of a small number of women who were marked out as being different and powerful. At times, researchers failed to identify these individuals as ones who held unexpected roles as they were caught up in prescribed views of gender and led by a focus on the accomplishments of men. Previous assumptions that all burials with weapons were 'male', whether in the absence of skeletal indications of sex or despite them, is a case in point. Many earlier studies carried out prior to the availability of aDNA analyses or in the presence of grave sets with poorly preserved or cremated bones, such those by Kristján Eldjárn (1956) in Iceland and Dommasnes (1991) in Norway, assigned burials to female or male categories based on the presence of jewellery and household goods, or weapons, respectively. But were these women buried with weapons, often labelled as 'exceptional', the only women in the Viking Age who led lives that today may be seen as norm breakers, or that do not fulfil the image of the farming woman or urban housewife?

Is it possible that our views of the past may be skewed through our own cultural preconceptions and experiences? Some evidence suggests that many of the women in the Viking Age were more equal to men than previously argued, working in partnership with men for their joint survival (see Sanmark and Athanasiou, and Riisøy, this volume). Many threads of evidence woven through this volume's chapters identify roles, activities, statuses, and objects once considered exclusively 'masculine' that were actually held, undertaken, or used by women as well as men, or were primarily occupied by women. Indeed, as shown by Unn Pedersen and Shane McLeod in this volume, roles and activities traditionally assigned to women as daughters, wives, mothers, etc., were, in fact, undertaken by women, but their lives were not limited to these roles and actions. This means that large parts of women's lives have not been discussed or examined in detail.

Who were the women that archaeology and history have traditionally not paid much attention to? Simply put, this book focuses on the hidden lives of Viking Age women, bringing out aspects of their lives that have not been fully understood or under-estimated. In each chapter, this volume's authors pull out details or social mechanisms that impacted women's lives in unexpected ways or find novel ways to illuminate surprising or under-researched roles that women held.

## Sources and source criticism

All of the authors in this volume have had to wrestle with issues of source criticism and the incomplete nature of the source material available to examine the lives of women in the Viking Age (*c.* AD 750–1050) and the subsequent Norse or Late Norse period (*c.* AD 1050–1250). This is due, in part, to the fact that much of our knowledge of Viking Age women is based on written sources composed within Scandinavia and Iceland after the end of the archaeologically and historically defined Viking Age. There are also written sources contemporary with the Viking Age that were produced by observers from communities that traded with or were in conflict with Viking Age Scandinavians, as well as evidence gained from archaeological sources (for an overview of these discussions, see the chapters in the section Language, Literature and Art in Brink and Price 2008). In Scandinavia, contemporaneous texts on rune stones and short runic inscriptions on items of archaeologically recovered material culture add to, and blur, the lines between written and archaeological sources, but these contemporaneous, written sources are themselves incomplete notations about individuals in the past rather than detailed narratives (see e.g. Williams 2008).

The history of source criticism regarding Eddic poems, Icelandic sagas, Norse histories, and law codes will not be repeated here, as the authors of the chapters included in this volume each address the nature of their source material adequately and, at times, from different academic or national perspectives that add flavour and nuance to the subject. However, it is worth reminding readers less familiar with studies of the Viking Age that many of the most richly detailed sources for life in this period, such as the Icelandic sagas, were written during the 12th–14th centuries and, therefore, incorporate not only 12th–14th century Icelanders' memories and beliefs about their ancestors' lives and activities but also settings, perspectives, and details that were familiar to their authors' medieval audiences at the times that the stories were written down and told. Their reliability and value as descriptions of actual events in the Viking Age have long been debated, but it is likely that they do capture the realities of life and cultural attitudes in earlier periods to some extent, if perceived as ethnographies rather than as direct accounts of life, and they certainly reflect 12th–14th century Icelanders' understandings of their own past (Miller 1996; Lönnroth 2008: 309–310). Similarly, the earliest Scandinavian law codes provide extremely valuable information about women's lives and roles, as well as their legal obligations, responsibilities, and opportunities but are not directly contemporary sources. Medieval Icelandic sources including *Íslendingabók* (Grønlie 2006) and *Landnámabók* (Hannes Finnsson 1774; Jakob Benediktsson 1968) state that the earliest Icelandic law codes available to us today only began to be written down in AD 1117 but incorporated orally transmitted laws that were originally based on Viking Age Norwegian law. However, the versions that exist today of both the Norwegian (Larson 1935; Simensen 2021) and the Icelandic law codes (Dennis *et al.* 1980; 2000; Gunnar Karlsson *et al.* 1992) were written down mainly in the 13th–14th centuries and enshrine a process of law making that allowed changes to be made to the law codes on an annual basis (Dennis *et al.* 1980; 2000; Gunnar Karlsson *et al.* 1992; Miller 1996). Unfortunately, it was not a part of the legal process in medieval Iceland or Scandinavia to record the dates at which changes were made to individual laws. The law codes, therefore, provide important information about medieval Norse society, much of which was likely developed from or remained comparable to earlier Viking Age law, but the degree to which changes were made, and when those changes were made, is difficult to entangle (see Miller 1996). Similarly, no court records are preserved from this period, as the proceedings were orally presented and determined. Therefore, aside from the saga narratives' many accounts of court cases, it is unknown to what degrees these laws were regularly enforced or what perceived transgressions they were created to regulate. They can, nevertheless, give an indication of perceived threats to the social balance of society (Ney 2002: 26). The degrees to which these sources provide accurate information about Viking Age and Norse society are frequently difficult to separate.

Similar issues surround historical accounts from Scandinavia, such as Saxo Grammaticus's *Gesta Danorum* (Davidson 1998), while accounts written by non-Scandinavians – for example the famous account of Ibn Fadlān (Lunde and Stone 2012) may provide accurate, and contemporaraneous, perspectives on how others saw Viking Age women but through lenses filtered through the cultural differences and agendas of their authors and intended audiences (see e.g. Montgomery 2008).

The archaeological record, in contrast, has the advantage of having been produced at a time contemporary with the issues discussed in this volume; yet the processes of decay and transformation that have affected the archaeological record over the past millennium have ensured that it is a partial record, at best. Differences over time in the research methods and excavation strategies through which archaeological data have been acquired, as well as differences through time and between different national or regional research cultures' approaches to interpreting the past, similarly affect the comparability of the archaeological data and interpretations with which we can build models of women's lives and roles across the vast geographical areas settled by Scandinavians during the Viking Age and Norse period.

However, through the judicious integration of both contemporary archaeological data and carefully considered documentary sources, the authors of the chapters in this volume have attempted to be both prudent in their use of sources and bold in their interpretations. That having been said, we recognise and look forward to the certainty that future scholarship and new sources of data will certainly challenge, may support, or will allow refinements of their visions.

## Review of current theoretical perspectives

### *Sex and gender*

Inevitably, any discussion of Viking Age and Norse women leads to considerations of not only biological sex and socially defined gender but also Old Norse terms and legal definitions, if only to determine who was considered biologically female (ON: *kvennkyn*) or a gendered woman (ON: *kona, kvenna*) in the Viking Age and how flexible that definition was. A wide range of definitions of sex and gender have been put forward in recent years. One of the most influential ideas that has emerged since the 1990s is that 'sex', in the same way as 'gender', should be seen as a social construct that cannot be treated as a constant over time and place, and is not strictly binary (male/female) but instead forms a spectrum (Butler 1990; Laqueur 1992; Clover 1993: 93; Fausto-Sterling 1993; Sørensen 2000: 42–48).

While such social constructionist ideas have been very influential, they have not been universally accepted, including in Viking Age and Norse studies – and biological sex continues to be featured in much recent research, particularly in connection to aDNA analyses and osteoarchaeology. One particularly well-known example is the proposed female warrior burial (Grave Bj.581) from Birka in Sweden, which was once known as the 'ultimate' Viking Age male warrior grave on the basis of the assemblage of objects interred with the deceased, but which has since been demonstrated through osteological examination and aDNA analyses to be the burial of a female (Hedenstierna-Jonson *et al.* 2017a; Price *et al.* 2019a). Marianne Moen, when discussing this burial, argued: 'What is fluid and negotiable is not here the physical sex of the deceased; it is the interpretations which modern archaeologists impose upon it' (Moen 2019: 214).

The concept of gender has also been subject to debate and renegotiation in recent scholarship. One of the areas of criticism concerns the ways in which gender roles have been closely mapped onto biological sex and have thus been seen as 'natural' and binary (Moen 2020: 621). Such discussions have highlighted problems in previous research and the need for more nuanced analyses. If, on a global scale, it is clear that gender cannot be, and was not, seen or defined in the same ways across time and place; neither sex nor gender should be used to distil 'assumed' or 'essential' characteristics of Viking Age women and men, with women perceived as inherently subordinate and tender and men as unwaveringly dominant and violent (Arwill-Nordbladh 1998: 73–75; Gilchrist 1999: 35, 37, 64; Croix 2015; Ljungqvist 2015; Raffield 2017; Raffield *et al.* 2017). Concepts of sex and gender are not a problem limiting more nuanced approaches to gender research, but rather that – with the right definitions and careful application – both can bring further insights into Viking Age and Norse society (cf. Sanmark 2024).

While we understand that there are divergent views of sex as either binary or a spectrum, we restrict the use of the terms 'sex' and 'biological sex' here to their use in the determination of skeletal sex based on the analysis and identification of preserved skeletal features that are conventionally used in osteological analyses to determine the sex of an individual's remains. We note, however, that aDNA analyses have made it possible, in recent years, to identify individuals – including notable examples in Viking Age and later periods – whose genetic constitution may have differed from the XX and XY female/male karyotypes, including individuals with Klinefelter (XXY), Turner (X), or Trisomy X (XXX) Syndromes. Whether these individuals may have been perceived, or self-identified, as being men, women, or belonging to another gender are questions that cannot be answered with skeletal or genetic data alone and are issues we briefly turn to below.

We recognise gender as a social construct, expressed in society by certain expectations of behaviour and roles, even though these roles in turn can be negotiated (Sørensen 2000: 60). We recognise, too, that as socially constructed and culturally specific concepts, gender categories current in the present day may not be directly transferrable to the past and that past societies may also have recognised genders or gender roles that are not equivalent to any present today. As such, a question for understanding women and their roles in the Viking Age and Norse period is whether socially defined genders were strictly defined, defended, and mapped onto physically or visibly defined (genetic) sexes or whether genders were more flexibly defined, with variations accepted.

## Third gender, queer theory, gods, goddesses, and the gendered role of magic

A discussion of gender in the Viking Age would be incomplete without the mention of third gender. Third gender is defined as a category of people that are permanently seen as 'neither male nor female' (Gilchrist 1999: 60). It is, therefore, quite different from the term 'gender non-conforming', which refers to gendered behaviour that is seen as breaking the social norms established by a given culture. Several recent studies have focused on applying queer theory to understanding the Norse pantheon or burial data through reference to third gender. Scholars such as Ármann Jakobsson (2011) and Brit Solli (2008) have defined the god Óðinn as a gender-fluid deity with no strong male or female associations.

However, gods are inherently different from humans, defined through their abilities to do things that humans cannot, and none of the extant sources underlying our knowledge about Viking Age belief and religious practice suggests that people were encouraged or expected to live their lives 'like the gods' in the same ways that later Christian belief encouraged practitioners to model their lives on Christ's. Neither is it clear that the activities and abilities of the Scandinavian pre-Christian goddesses and gods were directly modelled on humans' abilities and activities. Can we, therefore, extend this analysis of Óðinn as a deity able to occupy both 'male' and 'female' semantic spaces, as needed, to Viking society at large and to all, or even some, Viking Age men? Is this a matter in which we can assume the gods were a model for society or were based on social realities? Or, as gods, was their importance based on the fact that they were different from lived reality and not bound by its rules?

In terms of Viking Age and Old Norse society, third gender is often suggested in relation to *seiðmenn,* i.e. male practitioners of *seiðr* ('sorcery'), who are mentioned in sagas and Eddic poetry (Price 2019: 172; Bell 2021; Moilanen *et al.* 2022). *Seiðr* was, above all, seen as female magic that was taught to humans and even to Óðinn by the goddess Freyja, as described in *Ynglinga Saga* (Monsen and Smith 1990 [1932]: 5–6). Men who performed this type of sorcery could, therefore, be labelled 'unmanly' and accused of *ergi* (see below and Hayeur Smith, this volume). The Eddic poem *Hyndluljóð* contains the term *seiðberendr* ('*seiðr* practiser'), which has been interpreted as gender-neutral, possibly indicating a third gender (Solli 2008: 197; Larrington 2014: 249). However, it is not clear that the practice of sorcery by men or women inevitably involved gendered ambiguities, nor that only women were its practitioners.

Men who practised magic are well represented in the Icelandic Family Sagas (*Íslendingasögur*) and in *Landnámabók* ('the Book of Settlements'), where they are mentioned as frequently as women who practised magic. While many of the sagas' narratives associate magical practices with treacheries that ended in the sorcerers' or sorceresses' violent deaths, references to magical practitioners in *Landnámabók* more frequently note their power, refer to significant acts they did, or simply refer to them by terms relating to the kinds of magical practice they performed. None is linked to suggestions that they occupied third gendered spaces rather than being simply women or men who practised magic.

The terms used in the medieval literary sources for women who practised magic in Viking Age Scandinavia and Iceland include *seiðkona*, *spákona*, *spámeyja*, *spákerling*, *vísindakona*, *galdrakona*, *vitka*, and *fjolkyngiskona* as well as *vǫlva*, *húsfreyja (húsfrú)*, or *gyðja* (see Olof Sundqvist, this volume), while men represented in the written sources as part-time or full-time practitioners of magic are known by terms that include *seiðmaðr*, *seiðskatti*, *spámaðr*, *falsspámaðr*, *vísindamaðr*, *galdramaðr*, *galdrakarl*, *galdrasmiðr*, *galdmeisstari*, *vitki*, *fjolkyningsmaðr* that largely overlap with those used for female magical practitioners, as well as by the term *hamramr*, which implies the ability to change shape or to change the shape of things around them. This latter term is never used for female practitioners of magic in *Landnámabók* and, similarly, the term *vǫlva* never seems to be applied to men.

Rather than suggesting that magical ritual, prophesy, and other practices were innately 'female', the overlapping terms (Table 1.1) used for male and female magical practitioners suggest, instead, that there were *forms* of magic practised by both women and men. These were referred to by their expected actions or outcomes, including the conduct of *seiðr* rituals (*seiðkona*, *seiðmadr*, etc.), prophesy (*spá-*, *vísinda-*), the ability to create spells or curses intended to affect human interactions (*galdra-*), as well as forms of magic referred to by terms beginning with *vitk-* ('wisdom', implying knowledge of things hidden to most) or *fjolkynings-* (magic, witchcraft, sorcery, more generally) that suggest the ability to change nature or the materiality of things, create spells with stronger bonds, or lay curses of extreme power. The linkage of these terms with

*Table 1.1 Male and female terms for magical practitioners and their root word*

| *Root term* | *Female practitioners* | *Male practitioners* |
|---|---|---|
| *seið-* (oracle, incantation) | *seiðkona* | *seiðmaðr* |
| | | *seiðskratti* |
| *spá-* (sight, prophesy, foretelling) | *spákona* | *spámaðr* |
| | *spámeyja* | *falsspámadr* |
| | *spákerling* | |
| *vísinda-* (knowledge, wisdom) | *vísindakona* | *vísindamaðr* |
| *galdra-* (song, spell, witchcraft) | *galdrakona* | *galdramaðr* |
| | | *galdrakarl* |
| | | *galdrasmiðr* |
| | | *galdmeisstari* |
| *vitka* (to bewitch) | *vitka* | *vitki* |
| *fjölkyning-* (magical art, sorcery) | *fjölkyningskona* | *fjölkyningsmaðr* |
| Ritual/political leader | *gyðja* | *goði* |
| | *vǫlva* | |
| | *húsfrú* | |
| | | *skratti* |
| | | *hammrammr* |

both male and female designators suggests that none of these forms of magic was exclusively female or male gendered, although the more gender exclusive terms *vǫlva* and *húsfrúr*, like *skratti*, and *hamramr* (Ármann Jakobsson 2023) raise the possibility that certain forms of magic may well have been considered the specific province of female and male practitioners, respectively.

Archaeologically, more than 20 suggested burials of female *seiðr*-practitioners have been identified (Price 2002: 127–161), yet very few examples of possible *seiðmenn* have been identified. In large part this is due to the relatively recent discovery that *seiðkonur* may be identifiable in the archaeological record through the presence in their burials of specific tools associated with their roles (Price 2002; Gardeła, this volume). In contrast, very little comparable work has been undertaken to consider how one would recognise the burial of a male sorcerer or, specifically, a *seiðmaðr.* We have no reason to believe, for example, that *seiðmenn* would necessarily have used or been buried with the same kinds of implements as *seiðkonur*, given the symbolic associations of some of those tools with weaving, as Hayeur Smith and Gardeła discuss in their chapters. The identification of *seiðmenn* and other male magical practitioners in the archaeological record therefore remains an area open for more research. While not related directly to women, the absence of work on male ritual practitioners makes it hard to determine the degrees to which assigned gender or biological sex were (or were not) used to differentiate these 'extraordinary individuals' or whether overlaps in either the objects that marked their status or in the ways they were buried might imply that they occupied semantic spaces between the female and the male.

In the absence of such archaeological work, attention has been directed towards the possibility that male sorcerers may have been ambiguously, or third, gendered on the strength of *Ynglinga saga*'s statements that Óðinn practised *seiðr* (Monsen and Smith 1990 [1932]: 5) and through analogies with aspects of shamanic roles among the Sáami and other circumpolar peoples (Price 2002: 280–320). Yet, as noted above, it is not clear that the mythic nature of the gods directly influenced the ways that living humans dressed or were chosen for their roles. In this regard, it is notable that Óðinn is never represented, in dress or appearance, as anything other than male, while nonetheless practising magic that includes but is not limited to *seiðr*. Whether this means that Óðinn was the ultimate *seiðmaðr,* rather than a third gendered god, is a question worth considering along with the nature of *seiðmenn* in Viking Age society.

The suggestion that male seers and sorcerers may have crossed socially defined gender boundaries also derives from the suggestion that their prophetic knowledge and abilities to see the future necessarily placed them in the realm of 'female magic', through the association of the Norns and other females with fate (see Sundqvist, Gardeła, Hayeur Smith, Bek-Pedersen, this volume). However, given the very obviously incomplete record of pre-Christian Norse religion that we have available in the extant medieval written sources, and the use of similar terms regarding magic for both male and female practitioners in those sources, it is worth considering that in addition to 'female magic' there were also explicitly male gendered avenues for seeing and influencing the future.

*Ynglinga saga*, in fact, says that while the practice of *seiðr* was considered unmanly and was therefore taught to women, Óðinn also taught spells done with runes and songs, called *galdrar*, to men (Monsen and Smith 1990 [1932]: 5). Thus, as with so many other aspects of Viking Age and Norse culture and society explored in this volume, the limited information available to us regarding male and female magical practitioners and ritual specialists may well speak more to the existence of parallel 'female' and 'male' channels for contacting supernatural domains, influencing the present, or affecting fate than it does to the idea that men who performed magic necessarily intruded into 'female' spaces or that these practitioners necessarily occupied a liminal 'third gendered' space. Yet if it is questionable that all male practitioners of magic and prophesy were somehow considered 'female' or 'third-gendered', it is also evident that gender non-conforming individuals were present in Viking Age Scandinavia, even if they may not have been automatically associated with magical practices or given special status.

The burial of the biologically sexed woman with the trappings of a high status warrior in grave Bj.581 at Birka clearly shows that borders once considered impermeable by 19th–20th century scholarship could be, and were, crossed (Kjellström

2016; Hedenstierna-Jonson *et al.* 2017a; Price *et al.* 2019a). Even if we may not know how this individual fulfilled the roles implied by her burial's furnishings, there is nothing immediately apparent within her grave goods to imply that she was a sorceress rather than a warrior or leader.[1]

She may not have been alone in holding a role marked by weapons. Hedenstierna-Jonson *et al.* (2017b: 2–3) and Price *et al.* (2019b: 15–16), for example, describe two additional graves in Norway of individuals who have been identified as females on the basis of skeletal features and who were buried with full weapon sets. One, estimated to have been 18–20 years old at the time of her death, was buried beneath a mound in Hedmark with a sword (inverted, with the tip near her head), an axe, a spear, five arrows, a shield, bridles, a whetstone, and a possible file, with a horse at her feet (Hernæs 1984). The second grave, of a 20 year old female from Aunvollen in Nord-Trøndelag, was buried with a sword, perhaps a spear, nine gaming pieces, a sickle, a whetstone, a pair of scissors, a knife, a comb, one bead, and a dog (Stenvik 2005).

Interestingly, an 11th–13th century grave from Suontaka Vesitorninmäki, Finland (Moilanen *et al.* 2022), in which the fully articulated skeleton of an individual was buried with a silver inlaid, hilt-less sword blade and a sheathed knife directly associated with the body, was long considered to be a female leader or warrior. A second, complete sword decorated in Urnes style was either added to the grave as it was filled or was hidden in its upper layers at a later date (Moilanen *et al.* 2022: 4). Swords are normally associated with male graves in 13th century Finnish contexts, yet this individual also had two oval brooches dramatically displayed on the body, along with a twin-spiral chain-bearer, a small penannular brooch, and a sickle – all of which have been considered 'female' signifiers (Moilanen *et al.* 2022: 9). Analyses of fibre and hair from the grave's fill suggest that the person was laid on feather bedding or had a feather pillow under its head and was buried in woollen clothing, parts of which were dyed blue and may have had elements made from animal pelts.

Everything about this grave suggests that the person interred there was highly ranked and well respected. As Moilanen *et al.* note (2022: 1) the presence of both 'female' signifying jewellery and a 'male' signifying sword with the person buried at Suontaka Vesitorninmäki had been used for decades to suggest that this was a female warrior or leader comparable to the 'powerful women' known from the Icelandic sagas and other early medieval sources. However, analysis of DNA from one of the individual's femurs showed that this was actually the grave of a male born with an XXY karyotype – Klinefelter Syndrome –who may have developed female secondary sexual characteristics, including breasts, a gracile physique, and a high voice while retaining male genitals (Moilanen *et al.* 2022: 9). While this person was buried with both 'male' and 'female' material cultural signifiers,[2] nothing in this grave directly suggests that the individual from Suontaka Vesitorninmäki was a magical practitioner. The range and quality of the offerings, instead, suggest that this was the grave of an individual whose wealth, role, rank, or family connections made it possible to live, identify as, and be remembered visually at death in a space that existed between the standard mortuary representations of 'men' and 'women' in late Viking Age/early medieval Finnish society (Moilanen *et al.* 2022: 12).

Another individual with Klinefelter Syndrome was identified through aDNA analyses at Ytra-Garðshorn (Grave 2) in Svarfaðardalshreppur, northern Iceland by Sunna Ebenesersdóttir *et al.* (2018: 1028) during genomic analyses of a sample of 27 Icelandic Viking Age skeletons. In contrast to the example from Finland, however, this individual's burial was neither marked out as special in any way nor did it come from an unusually 'rich' cemetery (Kristján Eldjárn 2000: 153–162). The same paleogenetic study by Sunna Ebenesersdóttir *et al.* (2018) also determined that an individual buried at Öndverðarnes, western Iceland, who had been thought – on the basis of skeletal developmental features – to have been likely to be a man with Klinefelter Syndrome (Hildur Gestsdóttir 2000) was, in fact, a male with an XY, rather than XXY, chromosome set.

Comparisons among these five graves may provide some insights into how male and female genders were defined and how those whose roles crossed engendered norms or who might have been seen by their contemporaries as 'other' were treated. The burials from Birka, Hedmark, and Aunvollen suggest that women could occupy high status roles that have been assumed to have been exclusively 'male' or be buried with the markers of roles normally associated with males, even if such female 'warrior graves' are few in number. In contrast, aDNA analysis of the bones of the person buried at Suontaka Vesitorninmäki, previously thought to be a biological female, indicate that this was a male born with Klinefelter Syndrome. While we cannot know whether this person self-identified as male, female, or some other category that was relevant within local contexts and may not have any parallel in our own times, it is evident that those who chose the clothing and items to be displayed in that person's grave clearly treated them with respect, while perhaps recognising and marking the deceased as neither exclusively male nor exclusively female. On the other hand, the individual with Klinefelter Syndrome from Ytra-Garðshorn in Iceland was buried without any apparent special treatment or differentiation from others in this small 10th century household cemetery. These latter two cases from Finland and Iceland demonstrate that males with Klinefelter Syndrome, who may have developed both 'female' and 'male' secondary sexual characteristics, were present in the Viking Age, as in the modern day, but were not invariably regarded as magically potent, need not have been considered 'outsiders' in some way, and may not automatically have been viewed as 'exceptional' or 'spiritually gifted' people occupying positions of higher or lower rank or 'othered' statuses.

In contrast, most of the individuals identified archaeologically as potential 'seeresses' or *vǫlur* through the tools of the trade buried with them have been identified as biological females rather than as individuals who occupied third gendered spaces, while the woman buried in Birka's grave Bj.581 was buried with high status grave goods that suggest a military rather than magical role. However, as Price (2002) has argued, warfare and magic were deeply intertwined in the Viking Age, with women having active roles in what he called 'battle magic'. This woman, and others like her who were buried with weapons, may have occupied such a role but equally may have participated directly in warfare (Price *et al.* 2019a).

While there are more burials than these three from the Viking Age that blur the lines between graves of biological females buried with women's things and biological males buried with men's signifiers, it has to be noted that they are, overall, very few in number relative to the known corpus of all Viking Age burials assigned a sex either via aDNA or osteological features. As a result, comparing studies like that of Moilanen *et al.* (2022) and the individual from Ytra-Garðshorn requires citing examples thousands of kilometres apart and separated by generations or centuries in time. It may be, however, that renewed interest in such burials and the increasing use of aDNA studies will lead to the discovery of additional examples in older collections or that additional graves blurring the lens of gender assignment will be found as new sites are excavated, as Price and his colleagues have suggested (Price *et al.* 2019a: 194).

As much as contemporary media representations of the Viking Age encourage a belief in legions of shield maidens or of communities that honoured or accepted those who blurred the lines of male and female gender, the current archaeological record suggests that such individuals were rare and that most people who did not fit standard gender norms probably tried to fit in and meet traditional expectations. Alternatively, it is possible that some of those who did not fit into prescribed norms were buried in ways that have not allowed their recovery and identification. In this regard, the work done by Moilanen *et al.* (2022) with Suontaka Vesitorninmäki and by Hedenstierna-Jonsson *et al.* (2017a; Price *et al.* 2019a) with burial Bj.581 also suggests that the ability to cross gender boundaries may only have been possible for those who already had wealth, status, or prestige, whether that was gained by descent or through their own achievements in life (cf. Clover 1993). In contrast, the overwhelming majority of funerary representations made at the graveside for individuals at the time of their death suggest that the boundaries between males and females were relatively well defined and normatively prescribed by their living community members.

However, as the chapters in this volume suggest, it is important to look beyond the nature of biological sex and socially ascribed gender in order to determine what social, economic, and ritual roles Viking Age women performed and, through that examination, to review, revise, and perhaps discard ideas that certain activities were only the province of men and that women could only perform others. In order to continue to examine the many facets and expression of gender, and the lives of people in the Viking Age, including third gendered individuals, both sex and gender will continue to be relevant as part of the question regarding how gender was defined in Norse society.

## The unisexual, binary, or complementary nature of Viking Age society

Icelandic sagas and medieval Norse laws are among the main written sources used to investigate sex and gender in Viking Age and Norse society (Meulengracht Sørensen 1983; Mundal 1994b; 2001; Lloyd Evans 2019), although, as discussed above, these sources are all problematic in their own ways. One of the most influential and controversial ideas in Viking Age and Norse gender studies was presented in Carol Clover's 1993 article 'Regardless of sex: men, women, and power in early Northern Europe'. Clover argued that in Viking Age/medieval Iceland there was no defined femininity and that masculine qualities were seen as the reverse of 'unmanly' characteristics. Clover added that Icelanders distinguished between people labelled *hvatr* ('brisk, vigorous', able bodied men and exceptional women), and those classified as *blauðr* ('soft' or 'weak'), which encompassed the majority of women and children, as well as old or disabled men. There was, she implied, just one sex and also one gender to which men and women were assigned by the same norms: 'one standard by which persons were judged adequate or inadequate, and it was something like masculine' (Clover 1993: 379).

In recent years, this central concept of Clover's one sex model has been rather heavily criticised for giving the impression that 'sexual difference is of no consequence and gender performance is all' (Lloyd Evans 2019: 12). This was also argued by Henrik Bagerius who stated, 'of course sex was of great importance' (Bagerius 2009: 72–73). It is important to stress that Clover herself added that 'biological sex was known and accepted', but her emphasis on gender – indeed one gender – negates this (Clover 1993: 379).

The criticism of Clover's model was based on detailed studies of the Icelandic sagas and Norse laws. Bagerius and Gareth Lloyd Evans have both drawn attention to the many examples where clear distinctions were made between men and women, showing that not everyone was judged by the same 'masculine' standard (Bagerius 2009: 53–54; Lloyd Evans 2019: 12–13). *Grágás*, for example, clearly separates men and women, as seen in regulations stating that men have the right to carry weapons, cut their hair short, and wear breeches – rights that were expressly not extended to women (Bagerius 2009: 53–54). However, it is important to bear in mind that these analyses are taken from the Icelandic sources and in this volume Anne Irene Riisøy, working from Norwegian law codes and building on previous work by Else Mundal (Mundal 1994a; 1994b; 2001), suggests a different approach regarding the laws governing women. It is possible that the Icelandic sources were less tolerant of women, in part because they were written down later than the Norwegian law codes, and with amendments made throughout the Middle Ages. It may also be the case that the medieval Icelandic sources reflect specifically Icelandic cultural realities in a new colony that may have differed in varying degrees from Scandinavia and cannot be uncritically applied to all the Norse world.

It is, however, important to stress that Clover's work is valuable even without full acceptance of her one gendered society because of her emphasis on status and personal circumstances for social rank and advancement. She concluded that in medieval Iceland the decisive factor for a person was not whether they were male or female; rather, what was important were 'any number of other considerations – wealth, marital status, birth order, historical accident, popularity, a forceful personality, sheer ambition, and so on' (Clover 1993: 379). The application of this particular concept makes it one of the most important analytical tools for research into gender roles in Viking Age and Norse society (cf. Lloyd Evans 2019: 15; Moen 2019: 10–11, 70). Bagerius, moreover, emphasised that Clover's model was useful as it highlighted the *similarities* between women and men, an aspect that is usually ignored (Bagerius 2009: 53–54).

This is an important point that also relates to the ideas of strict divisions between male and female work and spheres of influence that characterised much previous research on Viking Age society (Clover 1993: 363–387; Ney 2002: 26; Moen 2020: 622 and 625). This perspective was based, for example, on selected parts of provisions in *Grágás* that stated that the wife should 'run the indoor household as she wishes', where indoor is defined as 'inside the threshold' (*innanstokks*) of the farm. Similar expressions also appear in a number of sagas (Hastrup 1985; Jochens 1995: 117–118, 169; Dennis *et al.* 2000: 66; Croix 2012; Sanmark and Athanasiou, this volume; Sanmark forthcoming). Such statements should not be interpreted to mean that women and men were confined to separate spheres, but they do suggest that people in Viking Age and Norse society had clear ideas about gendered work. Yet in practice, as part of the everyday life on the farm – and as suggested in the chapters in this volume by Pedersen, Sanmark and Athanasiou, and McLeod — there was a broader overlap between the work done by men and women than these sources, and 19th–20th century scholarship, might suggest.

This summary shows that, with the one sex/gender element removed, the overall framework of Clover's model is very useful and can be applied successfully, with refinement and additions, to the study of Viking Age and Norse society. Sex and gender are not the only stratifying element in society. Moving away from this focus is crucial, although it does not render sex and gender unimportant parts of an overall system.

## The negotiation of gender roles in a patriarchal society

Within the context of what has previously been discussed, the Icelandic written sources acknowledge that biological sex existed and that biological differences were ascribed different gendered meanings. These sources also suggest, in some circumstances, a certain unease with gender non-conforming dress or taking on engendered roles ascribed to the opposite sex. Cross-dressing, for example, was not condoned and in Iceland was punishable by lesser outlawry, although Agneta Ney has argued that this was a Christian reaction to practices that may have previously been accepted (Ney 2002). *Grágás* stipulates that 'if a man puts on a woman's headdress in order to beguile a woman then the penalty for that is lesser outlawry' (Dennis *et al.* 2000: 69) or 'If a woman becomes so deviant that they wear men's clothing or whatever male fashion they adopt in order to be different, and likewise if men adopt women's fashion, whatever form it takes, then the penalty for that whichever of them does it, is lesser outlawry' (*ibid.*).

This unease with the mixing of gender roles is further reinforced by the concepts of *ergi* and *níð*, explored in Gardeła's and Hayeur Smith's chapters in this volume. Women could frequently use the insults, *níð* or *níðingr*, to goad men into behaviours that they wanted by labelling or cursing them with terms employing the antithesis of the male ideal with the aim of spurring men into action by manipulating their fears of inadequacy through accusations of unmanliness (Hayeur Smith 2020: 26).

*Ergi*, when applied to men can be translated as 'cowardice', but contains hints of sexual non-conformity, of unconstrained and socially inappropriate sexuality, and of a concomitant loss of honour. This term implied that a man was the passive partner in a homosexual act. It could however also be applied to women, where it implied a heightened sense of sexuality, promiscuity, and even nymphomaniacal behaviour (Ström 1974; Meulengracht Sørensen 1983; Solli 2008: 197). Certain activities, such as *seiðr*, possessed a lot of *ergi* and were therefore, dangerous for men to engage in.

*Grágás,* as well as the earliest Norwegian laws, tend to focus on the biological and sexual rights of women but only sparingly, as women are rarely mentioned specifically in the law code. As discussed by Sanmark and Athanasiou in this volume, the term *maðr* occurs frequently throughout these laws but generally meant 'human' or 'person', and while it may often imply a relationship with the gendered concept of men, it can be assumed that women, too, were bound by laws using the term *maðr.* Regulations that needed to refer to women specifically used terms such as *kona* or *kvennmaðr* (Venås 1989; Mundal 1994a, 600–601). Women were specifically pinpointed in issues relating to marriage and betrothals, householders and their rights, inheritance of the chieftaincy, protection of a man's honour concerning sexual behaviour, the legitimacy of children, etc. (Dennis *et al.* 1980; 2000).

While the law codes are portrayals of Norse societies as they existed in the 12th–13th centuries, when extant versions were written down, they are assumed to incorporate aspects of law retained from earlier centuries when the law was orally transmitted (Dennis *et al.* 1980; 2000; Byock 1982; Gunnar Karlsson *et al.* 1992; Miller 1996; for an overview, see Sanmark 2004: 133–146 with references). Viking Age and Norse society, as reflected in these law codes, appears largely patriarchal and mostly focused on the lives of men. Yet, as several papers (see Pedersen, McLeod, Riisøy, Sanmark and Athanasiou, Bek-Pedersen, and Hayeur Smith) in this volume demonstrate, women were, at times, able to defy these patriarchal restrictions and negotiate new pathways affording status and authority without actually violating the laws, and some were able to go well beyond what might have been expected of them.

How they achieved this is the question. How did women become warriors? How could they inflict fear and control over men through witchcraft? How were they able to excel as tradeswomen? Gender and engendered restrictions, as we have seen, could be negotiated and these negotiations most likely occurred continually, in many different social arenas, varying according to social status (Clover 1993; Sørensen 2000).

The study of 'patriarchy' was a central topic of early feminist theory but fell out of favour in the 1980s and 1990s due to over-use of the term and, especially, its application to any culture or setting where men dominated women or exercised power over them (Mathews and Manago 2019: 3). The term was re-introduced into the social sciences in 2017, following a statement by the United Nations' Secretary General, Antonio Guterres, that violence towards women is a major barrier in the fulfilment of human rights. This violence is most prevalent in patriarchal societies and their practices. The term has thus been revived, aided by the #metoo movement.[3]

Patriarchal practices have been a significant contributor through which social order has been understood and reproduced (Miller 2017, in Mathews and Manago 2019), although historically patriarchy is not the same in all places but is culturally reconfigured. In the case of Viking Age patriarchy, clearly the masculine focus on society, as expressed in the preserved Icelandic laws and sagas, suggests that the system in Iceland as a whole was regulated and organised through a patriarchal lens. Can the same be said to be evident in Scandinavia or to have been consistent through time? Else Mundal has suggested that the weaker position of women in Icelandic law was largely due to the influence of Christianity on society after the island's conversion around AD 1000 (Mundal 1994a; 1994b; 2001).

In general, according to feminist theorist Kandiyoti (1988), the origins of patriarchal systems are thought to emerge from *familism*, where the needs of the family take precedence over the individual, and from notions of honour. According to Mathews and Manago (2019: 7), these are further cemented through the process of state formation and the consolidation of patriarchal systems associated with, for example, religion and militarism.

In the 1980s, Denys Kandiyoti, a key feminist theorist, introduced the phrase 'bargaining with the patriarchy' (1988; see Hayeur Smith, this volume) as a mechanism used by women in societies ruled by classic patriarchy to negotiate their rights and opportunities. According to her analysis and research in Middle Eastern societies, women traded submissiveness, virtuous behaviour, and deference for male protection (Kandiyoti 1988: 283).

In the Norse social context, women appear in some circumstances to be manipulating and constructing gender identities through their own agency. Perhaps Viking Age society, being more tolerant than their contemporary European counterparts and the Christian doctrines they later adhered to, allowed women the flexibility to bargain with the patriarchy in order to negotiate female gender and engendered roles in ways that are unexpected and rarely addressed. In many of the examples examined in this book, women functioned in areas where it has been assumed they held subservient positions, such as in the legal system, warfare, and trade. In each one of these circumstances, the evidence presented by this volume's authors suggest that they could circumvent society's gender expectations and perhaps especially rise above the expectations of 19th–20th century historians, saga scholars, and archaeologists, whose own views about women and society may have affected their views of women in the past.

A closer look at the papers in the volume reveal that women appear to have operated effectively in specific areas of society where they were able to manipulate social norms not only when men were absent due to raids, trade, travel, or death but also in areas which involved the survival and well-being of the community at large on a regular basis. In other instances, there are provisions in the law codes, mentions in the literary texts, and perhaps materialisations in archaeological data that have been overlooked by scholars and that imply women's rights were relatively equal to those of men or allowed them to gain authority and power in roles that were parallel to those more typically associated with men. Our chapters analyse women and the law, (Ch. 2, Riisøy), in war (Ch. 3, McLeod), trade (Ch. 4, Pedersen), the domestic sphere (Ch. 5, Sanmark and Athanasiou), the control of fate (Ch. 6, Bek-Pedersen), in the practice of magic (Ch. 7, Sundqvist, Ch. 8, Gardeła), and lastly in textile production (Ch. 9, Hayeur Smith).

If women did bargain with the patriarchy 1000 years ago, what remains today as material evidence in the form of objects, sites, documents, and the like to demonstrate their efforts? It is our job as archaeologists and historians to consider women when we consider the past, and to bring out the women archaeologically in the Viking Age, who were present all along but have escaped extended or open academic scrutiny over the course of decades of scholarship on the Viking Age that was written primarily by men, or mainly from a male perspective.

### Notes

1 It is worth noting that Androshchuk (2018) questioned the identification of burial Bj.581 as that of a female warrior given that two right femurs were present in the storage box that contained the skeletal material from this burial, as Vilkans (1975), Ardwisson (1989), and Kjellström (2012) had previously noted. This femur, identified by Ardwisson (1989: 144) as that of a male but by Price *et al.* (2019b: 13) as belonging to a female or possibly a teenager of indeterminate sex, was not analysed as a part of the study reported by Hedenstierna-Jonson *et al.* (2017a) and Price *et al.* (2019a). In their 2017 article, Hedenstierna-Jonson *et al.* (2017a: 855) noted that 'Stored with Bj.581 was also a femur belonging to another burial which was excluded'. Neither in that article nor its online supplementary material (Hedenstierna-Jonson *et al.* 2017a; 2017b) was any explanation provided for its exclusion, although in the online supplementary material they noted that 'All bone elements [from the chamber grave] have at one time been marked with the text 'Bj.581' in ink' (Hedenstierna-Jonson *et al.* 2017b: 3). However, in the online supplementary information to their 2019 paper, Price *et al.* (2019b) clarified this situation, noting that the third femur was labelled Bj.854, indicating that it was known to have come from another grave, unlike all the other bones in the storage box that were clearly marked Bj.581. It was, therefore, excluded on the basis of information suggesting that this femur had been inappropriately mixed into the assemblage from Bj.581 at some point after its excavation (Price *et al.* 2019b: 13, fig. S6).

2 In their article and its supplementary data files Moilanen *et al.* noted that the DNA strands on which their identification of Klinefelter Syndrome was based were so fragmented that novel approaches had to be employed to estimate the likelihood that the individual had an XXY

karyotype rather than this assignment being an ambiguous result due to the condition of the DNA or contamination (Moilanen *et al.* 2022: 48–52, Supplementary Material 2). On the basis of what they acknowledge was not a direct assessment of chromosomal sex, but rather a modelled assessment of probabilities, they concluded that 'despite the extremely low sequencing coverage, we found overwhelming evidence that the genetic data of the Suontaka individual most closely resemble an XXY karyotype' (*ibid.*, 50). They proceed on the basis that the XXY assessment is correct – in part because the burial also shows both 'male and female gendered' material culture.

3 Today a term such as 'patriarchy' is widely used in North America not only in the public realm but increasingly by feminist scholars. Its definition is well articulated in an article in *The Guardian* on the very use of the term: 'Part of the idea of "patriarchy" is that this oppression of women is multilayered. It operates through inequalities at the level of the law and the state, but also through the home and the workplace. It is upheld by powerful cultural norms and supported by tradition, education and religion. It reproduces itself endlessly through these norms and structures, which are themselves patriarchal in nature; and thus it has a way of seeming natural or inevitable, or else, in a liberal context, it is obscured by piecemeal advances in gender equality' (https://www.theguardian.com/news/2018/jun/22/the-age-of-patriarchy-how-an-unfashionable-idea-became-a-rallying-cry-for-feminism-today).

## Bibliography


Androschchuk, F., 2018. Female Viking revisited. *Viking and Medieval Scandinavia* 14: 47–60.

Ardwisson, B., 1989. Kommentar zu den Knochenfunden aus den Gräbern, mit einem Appendix. In *Birka, II.3: Systematische Analysen der Gräberfunde*, ed. Greta Ardwisson. Almqvist & Wiksell, Stockholm: 143–149.

Ármann Jakobsson., 2011. Óðinn as mother. The old norse deviant patriarch, *Arkiv för nordisk filologi* 126: 5–16.

Ármann Jakobsson., 2023. Watch out for the skin deep: Medieval Icelandic transformations. *Arts* 12.1: (5). https://doi.org/10.3390/arts12010005

Arwill-Nordbladh, E., 1998. *Genuskonstruktioner i nordisk vikingatid: förr och nu*, GOTARC/B, 9. Göteborg: Göteborgs Universitet.

Bagerius, H., 2009. Mandom och mödom: Sexualitet, homosocialitet och aristokratisk identitet på det senmedeltida Island. unpublished Ph.D. thesis, Göteborgs Universitet.

Bell, J., 2021. Magic, gender fluidity, and queer vikings, ca. 750–1050. *History Compass* 19.5: 1–9.

Brink, S. and Price, N. (eds), 2008. *The Viking World*. Abingdon, Routledge.

Butler, J., 1990. *Gender Trouble: Feminism and the Subversion of Identity.* Routledge, New York.

Byock, J.L., 1982. *Feud in the Icelandic Saga* 1. University of California Press, Berkeley CA/London.

Cleasby, R. and Vigfusson, G., 1984. *An Icelandic-English Dictionary, Based on the MS. Collections of The Late Richard Cleasby*. Clarendon Press, Oxford.

Clover, C.J., 1993. Regardless of sex: Men, women, and power in early Northern Europe. *Speculum: A Journal of Medieval Studies* 68.2: 363–387.

Croix, S., 2012. Work and Ritual Space in Rural Settlements in Viking-Age Scandinavia – Gender Perspectives. Unpublished PhD thesis, Aarhus University.

Croix, S., 2015. The Vikings, victims of their own success? A selective view on Viking research and its dissemination. *Danish Journal of Archaeology* 4.1: 82–96.

Davidson, H.R.E. (ed.), 1998. *Saxo Grammaticus's The history of the Danes, books I–IX* (trans. P. Fisher). D.S. Brewer Wadebridge/Rochester NY.

Dennis, A., Foote, P. and Perkins, R. (eds), 1980. *Laws of Early Iceland: Grágás I*. University of Manitoba Iceland Series 3, Winnipeg.

Dennis, A., Foote, P. and Perkins, R. (eds), 2000. *Laws of Early Iceland: Grágás II*. University of Manitoba Iceland Series 5, Winnipeg.

Dommasnes, L.H., 1991. Women, kinship and the basis of power in the Norwegian Viking Age. In *Social Approaches to Viking Studies,* ed. R. Samson. Cruithne Press, Glasgow: 65–73.

Fausto-Sterling, A., 1993. The five sexes: Why male and female are not enough. *The Sciences* (March/April): 20–24.

Gilchrist, R., 1999. *Gender and Archaeology: Contesting the past.* Routledge: London.

Grønlie, S. (ed.), 2006. Íslendingabók - *Kristni Saga: The Book of Icelanders and The Story of the Conversion* Vol. 18I. Viking Society for Northern Research, Text Series, London.

Gunnar Karlsson, G, Kristján Sveinsson and Mörður Árnason., 1992. *Grágás: Lagasafn* Íslenska Þjóðveldisins. Mál og Menning, Reykjavík.

Gunnell, T., 2018. II: 38 Ritual. In *Handbook of Pre-Modern Nordic Memory Studies*, eds J. Glauser and P. Hermann. De Gruyter, Berlin: 677–686.

Hannes Finnsson, 1774. *Islands Landnamabok: Liber Originum Islandiæ. Versione Latina, Lectionibus Variantibus, et Rerum, Personarum, Locorum, Nec Non Vocum Raøimarum, Indicibus Illustratus.* Augusti Friderici Steinii, Kopenhagen.

Hastrup, K., 1985. *Culture and History in Medieval Iceland: An anthropological analysis of structure and change.* Clarendon, Oxford.

Hayeur Smith, M., 2020. *The Valkyries' Loom: The Archaeology of cloth production and female power in the north Atlantic.* University Press of Florida Press, Gainsville FL.

Hedenstierna-Jonson, C., Kjellström, A., Zachrisson, T., Krzewińska, M., Sobrado, V., Price, N., Günther, T., Jakobsson, M., Götherström, A. and Storå, J. 2017a. A female Viking warrior confirmed by genomics. *American Journal of Physical Anthropology* 164.4: 853–860. DOI:10.1002/ajpa.23308.

Hedenstierna-Jonson, C., Kjellström, A., Zachrisson, T., Krzewińska, M., Sobrado, V., Price, N., Günther, T., Jakobsson, M., Götherström, A. and Storå, J. 2017b. Supporting information 2 for Hedenstierna-Joson *et al.* 2017a. ajpa23308-sup-0002-suppinfo2.docx

Hernæs, P., 1984. C22541 a-g. Et gammelt funn tolkes på ny. *Nicolay* 43: 31–39.

Hildur Gestsdóttir., 2000. Geldingurinn á Öndverðarnesi. *Árbók hins Íslenzka Fornleifafélags* 89: 143–150.

Jakob Benediktsson., 1968. *Landnámabók.* Vol. 1. Íslenzk Fornrit. Hið Íslenzka Fornritafélag, Reykjavík.

Jesch, J., 1991. *Women in the Viking Age.* Boydell, Woodbridge/Rochester, NY.

Jochens, J. 1995. *Women in Old Norse Society.* Cornell University Press, Ithaca NY.

Jochens, J. 1996. *Old Norse Images of Women.* University of Pennsylvania Press, Phildephia.

Jóhanna Katrín Friðriksdóttir., 2020. *Valkyrie: The women of the Viking world.* Bloomsbury, London.

Kandiyoti, D., 1988. Bargaining with patriarchy. *Gender and Society* 2.1 (special issue, ed. J. Lorber). Sage, London: 274–290.

Kjellström, A. 2016. People in transition: Life in the Mälaren Valley from an osteological perspective. In *Shetland and the Viking World,* eds V.E. Turner, O. Owen and D.J. Waugh. Lerwick, Shetland Heritage Publications: 197–202.

Kjellström, A., 2012. Projektet människor i brytningstid: skelettgravar I Birka och dess nära omland, In *Birka Nu: Pågående Forskning Kring Världsarvets Birka och Hovgården,* ed. C. Hedenstierna-Jonson. Historiska Museet, Stockholm: 69–80.

Kristján Eldjárn., 1956. *Kuml og Haugfé úr Heiðnum Sið á* Íslandi. Mál og Menning, Reykjavík.

Kristján Eldjárn., 2000. *Kuml og Haugfé* úr *Heiðnum Sið á* Íslandi (2nd edn, ed. A. Friðriksson). Mál og Menning, Reykjavík.

Larrington, C. (ed. and trans.), 2014. *The Poetic Edda.* Oxford University Press, Oxford.

Larson, L. (trans.), 1935. *The Earliest Norwegian Laws, Being the Gulathing Law and the Frostathing Law.* Columbia University Press, Columbia NY.

Laqueur, T., 1992. *Making Sex - Body and Gender from the Greeks to Freud.* Harvard University Press, Cambridge, MA.

Ljungqvist, F.C., 2015. Rape in the Icelandic Sagas: An insight in the perceptions about sexual assaults on women in the Old Norse world. *Journal of Family History* 40.4: 431–447.

Lloyd Evans, G., 2019. *Men and Masculinities in the Sagas of Icelanders*. Oxford University Press, Oxford, New York.

Lunde, P. and Stone C. (trans.), 2012. *Ibn Fadlan and the Land of Darkness: Arab travellers in the far north*. Penguin Classics, London.

Lönnroth, L., 2008. The Icelandic Sagas. In Brink and Price (eds): 304–322.

Mathews, H.F. and Manago, A.M. (eds), 2019. *The Psychology of Women under Patriarchy*, University of New Mexico Press, Albuquerque NM.

Meulengracht Sørensen, P., 1983. *The Unmanly Man: Concepts of sexual defamation in early Northern society*. Odense University Press, Odense.

Miller, W.I., 1996. *Bloodtaking and Peacemaking: Feud, law, and society in Saga Iceland*. University of Chicago Press, Chicago IL.

Moen, M., 2019. Challenging Gender. A Reconsideration of Gender in the Viking Age Using the Mortuary Landscape. Unpublished PhD Thesis, University of Oslo.

Moen, M., 2020. Ideas of continuity: Gender and the illusion of the Viking Age as familiar. In *Viking Encounter*, eds A. Pedersen and S.M. Sindbæk. Aarhus Universitetsforlag, Aarhus: 621–632.

Moilanen, U., Kirkinen, T., Saari, N.-J., Rohrlach, A.B., Krause, J., Onkamo, P. and Salmela, E., 2022. A woman with a sword? – weapon grave at Suontaka Vesitorninmäki, Finland. *European Journal of Archaeology* 25.1: 42–60. DOI:10.1017/eaa.2021.30.

Monsen, E. and Smith A.H., (trans. and eds), 1990 [1932]. *Snorri Sturluson: Heimskringla, or the lives of the Norse kings* (reprint). Dover Publications, New York.

Montgomery, J.E., 2008. Arabic sources on the Vikings. In Brink and Price (eds): 550–561.

Mundal, E., 1994a. Kvinner som vitne i norske og islandske lover i mellomalderen. In *Sagnaþing: Helgað Jónasi Kristjánsyni Sjötugum 10. Apríl*, eds G. Sigurðsson, G. Kvaran and S. Steingrímsson. Hið íslenska bókmenntafélag, Reykjavík: 593–602.

Mundal, E., 1994b. The position of women in Old Norse society and the basis for their power. *NORA – Nordic Journal of Feminist and Gender Research* 2.1: 3–11.

Mundal, E., 2001. The double impact of Christianisation in Old Norse culture. In *Gender and Religion: European studies*, eds K.E. Børresen, S. Cabibbo and E. Spech Carocci, Rome: 237–253.

Ney, A., 2002. Myter, ideologi och ogifta kvinnor: Mö-traditionen i fornnordisk myt och verklighet. In *Makalösa kvinnor: Könsöverskridare i myt och verklighet*, ed. Eva Borgström. Alfabeta/Anamma:, Stockholm: 25–61.

Price, N., 2002. *The Viking Way: Religion and war in Late Iron Age Scandinavia*. Uppsala University Press: Uppsala.

Price, N. 2019. *The Viking Way: Magic and Mind in Late Iron Age Scandinavia*. Oxford: Oxbow Books.

Price, N., Hedenstierna-Jonson, C., Zachrisson, T., Kjellström, A., Storå, J., Krzewińska, M., Günther, T., Sobrado, V., Jakobsson, M. and Götherströ, A., 2019a. Viking warrior women? Reassessing Birka chamber grave Bj.581. *Antiquity* 93(367): 181–198. DOI:10.15184/aqy.2018.258.

Price, N., Hedenstierna-Jonson, C., Zachrisson, T., Kjellström, A., Storå, J., Krzewińska, M., Günther, T., Sobrado, V., Jakobsson, M. and Götherströ, A., 2019b. Online supplementary materials 1 for Price *et al.* 2019a. https://doi.org/10.15184/aqy.2018.258

Raffield, B., 2017. Male-biased operational sex ratios and the Viking phenomenon. *Evolution and Human Behavior* 38.13: 315–324.

Raffield, B., Price, N. and Collard, M. 2017. Polygyny, concubinage, and the social lives of women in Viking-Age Scandinavia. In *Viking and Medieval Scandinavia* 13: 165–209,

Roesdahl, E., 1998. *The Vikings*. Penguin, London.

Sanmark, A., 2004. *Power and Conversion. A Comparative Study of Christianisation in Scandinavia*. OPIA, Uppsala University: Uppsala.

Sanmark, A., 2024. An examination of the concepts of sex and gender and their application to Viking-Age and Old Norse Society. In *Women of the Past, Issues for the Present*, eds N.J. Koefoed and R. Raja. Brepols: Turnhout: 83–98.

Sanmark, A., forthcoming The role of women in Viking Age society: An evaluation of previous research. In *Viking Women*, eds J. Morawiec, A. I Riisøy and C. Hedenstierna-Jonsson. Brepols: Turnhout.

Simensen, E. (trans.), 2021. *The Older Gulathing Law*. Routledge, Abingdon.

Solli, B., 2008. Queering the cosmology of the Vikings: A queer analysis of the cult of Odin and 'Holy White Stones'. *Journal of Homosexuality* 54.1–2: 192–208.

Sørensen, M.-L. S., 2000. *Gender Archaeology*. Polity Press, Cambridge.

Stenvik, L., 2005. Sosiale forskjeller. In *Trøndelags Historie. Landskapet blir landsdel. Fram til 1350*, ed. I. Bull. Tapir, Trondheim: 147–157.

Ström, F., 1974. *Nið, Ergi and Old Norse Moral Attitudes: The Dorothea Coke Memorial Lecture in Northern Studies Delivered at University College London 10 May 1973*. London: Viking Society for Northern Research.

Sunna Ebenesersdóttir, S., Marcela Sandoval-Velasco, Ellen D. Gunnarsdóttir, Anuradha Jagadeesan, Valdís B. Guðmundsdóttir, Elísabet L. Thordardóttir, *et al.*, 2018. Ancient genomes from Iceland reveal the making of a human population. *Science* 360(6392): 1028–1032. DOI:10.1126/science.aar2625.

Thedéen, S., 2012. Box brooches beyond the border. Female Viking Age identities of intersectionality. In *To Tender Gender: The pasts and futures of gender research*, eds I.-M. Back Danielsson and S. Thedéen. Stockholm University, Stockholm: 63–81.

Venås, K., 1989 Kvinne og mann i Gulatingslova: Etter ein idé av Lis Jacobsen. In *Festskrift til Finn Hødnebø 29. Desember 1989*, ed. B. Eithun. Novus, Oslo:. 258–303.

Vilkans, B., 1975. 101 gravar från Björkö, Adelsö sn. Uppsala Osteologisk Undersökning. Osteological archive report. National Historical Museum, Stockholm.

Williams, H., 2008. Runes. In Brink and Price (eds): 281–290.

# Chapter 2

## Aspects of violence connected to women in the Old Norse legal systems

*Anne Irene Riisøy*

As an historian working predominantly with texts, I would initially like to draw attention to, and offer new thoughts on, the legal regulations regarding violence committed by women in 'Old Norse society', a catch-all term designating Norway and Iceland, that includes the Viking Age until the mid-13th century. Violent women are discernible in the earliest Norwegian laws, for instance, if a woman kills a man or another woman, then 'she is an outlaw' (the *Frostathing Law*, henceforth abbreviated *F*, V 31, see Keyser and Munch 1846–1849 henceforth abbreviated *NgL* I: 267, Table 2.1, no. 3). A person, whether a man or a woman, may also fall victim to violence for which they had a right to compensation. However, there was a limit – three times – for which compensation could be claimed, before revenge was required (the *Gulathing Law*, henceforth abbreviated *G*, 186, *NgL* I:68, table 1, no. 6). These regulations raise some intriguing thoughts, for example, did women kill using fighting weapons? And did they have sufficient resources and control over people and property to receive legal support in order to pay compensation or to hire someone to exact vengeance on their behalf?

In 1993 two seminal articles on the position of women in Viking and medieval Scandinavian society were published by Jenny Jochens and Carol Clover respectively. For example, Jochens found that gender symmetry in the Icelandic law book *Grágás* was virtually non-existent and could be found in two areas only: 1) property transactions and 2) more recent rules enacted in the Christian law section (Jochens 1993: 51). Jochens' great divide between women and men was repeated two years later in her influential book on *Women in Old Norse Society*, where women operated inside the threshold (*innan stokks*), and men, who were in charge of everything outside the threshold (*útan stokks*) (Jochens 1995: 113–117, 163, for further discussion, see Sanmark and Athanasiou, this volume). In contrast to an overly schematic partition between an important and public male oriented sphere, and the privately confined spaces of women inside the threshold, Clover's one sex model was basically 'male', because 'there was finally just one "gender", one standard by which persons were judged adequate or inadequate, and it was something like masculine' (Clover 1993: 379). However, if the standard is 'masculine', at the same time women are downplayed, and they risk being portrayed as mere substitutes for men (Sanmark forthcoming).

Otherwise, I agree with Clover's assessment that factors such as social status, wealth, and personality may have been more important determining factors than whether a person was a woman or a man. Along these lines, I have found inspiration in Nira Gradowicz-Panzer's study on 'Merovingian female honour as an exchange of violence' (2002). Gradowicz-Panzer persuasively argued that among the upper echelons of early Merovingian society, men and women shared the same *habitus*; from childhood, they were socialized into the same code of honor characterized by aggressiveness and physical violence (Gradowicz-Panzer 2002: 5). Gradowicz-Panzer draws of narrative texts such as the 6th century *Historia Francorum* by Gregory of Tours, that depict women as perpetrators, and who also retaliated against male counterparts (Gradowicz-Panzer 2002: 9–11 with examples from *Historia Francorum* (*HF*) involving Chlothild, King Charibert's daughter, *HF* X 16; two examples involving Queen Fredegund, *HF* VII 15; *HF* VI 23). Violence or threats of violence were often crucial in various social interactions, in other words, the key issue was whether the family was omnipresent and able to defend its position in the social hierarchy (Gradowicz-Panzer 2002: 6). Thus, men and women of the elite had much more in common than an aristocratic woman with a female serf or slave.

When focusing on Old Norse Society, it is necessary to note that Jochens's study, where she applied the Icelandic law *Grágás*, may not adequately describe the legal situation for women in Norway, as there were some important differences. For example, the earliest Norwegian laws granted free women relatively wide-ranging legal capacities, as they could attend assemblies, raise and prosecute cases, and serve as witnesses, *Grágás* excluded women in such instances (Mundal 1994a, but see Mundal 2015: 237 who noted that, in practice, the situation for women in Iceland from a 'foreign culture' and of low status would probably be different from free women of Norwegian background; Sanmark 2014). The settlers of Iceland made laws and created assemblies modelled on those of their homelands (Gudmundur Ólafsson 1987; Gunnar Karlsson 2009; Riisøy 2014: 104–105), however, from a gender perspective the settlement period was distinct, and may have negatively affected the legal standing of women (Mundal 2015: 235–236). Among first generation settlers there were fewer women than men, and DNA studies indicate that Iceland was settled by a group consisting of primarily Norse men whereas most Icelandic foremothers came from the Western Isles of Scotland, many of whom women may have arrived as slaves (Agnar Helgason *et al.* 2000; Mundal 2015: 236). Although only a small proportion of the total colonising population is mentioned in the Icelandic *Lándnamabók* ('Book of Settlements') a similar pattern is indicated here, because of the 48 women whose origin is recorded, 16.7% have British ancestry, whereas 4.7% of the 220 men whose genealogy is recorded have British ancestry (Jón Steffensen 1975; Agnar Helgason *et al.* 2000: 697). As Mundal (2015: 236–237) pointed out, although some of the women who came from the British Isles as slaves received free status when they married, their different cultural and social backgrounds would put them at a disadvantage and, therefore, the average woman may have possessed less relevant legal knowledge than the average man and therefore had less scope for legal manoeuvres. The political context is another noteworthy difference between Iceland and Norway. Before the subjection to Norway in 1262–1264, Iceland had 'no king, but only law', as Adam of Bremen famously noted in the late 11th century (Tschan and Reuter 2002: 217). In addition to laws, Norway had kings who aspired to exact punishment and collect fines and, in contrast to *Grágás*, the earliest Norwegian laws pay great attention to social stratification, which has a bearing on violence, and related issues such as honour, revenge, and compensation (Riisøy 2003).

On the topic of Old Norse women, violence, and the law, I will balance earlier studies where Iceland has been in focus; place a greater focus on Norway; use the earliest laws to tease out women as perpetrators of violence; and also examine the scope for action available to women seeking redress for violence and wrongs committed against them.

## Material, methods, and methodological issues

My point of departure is the relevant chapters in the earliest Norwegian laws. Before the codification of the *Laws of the Land* in 1274, there were four large legal provinces within the area that approximately corresponds to present-day Norway: the Gulathing, Frostathing, Eidsivathing, and Borgarthing. From the Borgarthing and the Eidsivathing law provinces of south-east Norway, except from a handful of chapters, only the Christian law section has been preserved (Riisøy 2003). The most relevant regulations are therefore to be found in the section on 'Personal Rights', regulating violence, in the *Frostathing Law* and the *Gulathing Law* that have been preserved in manuscripts and fragments, the earliest from *c.* 1200 (see Gustav Storm, *NgL* IV: xiv–xv). Parts of these laws may have been written down in the 11th century, whether early (Rindal 2004) or late (Helle 2001: 21–23), is still open to debate. Rune Røsstad (1997) found that stylistic variation in medieval Norwegian legal language correlates somewhat with chronology, implying that the secular law sections contain Viking Age law. I will occasionally draw on *Grágás* for comparison and this law, which originated before Iceland's submission to the Norwegian crown in 1262–1264, also contains rules from different time periods, some of which go back to the Viking Age (Foote 1987). Rules that originated in pre-Christian times include paragraphs that apply 'ring' (*baugr*) terminology, such as designating a woman who had the right to receive and pay compensation as a *baugrýgr* 'ring-woman' and the payment of compensation in rings. These topics will be discussed further below. Moreover, chapters that stipulate revenge as a legal option in cases such as manslaughter and various personal affronts, reflect a legal principle that originated before the arrival of Christianity (Riisøy 2020: 259–262).

My approach to aspects of violence connected to women therefore includes the Viking Age, and thus chronologically earlier than a recent article on 'Gendered punishments in Nordic medieval legislation ca. 1100–ca. 1300' (Tveit *et al.* 2022) published after I wrote my first draft of this chapter.

Contemporary evidence, such as runic inscriptions from Scandinavia and skaldic poetry (Johnsen 1969; Brink 2002) and documents such as peace treaties and sporadic notations in various chronicles, written down by Carolingian, Byzantine, Scottish, and Anglo-Saxon scribes (Stein-Wilkeshuis 2002; Riisøy 2016a; Sanmark 2017: 8–9), support the fact that Viking Age Scandinavia had a well developed legal culture long before the arrival of Christianity and before the introduction of stylus and parchment.

Some chapters of the laws specifically mention men or women, whereas others apply the neuter term *maðr* ('person' or 'human'), but relevant information can disappear when *maðr* is wrongly translated as a member of the male sex (Venås 1989). Kjell Venås also pointed out, that the pronoun *hann* 'he' or 'his' may occasionally be used without regard to gender (Venås 1989: 294). Translations may also be influenced by pre-conceived views on the respective roles of men and women in past societies, typically that heads of households had to be men, and only in the absence of a man, unmarried women or widows, may step into a man's shoes. One such example concerns the 'coastal defence', the leiðangr. Assembly attendance to prepare the muster roll included '[unmarried] women who are in charge of a household' (*F* VII 8, *NgL* I: 199; Larson 1935: 316). In this case the translator assumed that a woman in charge of running a farm is unmarried, whereas no such distinction is made, as *konor* in the legal manuscript simply means 'women' (*NgL* I: 199).

In the following analysis I have confined myself to chapters where women are explicitly mentioned, as considerably more work is required to analyse all potentially relevant, but gender ambiguous paragraphs to decide whether they encompass both men and women.

## Violent acts

Several chapters of the laws take it for granted that women could kill (Table 2.1, nos 1–3). Whereas nos 1 and 3 in Table 2.1 concern manslaughter without further specification, no. 2 deals with women who killed their own husbands because they had a lover or intended to take one, which may reflect different gendered norms. Relations with several women and polygamy by the male elite were rather common in pagan and early Christian times in Scandinavia as indeed in the rest of Europe (Clunies Ross 1985; Riisøy 2009: 70–71). Therefore, a married man may not contemplate to kill his spouse to accommodate a lover, he could simply take on a second wife or a concubine without risks of moral condemnation. I have not seen any chapters that specifically deal with husbands who kill their wives, however, there are chapters in the earliest Norwegian laws concerning husbands who beat their wives in public. Beatings and

Table 2.1. *Manslaughter and maiming*

| No. reference | Old Norse | Translation |
|---|---|---|
| 1. *F* IV 33, *Ngl* I:168, Larson 1935: 271 | Ef kona vegr mann | If a woman slays a man |
| 2. *F* IV 35, *NgL* I: 168, Larson 1935: 271, Hagland and Sandnes 1994: 68 | En ef kona ðrepr búanða sinn | If a woman kills her husband |
| 3. *F* V 31, *NgL* I: 267, Hagland and Sandnes 1994: 92 | Ef karlmaðr ðrepr kono þa er hann utlægr oc sua ef kona ðrepr karlmann þa er hon utlæg oc sua ef kona ðrepr kono þa se hon utlæg | If a man kills a woman, he is outlawed, and likewise, if a woman kills a man. Then she is an outlaw, likewise if a woman kills a woman, she is an outlaw |
| 4. *G* 190, *NgL* I: 69, Larson 1935: 141 | Nu ef karlmaðr ðrepr kono æda kona karlmaðr | If a man strikes a woman or a woman [strikes] a man |
| 5. *G* 196, *NgL* I: 70, Larson 1935: 143 | fullrettes orð | Insult that calls for full compensation |
| 6. *G* 186, *NgL* I: 68, Larson 1935: 40 | Nu a engi maðr rett a sér oftarr en þrysvar hvarke karl ne kona ef hann hemnisc cigi a milli | No one, either man or woman, has a right to claim compensation more than three times, unless he has taken revenge in the meantime |

abuse constitured gross assault on a free person, and being struck with horns or fists at an ale feast, for example, made the abuse visible and therefore known to everyone in the local community. Accordingly, damage to the wife's honour was greater than if the abuse had taken place in private, and in such cases the wife's options were a hefty compensation and divorce.[1]

Women could of course also be physically abusive, which requires a comment on *ðrep*, a term that has a wide meaning, from hitting to killing someone (*NgL* V: 139 *ðrep*, *NgL* V: 140 *dræpr*). Thus, *ðrep* is translated as manslaughter (*F* V 31, *NgL* I: 267; Table 2.1, no. 3) or striking someone (*G* 190, *NgL* I: 69; Table 2.1, no. 4, cf. Robberstad 1969: 193), although I will not rule out that in both cases manslaughter may be included.

## Reactions to violence

Women who killed or physically abused someone were treated as legal subjects and had to face the consequences: fines payable to the king, outlawry, compensation to the victim, or being killed as part of revenge (Table 2.1, no. 1; *F* IV 33, *Ngl* I: 168; no. 2. *F* IV 35, *NgL* I: 168; no. 3, *F* V 31, *NgL* I: 267; no. 4. *G* 190, *NgL* I: 69).

As noted above, the Norwegian provincial laws of the Gulathing and the Frostathing show that there were kings who aspired to exact punishment. No. 4 in Table 2.1 also stipulates a *baugr* 'ring' as a fine to the king for physical abuse and perhaps also manslaughter (*G* 190, *NgL* I: 69). In any case, it is reasonable to assume that the king was also entitled to fines in cases of manslaughter, which were more serious.

As items for compensation, rings constitute a definite pre-medieval feature that also had pagan mythological associations (Hafström 1957; Engeler 1991: 85–114; Kilger 2008: 292–293; Riisøy 2016a: 144; 2016b: 165). For example, in Norwegian medieval laws the *baugr* occurs as a fine to the king, never to the bishop, which shows the pre-Christian origin of the *baugr* (Hafström 1957: 2) and when the Norwegian *Laws of the Land* was codified the term *baugr* was not applied as a unit of account to signify fines or compensation. Dagfinn Skre (2017) argued regulations in the *Frostathing Law* and the *Gulathing Law* that stipulate that the *baugr* 'ring' should be of gold may originate in the Migration Period (*c.* AD 400–550), the only gold-rich period in western Scandinavia. In contrast, regulations that specify rings of silver were either codified or adjusted during the Viking Age when silver was common and gold had become rarer (Skre 2017: 292–293).

Whether *baugr*, as an early word for punishment designating a fine to the king, is older than the Viking Age is hard to say. It is not unreasonable to assume so, since there were larger political units and rulers in Norway, as elsewhere in Scandinavia during that time (Andersen 2017; Iversen 2020; Skre 2020). Otherwise, the earliest attestation of 'a ring to the lord' (*drihtinbeage*) appears in the earliest Anglo-Saxon law of Æthelberth of Kent of *c.* AD 600, which is preserved in *Textus Roffensis* of the early 1120s. This law contains several chronological stages, of which the section on personal injury in Æthelberth's law is the oldest, as for example it has some archaic terms (*drihtinbeage* being one of them) and archaic syntax (such as the 'dative of quantity'), which suggests that it had been preserved from an oral transmission pre-dating AD 600 (Oliver 2002: 25–51, see also Lambert 2017: 32–33). Here the king was entitled to 50 shillings as *drihtinbeage*, a compound of 'lord' and 'ring' if a freeman was killed (Oliver 2002: 62–63, rule 12, translated as 'lord-payment'). Daniela Fruscione (2014: 37) suggested that the *drihtinbeage* emerged in the Migration Period when the size of a lord's retinue was of great importance, and where the interests of *drihtin* (military lordship) were relevant to a larger community. Hence *drihtinbeage* in Æthelberht may have been part of the orally transmitted legal heritage the settlers brought from their homelands, which also included Scandinavia.

During the late Viking Age, the discontinuation of the *baugr* commenced, most likely due to monetary and religious changes. New Christian ideals were gradually introduced, hack silver started to appear, a different principle of reckoning and valuation gradually developed, as well as the usage of coins (Kilger 2008: 318–325).

In cases of manslaughter, men, and women alike risked outlawry (*útlegð*, *F* V 31, *NgL* I: 267, Table 2.1, no. 3). Unfortunately, this chapter does not further specify the extent of the outlawry, but it would normally include confiscation of property to pay compensation to the victim's kin and a fine to the king, banishment, and the risk of being killed. In some cases, if the outlawry was not irredeemable, the outlaw could pay the king a price for release (Riisøy 2014: 106–107).

Revenge was also a legal option for manslaughter. If a woman *vegr mann* 'slays a man', *þá eigu frænðr hins dauða kost at drepa hana ef þeir vilia* 'his kinsmen have the right to kill her if they wish', the killer was however granted a respite, she should leave the land within five days in the summer and half a month in the winter (*F* IV 33, *Ngl* I: 168, Table 2.1, no. 1). In cases where women killed their own husbands the relatives of the slain man could legally *meiða hana eða ðrepa* 'maim her or kill her' (*F* IV 35, *NgL* I: 168, Table 2.1, no. 2). These examples show that also women risked prosecution to the full extent of the law, the offended party had legal backing to kill them to settle scores.

In addition to paying a ring as a fine to the king, no. 4 in Table 2.1 stipulates compensation to the offended party: *þa scal bæta slicum retter sem hann a af taca er uvæne* 'the offender shall pay such compensation as the injured person has a right to claim' (*G* 190, *NgL* I: 69). Recompense was therefore accentuated according to the rank of the wounded person, higher rank entails higher payment, a principle that is otherwise well attested in the earliest Norwegian laws. Compensation is also stipulated in Table 2.1, nos 2 (*F* IV 35, *NgL* I: 168) and 5 (*G* 196, *NgL* I: 70). In no. 2 it covers remuneration for manslaughter and is therefore translated 'wergild', a modernisation and standardisation of **wira-gelda* 'remuneration for a man (human)' that is first found in Merovingian legal texts (Haubrichs 2021: 94–95; Siems 2021). Compensation for wrongs is a hallmark of Germanic law, and therefore originated before the arrival of Christianity and influences from Roman and Canon law (Wormald 2003: 47–53; Oliver 2011: 10). No. 6 in Table 2.1 gives a maximum for the number of times a person (man or woman), could receive compensation for wrongdoings, that maximum was three, before revenge should be exacted (*G* 186, *NgL* I: 68). This explicit endorsement of vengeance is rooted in a pre-Christian moral code of honour. The expectation to exact vengeance was highest at the top level of society, because being able to pursue revenge was a way to display strength, power, and superiority and therefore affected a person's social standing (Riisøy 2020: 260–269). The wrongdoing is not specified but, in addition to manslaughter and various forms of physical abuse, it probably included slanderous words that could cause great harm to someone's honour. For example *fullréttisorð* was an insult that called for full compensation and often had sexual overtones that demanded a response (*G* 196, *NgL* I: 70, Table 2.1, no. 5). Typically, any accusations that refers to men as 'effeminate' or with female behavioural characteristics (*G* 196, *NgL* I: 70), and in the eyes of his peers therefore became *The Unmanly Man* (Meulengracht Sørensen 1983) and a woman who is accused of being a whore (*G* 196, *NgL* I: 70). It was possible to seek redress to rectify the damage a *fullréttisorð* did to someone's honour and presumably, in such cases, women had the same courses of actions available as men: to demand *fullum rette* 'full compensation' or *viga um at utlogum* 'satisfaction in blood and outlawry' (*G* 186, *NgL* I: 68, Table 2.1, no. 6).

Revenge was often set in motion through goading, where a certain character incited (Old Norse verbs *eggja* or *hvetja*) someone else. Scenes of goading frequently appear in the family sagas (*Íslendingasögur*) written down in the 13th and 14th centuries and describe events from the late 9th to the early 11th centuries. Goading also appears in other sources, such as the Kings' sagas, that principally involve various Norwegian kings, and Eddic poetry, where pagan gods and goddesses as well as heroes and heroines are the main protagonists (Riisøy 2016b: 165–166). Goading may have been a common Germanic legal institution, and Else Mundal found traces as far back as Tacitus *Germania* (Mundal 1994b: 3–11). Tacitus, the Roman politician and historian who wrote about the Germanic tribes in the 1st century AD, remarked that women are each man's sacred witnesses, that women rally armies, and that it was a firm obligation to take on family enmities (*Germania*, 7.2, 8.1, 21.1: Rives 1999: 80, 86). Goading is also depicted, for example, in Anglo-Saxon and Frankish sources (Enright 1996: 42–48, Gradowicz-Panzer 2002: 7). Whether goading existed outside the minds of Christian male authors has been debated. In a classic study of the role of the *Hetzerin* ('female inciter'), Rolf Heller (1958) argued that whoever created this literary motif established a pattern that later authors have borrowed (for a similar view see Jochens 1986). On the other hand, as Miller (1983: 160–161) and Clover (1987: 158) argued, goading, which was often accompanied by a so-called 'bloody token', typically blood-stained clothes representing the corpse, was a genuine legal procedure. In other words, legal procedures are methods by which legal rights are enforced and they are characterised by formal and set expressions, often accompanied by specific objects. Legal procedures were thus crucial in early law as in this way law was seen, heard, comprehended, and remembered (Riisøy 2016a; Sanmark 2017: 82–116).When a killing had taken place, the inciter acted on behalf of the corpse, and it was normally the role of women to remember and remind relatives of the injustice that had taken place, and to the role of men to act and exact vengeance (Mundal 2009). In the sagas it is possible to discern a link between the people who goaded, exacted revenge, and inherited, which supports arguments that goading was used in real life. Relatives with a claim to inheritance were obliged to help avenge a killing and the goading woman herself, or the man she goaded – or often both – were at or near the top of the legal list of heirs (Sommerfelt 1974: 145; see also Riisøy 2009: 64 who noted that in the early Middle Ages sexuality was regulated by comparable rules).

Goading gave women a real position of power as guardians of the family honour (Mundal 1994b: 3–11). From a gender perspective it is important to point out that goading may not have been a role exclusively reserved for women (Riisøy 2016b: 165–166). I have not come across any studies on the relative frequency of women versus men as inciters in the various categories of sources, however, in my studies of pre-medieval law and legal practice in the Eddic poems, I have found that also male characters incited others to take revenge (Riisøy 2016b: 165–166, with specifications in table 5, p. 166, five examples of goading, two cases involving women, and three cases involving men). For example, in the Eddic poem *Reginsmál*, Reginn goaded Sigurðr to kill Fáfnir (*eggjaði Reginn Sigurð at vega Fáfni*) because it would cause laughter if Sigurðr *munur at sækia hringa rauða enn hefnd föður* 'had a greater lust to gain red gold than to avenge his father' (Larrington 1996: 154, prologue and stanza 15; Neckel and Kuhn 1983: 177). In addition to showing goading, also by men, as a prelude to revenge, *Reginsmál* also stressed an important pre-Christian ethic, that it was more honourable to exact revenge than settle for compensation (see Riisøy 2020: 255–261).

The term *baugrýgr* occurs in these three laws only, *Grágás*, the *Frostathing Law*, and the *Gulathing Law* (https://onp.ku.dk/onp/onp.php?o7365). Whereas the term *baugr* 'ring' frequently appears alone or as a compound word in the earliest laws, in sagas and in poetry the second element *rýgr* is very rare. According to *Skáldskaparmál* in *Snorri's Edda* a handbook for aspiring poets written by Snorri Sturluson around 1220, a *rýgr* is not any woman, but a woman who is rich, powerful, and raised above others, *heitur sú kona, er rikust er* (Jónsson 1900: 145; Fritzner 1973.I: 141, cf. *rikr* in III: 112; *Dictionary of Old Norse Prose*).

According to *Grágás*, a *baugrýgr* is the daughter of the dead man (*hon er dottir ens davða*), and as such she was given rings providing that no official receiver of the main ring existed; alternatively, she was the daughter of the killer and as such paid in rings (*Grágás* Ia: 200–201; Dennis *et al.* 1980: 181; Table 2.2, no. 1). This passage has been used as evidence for female warriors, i.e. unmarried women who took on a male vengeful role in the absence of brothers (Clover 1987) and Jochens (1993: 51–52) saw the *baugrýgr* in *Grágás* as 'a channel through which important payments for dead bodies were transmitted to living relatives ...'. This *Grágás* regulation has received more attention than the comparable Norwegian ones, but it should be noted that the *baugrýgr* is defined differently in the three laws.

In the *Frostathing Law* the *baugrýgr* is a *mær* 'unmarried woman' (Fritzner 1973.II: 769), whereas *Grágás* and the *Gulathing Law* use the term *kona* (f.) 'woman', which has a wider meaning, including unmarried and married women and widows (Fritzner 1973. II: 325). The context of the regulation in *Grágás* shows that in this case, *kona* means

*Table 2.2 The baugrýgr 'ring-lady'*

| *Reference and source* | *Old Norse* | *Translation* |
|---|---|---|
| 1. Grágás, *baugatal* section in the *Konungsbók* version (1852), *Grágás* Ia: 200–201, Laws of Early Iceland. *Grágás* I, Dennis *et al.* 1980: 181 | *... kona ein er bæðe scal bauge bøta oc baug taca er einbærne en su kona heitir baugrygr* | ... one woman who is both to pay and to take a wergild ring, given that she is an only child, and that woman is called 'ring-lady' |
| 2. *F* VI 4, *NgL* I: 184–185, Larson 1935: 294, cf. *NgL* V: 93, *baugrygr* | *Nú er mær ein er baugýgr er callað hon scal bæði baugum bæta oc svá taca er hon er einberni oc til arfs komin* | Now, there is one maiden who is called a *baugrygr*; she both pays into the *baug* and receives payment from it, if she is an only child and has come into an inheritance |
| 3. *G* 275, *Um baugrygi*, *NgL* I: 92, Larson 1935: 180 | *Nv verðr kona baugrygr* | A woman is a *baugrygr* |

unmarried woman, whereas according to the *Gulathing Law* this is not obvious. There are notable similarities between the *Frostathing Law* and *Grágás* where the *baugrýgr* is an only child (*einberni*, n., Fritzner 1973.I: 304), and her status as a *baugrýgr* ceases upon marriage, henceforth her kinsmen take over her responsibilities: *þa kastar hon giolldom i kne frændo* (*Grágás* Ia: 200–201, Dennis *et al.* 1980: 181, Table 2.2, no. 1), *þa castar hon giölldum aptr i cné frenðom* (*F* VI 4, *NgL* I: 184–185, Table 2.2, no. 2). No. 2 in Table 2.2 further underlines that, after marriage, she shall *hvárki síðan baugum bæta ne taca* 'neither pay into, nor receive payments from, the baug' (*F* VI 4, *NgL* I: 184–185, Larson 1935: 294).

In important ways the *Gulathing Law* (*G* 275, *Um baugrygi*, *NgL* I: 92, Table 2.2, no. 3) stands apart. A *baugrýgr* is said to include more women than a daughter who was an only child and marriage is not stipulated as a threshold when relatives would take over responsibilities. Moreover, in addition to receiving and paying wergild rings, the *Gulathing Law* connects a *baugrýgr* to inheritance of *oðals oc aura*, 'allodial and all other property'.[2] *Oðal* was elevated above other kinds of property and it was protected in law from falling into the wrong hands when transferred (Ruthström 2003: 171, *oðal* means 'the best of something', cf. Iversen 2008: 66 for a discussion of etymology). A *kona* 'woman' was a *baugrýgr* if she was an heiress to *oðals oc aura*. The chapter lists the so-called *oðals konor*: a daughter, a sister, a father's sister, a brother's daughter, and a son's daughter. There is however a contradiction in the same chapter since a *baugrýgr* who received or paid wergild rings states daughter and sister only: *þær ero baugrygiar tvær dotter oc syster þær scolo baugum bæta oc sva taca sem karlmenn oc sva eigu þær boð a iorðum iamt sem karlar* 'There are two baugrygjar, a daughter and a sister, who shall contribute to the wergild and shall share in the wergild, just as men do, and they have the right to redeem land, just as men have'. The Gulathing chapter is not consistent as the *baugrýgr* includes five, or alternatively two women, which begs the question whether this rule was adjusted at some point, but not accurately captured by later scribes.

We do not know when *baugrýgr* was coined, however, a term that links certain rights and duties specifically to women suggests that at some point in time a legal distinction between men and women was discussed. For example, when rings of gold became standardised items of payment, perhaps already in the Migration period, did men and women have the same rights and duties connected to paying and receiving compensation? Considering such a scenario, it would not be necessary to have a separate term: *baugrýgr*. If, however, from the onset women had different rights and duties connected to compensation and *oðal*, or if changes were introduced over time, it would make sense to single out women *qua baugrýgr*. Moreover, the earliest laws define the *baugrýgr* differently, the *Gulathing Law* differs from the *Frostathing Law* and *Grágás*. This suggests regional variation, either from the beginning, or adjustments that may have been introduced over the centuries, such as the categories of women involved, and how their status as maidens or married women had a bearing on their rights and duties.[3] I would like to suggest that these changes took place when rings were still used and, therefore, prior to the Middle Ages.

Rings circulated in the upper strata of society and, as noted above, the people who paid and received rings were gone by the time of the Norwegian *Laws of the Land*. The people of the rings were elevated above the ordinary free farmers, and they owned the most prestigious category of property: *oðal*.[4] In the *Gulathing Law* the *baugrýgr* was explicitly linked to possession of *oðal*, and such property is connected to the social class of the *höldr*, who were probably regarded as nobles during the Viking Age (Ugulen 2012).The definition of *oðal* and who could inherit it may have had regional differences and changed over time. Already in the elder *fuþark*, used until the 7th century, an *óðal*-rune appeared (proto-Scandinavian **õþila*, Old Norse *óðal* n. 'property under an allodial system'; Grønvik 1982: 25). In pre-medieval Scandinavia runic inscriptions documented ownership and inheritance (Johnsen 1969), although on late Viking Age runestones women appear with less frequency than men (Sawyer 2000: 111–116). Based on Danish runic inscriptions, Ingrid Sanness Johnsen found that the reduction of female names in the late 10th century is concomitant with the arrival of Christianity and the establishment of the Church (Johnsen 1969; 12–13). Johnsen drew attention to several pre-medieval runic inscriptions from across Scandinavia that attest to female inheritance. The most famous example is also the oldest, i.e. the late 4th century Tune-stone from south-east Norway, which was raised to commemorate WoduridaR. WoduridaR's three daughters who arranged the funeral feast and who were also the heirs (Johnsen 1969: 40–43, Spurkland 2005: 37–41). The duty of the heir to hold a funeral feast was part and parcel of the right to take possession of the inheritance (Grønvik 1982: 7–9, 18). The deceased was a *witadahalaiban* 'one who provides bread', and as such presumably a powerful farmer or chieftain with many subordinates (Spurkland 2005: 38, *witadahalaiban*, **witan* – 'to provide', and *halaiban* 'bread'; cf. Old English *hlãford* 'lord', and *hlæfdige* 'lady'). Perhaps the three heirs took over their father's title as 'bread-guardians', and in this capacity presided over ceremonial feasts and controlled a redistributive system based on access to and distribution of grain and bread (for such practices see Sundqvist 2011: 185–186). Burial mounds also recorded ownership, and according to law, reciting one's ancestors back to the person in the mound was one way to inherit *óðal* (*haugóðal* Fritzner 1973.I: 743, Iversen 2008: 66–71; see also Zachrisson 1994; 2017: 120–121). Frode Iversen drew attention to a few documents from western Norway which offer evidence that this rule was applied in legal practice to women and men alike. In the early 1300s witnesses confirmed a woman named Ingrid's pedigree back to the mound (*Diplomatarium Norvegicum* (*DN*) III no. 122, for further references see Iversen 2008: 66–71. In addition to the manuscript AM 22b, the following documents refer to burial mounds in connection to inheritance: *DN* II 694, *DN* X 257).

As Birgit Sawyer noted, 'to raise a stone was a costly business' (Sawyer 2000: 111) and it was also very much a costly business to build burial mounds, so such practices were therefore reserved for a select few, also including women. In the famous Oseberg burial for example, two women lay interred.

## Property for payment and power

Some women inherited and owned property, including the prestigious *óðal*, which enabled them to pay compensation and fines in rings if they had killed or maimed someone, or alternatively provided them with resources for legal support or to hire help to settle scores. This reflected honour and having sufficient power and authority to be able to take vengeance.

As noted above, *rýgr* designated such a rich and powerful woman, and she may also have been titled *húsfreya* ('Lady' and 'ruler') derived from the name of the goddess Freyja (Green 1965: 19–55). As the *Ynglinga saga* noted, everyone who was a mistress over her property *yfir sinni eigu* is called *freya* and *húsfreya* was someone who 'owns an estate' *er bú á* (Hollander 1964: 14). Runic inscriptions bear contemporary evidence to such women, and a bereaved husband honoured his deceased wife Oðindisu, who was also called *hifreya*, on a late 11th century praise poem inscribed in runes on a stone from Hassmyra in Västmanland, Sweden. As her name implies, Oðindisu may have had an important role in cultic matters, as a *húsfreya*, she oversaw the estate, and she *byi raðr* 'ruled' (verb *ráða*) the *by*, a term designating anything from a farm to a larger settlement (Jansson 1964, Vs 24; Sundqvist 2002: 79–80; Jesch 2011: 38; see also *hús-freyia* in Fritzner 1973.III: 141). Oðindisu is therefore an example of a woman who was not a substitute man, she had a powerful position in her own right, even during her husband's lifetime, which is evidenced in the inscription commissioned by said husband who outlived her.

Women in charge of their property appear in a unique chapter in the *Frostathing Law* which stipulates that *svá cona sem carlmaðr* 'a woman as well as a man', should have free disposal of his or her *fé* 'property', if she or he is able to sit in the *ǫndvegi* 'high-seat', and have the mental capacity to administer said property (*F* IX 20, *NgL* 1: 213, *fé* is a pre-medieval term for property in general; Ruthström 2003: 61, 153–154). Thus, in addition to social status, factors such as old age and feeble minds had an impact on control of property, not whether the person was a man or a woman. Moreover, this rule exemplifies that a distinction between *innan stokks* and *útan stokks* along lines of gender, publicity, and importance, not necessarily holds, because the hall represented the centre of leadership, and the high-seat was the absolute locus *innanstokks* (Herschend 1997; Sundqvist 2016: 219–249; Jessen and Majland 2021: 6; Sanmark forthcoming).

## Weapons and women

Because weapons are commonly associated with manslaughter as well as revenge, a further question is whether women wielded weapons. According to a chapter in *Grágás*, under the threat of lesser outlawry, a woman was prohibited to dress in men's clothes, cut her hair short and 'carry weapons' (*feR með vápn*), unfortunately the kinds of weapons are not specified (Vilhjálmur Finsen 1852: 203–204; Dennis *et al.* 2000: 219). This is a strong indication that some women in fact did carry weapons, presumably not only for display but also to use them, either for defence or deliberately to kill someone. In a groundbreaking study of 2007, Lydia Klos drew attention to various sources, originating both within and outside Scandinavia, that support this supposition (Klos 2007). For example, one of the Irish *Annals* noted that the leader of a Viking expedition in AD 914 was led by a woman (*Cogadh Gaedhel re Gallaibh* 41; Klos 2007: 75), and the Oseberg tapestries depict men and women carrying weapons (Klos 2007: 77–78)

The Eddic poem *Rígsþula*, probably composed in the mid-Viking Age (Amory 2001), describes habits and suitable activities for people from various social strata. According to stanza 42, the *bornir* 'children' of the earl/*hesta tomðo, hlífar bendo/sceyti scófo, scelfðo* acsa/ '/tamed horses, brandished shields/ practiced shooting, used ash spears' (Larrington 1996: 251; see also Neckel and Kuhn 1983: 286). Women buried with a full set of weapons in graves from Aunvollen in North Trøndelag and Nordre Kjølen in Hedmark, both in Norway (Moen 2019: 50–53; Gardela 2021: 149–160; see also the famous 'Birka-Warrior' that sparked worldwide interest: Price *et al.* 2019), may have been born into, and were raised in the social strata described in *Rígsþula* stanza 42. Women associated with a full set of weapons, which in Norway included a sword or broadaxe, a spear, and a shield, belonged to the upper echelons of society. Social stratification had a bearing on what kind of weapons a person was in possession of and it should be noted that not all free men were owned of a full range of weapons either (Solberg 1985).

As I have previously argued, goddesses and heroines in Old Norse mythology, who appear above all in the Eddic poems, demonstrated to women that in this world they need not be the victims of violent men but may themselves be violent and pursue vengeance (Riisøy 2016b: 165–166). The Eddic poems present revenge as a pressing moral duty, and the most noteworthy avenger is Guðrún in *Atlakviða*. When Guðrún's husband Atli instigated the killing of her brothers, Guðrún spared no costs to settle this grave insult to the family honour, and in this case the family was not defined by Christian standards whereby a wife was joined to her husband for better or for worse. Guðrún's loyalties lay with her own kin and Guðrún therefore killed Atli and the sons she had with him, to extinguish Atli's line. As a final touch, Guðrún burned down Atli's hall, an action that marked the end of his dynasty's rule (Neckel and Kuhn 1983: 240–247; Larrington 1996: 210–216; Riisøy 2016b: 165–166). The emphasis on revenge above (particularly *G* 186, *NgL* I:68, Table 2.1, no. 6), reflects this pre-Christian moral code of honour which applied to people of high social standing. Similar observations have been made for Merovingian society, for powerful magnates, men, and women alike it was honourable to exact revenge and the greater success, the more influence and power the person acquired (Gradowicz-Panzer 2002: 16).

On the topic of violent women and the law, there are important avenues for further research, such as analysing gender ambiguous paragraphs that may also include women. Another pressing task is to examine the relationship and chronological ranking between the several systems of wergild and injury tariffs for wounds that appear in the earliest Norwegian laws, and which became obsolete in the *Laws of the Land* of 1274 (Philpotts 1913: 68; Robberstad 1969: 370–375).

## Concluding remarks

Violence in the past should be studied in its specific historical contexts and include the assumption that the earliest Norwegian and Icelandic laws also contain pre-medieval regulations. I have argued that, on the basis of the earliest Norwegian laws, there were no absolute formal dividing lines between men and women. Some chapters in the laws regulate women who committed violent acts, including manslaughter, and women exacting revenge, demanding, or paying compensation. The few chapters that have survived show that violent women had to face the same consequences as men: paying compensation to the offended party, or being killed as revenge, and additionally they had to face public punishment: to be declared outlaws at the assembly and/or pay fines to the king. Moreover, according to law, women who were victims to various wrongs could receive compensation or exact revenge.

There were regional differences concerning women's rights, duties, and scope for operation within Scandinavia (Tveit *et al.* 2022). Moreover, there were changes over time and the arrival of Christianity made great impact on society. Christianity was accompanied by new legal principles and laws, that changed society, including gender roles. Some roles and behaviours for women became obsolete and outlawed, and perhaps when *Grágás* prohibited women from carrying weapons, curtailing earlier practices, this was due to Christian influence. On the other hand, we should bear in mind that some practices and principles related to the topic of 'violence' lived on for a long time. In Norway, for example, it took several centuries of Christian teaching, combined with royal law enforcement, to uproot the practice of exacting revenge (Mundal 2009: 148–151; Riisøy 2020: 262).

Viking Age society was socially stratified, which is reflected in burial practices and written sources. Social status therefore had a huge impact on a person's scope of operation within the law and obtaining satisfaction for wrongdoings. It also had an impact on violent acts, whether the violence was illegal or sanctioned by law, and bearing in mind that in many cases revenge was a legal and even expected option. Revenge was governed by a set of duties and standards and it showed that the wronged person, or his/her family, were able to settle scores. People who belonged to the upper echelons of society, were raised in a culture that stressed the importance of upholding the family honour at all costs and this honour culture was the same for men and women. The codification and execution of law were in the hands of heads of important households, who also controlled land and people, and women may well have been included here. Regardless of gender, people from the lower echelons of society, the slaves and the semi-free, had considerably less scope for violence, they had little or no legal power, and the same restrictions probably also applied to free people who were excluded on grounds of poverty.

### Notes

1 The *Gulathing Law* and the *Borgarthing Law* both allowed the wife divorce and compensation: in the *Gulathing Law* the husband had to pay the wife the same compensation as he himself would be entitled to if he was beaten (*bœta henne slicum rette sem hann a at taca a silfum ser*), i.e. graded according to social status; and three marks, the equivalent of 10–12 cows, in the *Borgarthing Law* (*G* 54, *B* II 8, *NgL* I: 29, 356; Riisøy 2003: 159–160). The amount of three marks is interesting, it often occurs in the Norwegian laws, and in the Danish provincial laws *tremarksmanden* originally designated someone who was able to raise this substantial amount, 12 bulls (Fenger 1985). The concept of 'public knowledge' had interesting facets, see Sanmark (2006: 37–40).

2 *Oðals oc aura* is translated as 'odal and movables' (Larson 1935: 180, cf. Robberstad 1969: 275 '*odelsjord og til lausøyre*'). This expression may go back to the Viking Age, and, if so, *aura* cannot mean movables, because the antithetical and juridical distinction between movable and immovable property (*res mobiles et immobiles* since the days of the Roman empire) did not yet exist in Scandinavian law. The *oðal* was *allodium*, closely attached to the homestead, it was inherited land, and the opposite of 'purchased land' *kaupland*. The term *aurar* (pl.) refers to property that was not *oðal* in the pre-medieval legal terminology (Ruthström 2003: 22–24, 122–123).

3 The Gulathing regulation stands apart, and the similarities between the Icelandic and the Frostathing *baugrýgr* regulations suggest that the *Frostathing law* formed the basis of the Icelandic one, as legal transfer seems to have taken place from Norway to Iceland and not the other way round.

4 The *Gulathing Law* stipulated that the most valuable 'main ring' *hofuð baugr* to be paid in compensation should be 10 marks, equaling a staggering number of 32 cows, if the person killed was born to *oðal* (*G* 218, *NgL* I: 74).

## Bibliography

Note: primary source citations appear only in the text and are not duplicated below


Agnar Helgason, Sigrún Sigurðardóttir, Nicholson, J., Sykes, B., Hill, E.W., Bradley, D.G., Bosnes, V., Gulcher, J.R., Ward, R. and Stefánsson, K., 2000. Estimating Scandinavian and Gaelic ancestry in the male settlers of Iceland. *American Journal of Human Genetics* 67: 697–717.

Amory, F., 2001. The historical worth of Rígsþula. *Alvíssmál* 10: 3–20.

Andersen, K.H., 2017. *Dansk etnicitet og identitet til ca. år 1000*. Aarhus University Press, Århus.

Brink, S., 2002. Law and legal customs in Viking Age Scandinavia. In *The Scandinavians. From the Vendel Period to the Tenth Century*, ed. J. Jesch. Boydell, Woodbridge: 87–127.

Clover, C.J., 1987. Hildigunnr's lament: Women in bloodfeud. In *Structure and Meaning in Old Norse Literature*, eds J. Lindow, L. Lönnroth and G. Wolfgang Weber. Odense University Press, Odense: 141–183.

Clover, C.J., 1993. Regardless of sex: Men, women, and power in early Northern Europe. *Speculum: A Journal of Medieval Studies* 68.2: 363–387.

Clunies Ross, M., 1985. Concubinage in Anglo-Saxon England. *Past & Present* 108.1: 3–34.

Dennis, A., Foote, P. and Perkins, R. (eds), 1980. *Laws of Early Iceland: Grágás I*. University of Manitoba Iceland Series 3, Winnipeg.

Dennis, A., Foote, P. and Perkins, R. (eds), 2000. *Laws of Early Iceland: Grágás II*. University of Manitoba Iceland Series 5, Winnipeg.

*Dictionary of Old Norse Prose*. https://onp.ku.dk

Engeler, S., 1991. *Altnordische Geldwörter*. Peter Lang, Frankfurt am Main.

Enright, M.J., 1996. *Lady with a Mead Cup: Ritual, prophecy, and lordship in the European warband from La Tène to the Viking Age*. Four Corts Press, Dublin.

Fenger, O., 1985. Tremarksmanden. In *Festskrift til Troels Dahlerup på Tresårsdagen*, eds A. Andersen, P. Ingesman and I. Ulsig. Aarhus University Press, Århus: 243–356.

Foote, P., 1987 Reflections on Landabrigðisþattr and Rekaþattr in Grágas. In *Tradition og historieskrivning: kidlerne til Nordens ældste historie*, eds K. Hastrup and P. Meulengracht Sørensen. Aarhus University Press, Århus: 53–64.

Fritzner, J., 1973. *Ordbog over det gamle norske sprog. Omarbeidet, forøget og forbedret udgave.* Universitetsforlaget, Oslo.

Fruscione, D., 2014. Beginnings and legitimation of punishment in Early Anglo-Saxon legislation from the seventh to the ninth century. In *Capital and Corporal Punishment in Anglo-Saxon England*, eds J.P. Gates and N. Marafioti. Boydell, Woodbridge: 34–47.

Gardela, L., 2021. *Women and Weapons in the Viking World: Amazons of the North*. Oxbow Books, Oxford.

Gradowicz-Panzer, N., 2002. Merovingian female honour as an 'exchange of violence. *Early Medieval Europe* 11: 1–18.

Green, D.H., 1965. *The Carolingian Lord: Semantic studies on four Old High German words: Balder, Fro, Truhtin, Hero*. Cambridge University Press, Cambridge.

Grønvik, O., 1982. *The words for 'heir', 'inheritance' and 'funeral feast' in early Germanic: An etymological study of ON arfr m, arfi m, erfi n, erfa vb and the corresponding words in the other Old Germanic dialects.* Det Norske Videnskaps-Akademi: Avhandlinger 2/Historisk-Filosofisk Klasse Ny Serie 18, Oslo/Bergen/Tromsø.

Gudmundur Ólafsson., 1987. Tingnes by Elliðavatn: The first local assembly in Iceland? In *Proceedings of the Tenth Viking Congress*, ed. J.E. Knirk. Universitetets oldsaksamlings skrifter Ny rekke 9, Oslo: 343–349.

Gunnar Karlsson., 2009. Was Iceland the Galapagos of Germanic political culture? *Gripla* 20: 77–91.

Hafström, G., 1957. Böter och baugar. In A. Bandert, *Rättshistoriska studier, andra bandet*. A-B. Nordiska, Stockholm: 1–7.

Hagland, J.R. and Sandnes J. (trans.), 1994. *Frostatingslova*. Det Norske Samlaget, Oslo.

Haubrichs, W., 2021. Wergeld: The germanic terminology of *Compositio* and its implementation in the early Middle Ages. In *Wergild, Compensation and Penance. The Monetary Logic of Early Medieval Conflict Resolution*, eds L. Bothe, S. Esders and H. Nijdam. Brill, Leiden: 92–112.

Helle, K., 2001. *Gulatinget og Gulatingslova*. Skald, Leikanger.

Heller, R., 1958. *Die literarische Darstellung der Frau in den Isländersagas*. Niemeyer, Halle.

Herschend, F., 1997. *Livet i hallen: Tre fallstudier i den yngre järnålderns aristokrati*. Institutionen för arkeologi och antik historia, Universitetet i Uppsala, Uppsala.

Hollander, L.M. (trans.), 1964. *Heimskringla: History of the Kings of Norway*. University of Texas Press, Austin.

Iversen, F., 2008. *Eiendom, makt og statsdannelse. Kongsgårder og gods i Hordaland i yngre jernalder og middelalder*. Universitetet i Bergen Arkeologiske Skrifter, Bergen.

Iversen, F., 2020. Between tribe and kingdom – people, land, and law in Scandza AD 500–1350. In *Rulership and Ruler's Sites in 1st-10th-century Scandinavia. Royal Graves and Sites in Avaldsnes and Beyond*, ed. D. Skre. De Gruyter, Berlin: 245–304.

Jansson, S.B.F., 1964. *Västmanlands runinskrifter. Granskade och tolkade. Sveriges.* Runinskrifter 13, Stockholm.

Jesch, J., 2011 Runic inscriptions and the vocabulary of land, lordship, and social power in the Late Viking Age. In *Settlement and Lordship in Viking and Early Medieval Scandinavia*, eds B. Poulsen and S.M. Sindbæk. Brepols, Turnhout: 31–44.

Jessen, M.D. and Majland, C.R., 2021. The sovereign seeress – on the use and meaning of a Viking Age chair pendant from Gudme, Denmark. *Danish Journal of Archaeology* 10: 1–23.

Jochens, J., 1986. The Medieval Icelandic Heroine: Fact or Fiction? *Viator* 17: 35–50.

Jochens, J., 1993. Gender symmetry in law? The CASE OF Medieval Iceland. *Arkiv för nordisk filologi* 108: 46–67.

Jochens, J., 1995. *Women in Old Norse Society.* Cornell University Press, Ithaca NY.
Johnsen, I.S., 1969. Kan runeinnskrifter bridra til å belyse kvinnene stilling i det førkristne Norden? *Arkiv för Nordisk Filologi* 84: 38–55.
Jónsson, J., 1900. *Snorri Sturluson Edda.* Universitetsboghandler G.E.C. Gad, Nielsen, & Lydiche, København.
Jón Steffensen, J., 1975. *Menning og meinsemdir: ritgerðarsafn um mótunarsögur íslenzkrar þjóðar og bárattu hennar við hungur og sóttir.* Sögufélagið, Reykjavík.
Keyser, R. and Munch, P.A. (eds), 1846–1949. *Norges Gamle Love Indtil 1387.* Grondahl, Christiania.
Kilger, C., 2008. Wholeness and holiness: Counting, weighing, and valuing silver in the Early Viking period. In *Means of Exchange: Dealing with silver in the Viking Age*, ed. D. Skre. Aarhus University Press, Århus: 253–325.
Klos, L., 2007. Lady of the rings. In *Kult, Guld, och Makt. Ett tvarvetenskapligt symposium i Gøtene*, ed. I. Nordgren. Historieforum Västra Götaland, Skara: 70–86.
Lambert, T., 2017. *Law and Order in Anglo-Saxon England.* Oxford University Press, Oxford.
Larrington, C., 1996. *The Poetic Edda.* Oxford University Press, Oxford.
Larson, L. (trans.), 1935. *The Earliest Norwegian Laws, Being the Gulathing Law and the Frostathing Law.* Columbia University Press, Columbia NY.
Meulengracht Sørensen, P., 1983 *The Unmanly Man:* Concepts of sexual defamation in early northern society. Odense University Press, Odense.
Miller, W.I., 1983. Choosing the avenger: Some aspects of the bloodfeud in medieval Iceland and England. *Law and History Review* 1.2: 159–204.
Moen, M., 2019. Challenging Gender. Reconsideration of gender in the Viking Age using the mortuary landscape. Unpublished Ph.D thesis University of Oslo.
Mundal, E., 1994a. Kvinner som vitne i norske og islandske lover. In *SagnaÞing helgað Jónasi kristjánsyni sjötugum 10. apríl*, ed. G. Sigurðsson. Hið íslenska bókmenntafélag, Reykjavík: 593–602.
Mundal, E., 1994b. The position of women in Old Norse society and the basis for their power. *NORA - Nordic Journal of Feminist and Gender Research* 2.1: 3–11
Mundal, E., 2009. The view of blood vengeance in medieval Norwegian sources. In *Approaching the Viking Age.*, eds E. Sausverde and I. Steponoviciute. Vilnius University Publishing House, Vilnius: 139–152.
Mundal, E., 2015. 'svá kona sem karlmaðr.' Women in Old Norse society. In *Nordic Middle Ages - Artefacts, Landscapes and Society. Essays in Honour of Ingvild Øye on her 70th Birthday*, eds I. Baug, J. Larsen and S. Samset Mygland. University of Bergen Archaeological Series, Bergen: 227–239.
Neckel, G. and Kuhn, H. (eds), 1983. *Edda: Die Lieder des Codex Regius nebst verwandten Denkmälern. Text* (5th edn, original publication 1899). Heidelberg: Winter
Oliver, L., 2002. *The Beginnings of English Law.* Toronto University Press, Toronto.
Oliver, L., 2011. *The Body Legal in Barbarian Law.* University of Toronto Press, Toronto.
Phillpotts, B.S., 1913. *Kindred and Clan in the Middle Ages and After.* Cambridge University Press, Cambridge.
Price, N., Hedenstierna-Jonson, C., Zachrisson, T., Kjellström, A., Storå, J., Krzewińska, M., Günther, T., Sobrado, V., Jakobsson, M. and Götherströ, A., 2019a. Viking warrior women? Reassessing Birka chamber grave Bj.581. *Antiquity* 93(367): 181–198. DOI:10.15184/aqy.2018.258.
Riisøy, A.I., 2003. Komparativt blikk på 'verdslig' rett i Eldre Borgartings kristenrett. In *Østfold og Viken i yngre jernalder og middelalder*, eds J.V. Sigurðsson and P.G. Norseng. Senter for studier i vikingtid og nordisk middelalder, Oslo: 155–177.
Riisøy, A.I., 2009. *Sexuality, Law and Legal Practice and the Reformation in Norway.* Brill:Leiden.
Riisøy, A.I., 2014. Outlawry: From western Norway to England. In *New Approaches to Early Law in Scandinavia*, eds S. Brink and L. Collinson. Brepols, Turnhout: 101–120.
Riisøy, A.I., 2016a. Performing oaths in Eddic poetry: Viking Age fact or medieval fiction? *JONA Journal of the North Atlantic* Special Volume 8: 141–156.

Icelandic texts written after the Viking Age which *may* preserve evidence from the Viking Age.
3. Speculation extrapolated from the surmises in category 2, often with little regard to the evidence from category 1.

This paper will briefly outline the evidence from category 1 and use it to make surmises belonging in category 2.

## Viking women in Britain: Primary written sources

The coverage of primary written sources in Britain during the Viking Age varies considerably: England is comparatively well served, especially southern England (Swanton 2000); likewise, Wales is well served (Ithel 1965); most of Scotland has little local coverage for most of the period, but its southern half had a chronicle up to *c.* 973 (Hudson 1998). For the Isle of Man, the *Chronicles of the Kings of Mann and the Isles* only recorded information back to Knut becoming King of England in 1016 and will therefore not be discussed (Broderick 1995). Most of the primary written sources come in the form of annals or chronicles: a few sentences outlining the major events of the year, and Vikings are mentioned in the chronicle material from Britain. However, even for England and Wales the available information on Viking activities is brief, mostly consisting of notices of raids and battles. In such circumstances, it is only Viking leaders who are mentioned by name, all of whom are male, and women rarely appear. In addition, there are occasionally other primary written sources from the period, such as charters and wills, but the non-narrative nature of these sources makes the mention of Viking women very unlikely.

In England, what may be considered 'Viking' women, and children, first appear in the *Anglo-Saxon Chronicle*, the main historical source for the Viking Age, as part of a Viking army that has crossed the Channel. They are not mentioned as combatants, but as people who were captured by King Alfred in AD 893, and they are again mentioned in 893 and 896 when they were left in a Viking controlled kingdom as the army campaigned elsewhere (Swanton 2000: 86, 88, 89). Although there are other entries in the *Anglo-Saxon Chronicle* that may relate to Viking women, these are the only times that they are explicitly mentioned. In other instances it is reasonable to assume that Viking women were part of 'the people' referred to in texts. For example, women would have been part of 'the people' and 'their subjects' that agreed to the treaty between King Alfred and the Viking king Guthrum of East Anglia (Keynes and Lapidge 1983: 171); the Vikings with enough money who settled in eastern England in 896 probably included some of the women and children mentioned earlier (Swanton 2000: 89); when Viking controlled Colchester, Essex, was conquered in 917 and the Anglo-Saxons 'killed all of the people', it is reasonable to assume that women were amongst those killed (Swanton 2000: 102); similarly, the victims of the St Brice's Day massacre in 1002, when King Æthelred II ordered the death of all of the Danes living in England, probably included women (Swanton 2000: 135). Other than the *Chronicle*, there is a rather curious reference to Viking women by Archbishop Wulfstan II of York in his *Sermo Lupi ad Anglos* ('Sermon of the Wolf to the English'), composed and edited between 1010 and 1014, that is, during the period of intense Viking incursions in the reign of Æthelred II that culminated in the Danish prince Knut becoming king of England in 1016 (Godden 1994). In the sermon, Wulfstan refers to a very specific type of Viking woman, a *wælcyrian*, the Old English version of valkyrie. In Wales and Scotland, Viking women are not mentioned in the chronicle sources.

Another form of primary written source is runic inscriptions in ON, and some of these record the names of women. These are clearly important as texts written by Vikings. Due to the inscriptions being carved into a hard surface, the texts are short and therefore have minimal information about the women, but they do preserve the names of some authentic Viking Age women. For example, the inscription on the 10th century Kilbar cross, Barra, Outer Hebrides, Scotland, appears to commemorate Þorgerðr, the daughter of Steinar (Barnes and Page 2006: 226–232). An inscription at Thurso, northern Scotland, mentions the wife Gunnhildr (Barnes and Page 2006: 250). Occasionally, as on the Hunterston brooch, it is uncertain if the name recorded is for a man or women. The brooch is also interesting in that the inscription is in ON runes, but the name is Gaelic, reminding us of the mix of cultures in Britain during the Viking Age (Barnes and Page 2006: 219). The runic inscriptions from the Isle of Man include the names of ten women, representing one quarter of the names recorded there, and include both Scandinavian names such as Friða (Barnes 2019: 190), and Gaelic names such as Muirgheal (Barnes 2019: 234). Nine of the ten women are commemorated as wives, mothers, daughters, and even a foster mother, perhaps highlighting the female roles valued by the community, but the tenth is a rare example of a woman, Þúríðr, carving/inscribing runes (Barnes 2019: 235).

A final form of written evidence that needs to be considered is that of names. As we have seen, some female names are preserved in runic inscriptions, but more are known from place names. For example, Raventhorpe in Yorkshire and Lancashire is derived from the ON female name Ragnhildr +thorpe, Ragnhildr's farmstead (Jesch 1991: 78). These names suggest 'independent landholding by women bearing Scandinavian names' (Kershaw 2022: 105). Unfortunately, place names that include Viking women's names are usually impossible to date, and many of them were first recorded after the Viking Age, making it difficult to know if they represent the names of original immigrants from Scandinavia, later descendants, or even non-Vikings who bore a Viking name as such names became popular (Jesch 1991: 78).

Based on the primary written evidence discussed above, it is clear that Viking women lived in Britain during the Viking Age: we know some of their names and, thanks to the locations of the runic inscriptions and perhaps the place names, we have a rough idea of where they lived. Beyond that little can be said with certainty. Viking women were first mentioned in England in 893 but no mention is made of any arriving earlier. For Scotland and the Isle of Man, Viking women are not mentioned in chronicle sources, but they do appear in runic inscriptions. For Wales, there is no written evidence for Viking women at all. Bearing this in mind, it is hardly surprising that Viking women were rarely mentioned by historians of the Viking Age in Britain, who worked primarily from written sources, before the 1990s.

## Viking women in Britain: Archaeological evidence

In contrast to the written sources, there is ample evidence for Viking women in the archaeological record. The surest archaeological evidence is female skeletons buried in a culturally Scandinavian manner, but the discovery of such things as Viking female jewellery, and perhaps household implements associated with Viking women, may also indicate their presence. However, clearly a note of caution is required. Ideally, skeletons need to have been scientifically tested to determine if they were female and if the person buried grew up in either Scandinavia or an area with known Viking settlements, and/or was genetically Scandinavian. With finds of personal items, it is possible that Viking female jewellery was worn not just by Viking women. However, the culturally distinct oval brooches may have only/predominantly been worn by Viking women and they are accepted here as evidence for Viking women, especially when they were discovered *in situ* on a skeleton that has not been scientifically sexed. Similarly, there is nothing to discount household objects traditionally associated with Viking women, such as spindle whorls, being used by women from other cultural backgrounds in Britain, or indeed by men, and such objects do not feature in the following discussion (Kershaw 2022: 103; but see Hayeur Smith, this volume).

In Wales, the archaeological evidence for Viking women is currently minimal. A fragment of an oval brooch was found during excavations at Llanbedrgoch, Anglesey (Redknap 2000: 82). As noted, oval brooches are culturally distinctive to Viking women, but as only a fragment was found it is possible that it had travelled as scrap metal to be melted down and is not necessarily indicative of a Viking woman. A young adult female not native to Anglesey has been identified as one of six Viking Age burials found in the ditch around the settlement at Llanbedrgoch, but until the full publication of the scientific report into the remains has been published, it is unwise to consider her to have been a Viking (Redknap 2020; in prep.). Additionally, the skeleton of a young woman buried with a comb and possibly in a coffin or chest was discovered at Benllech, Anglesey (Redknap 2000: 97).

The Isle of Man has a number of prominent Viking burials, but all of those in mounds, other than a probable female sacrifice victim, are men (Wilson 2008: 27–29). However, amongst the flat graves in the cemetery on St Patrick's Isle was the richly furnished mid-10th century burial of a middle-aged woman (Wilson 2008: 48–50). Another female burial, which included a pair of oval brooches provisionally dated to *c.* 900–950, was discovered by metal detectorists in 2018, but the full report of the find has yet to be published (Cipirska 2021).

England also has burial evidence for Viking women. Although they were first mentioned in the *Anglo-Saxon Chronicle* in 893, the earliest burials are dated to the campaigns of conquest of the great army between 865 and 878 (McLeod 2011: 350–351).

Of particular note is the cremation burial of a woman and unsexed infant or juvenile under a mound with a sword and shield found at Heath Wood, Derbyshire (Richards *et al.* 2004: 91). There are two other burials that may also qualify as 'warrior women' that will be discussed below. In all, there are six osteologically sexed female burials known from England, and numerous others that have not been scientifically tested but are assumed to be female due to the grave goods present (Alexander 1987; Budd *et al.* 2004: 137–138; Richards *et al.* 2004: 33–34, 77, 91; Speed and Walton Rogers 2004: 60–61). Although the latter will be excluded due to the inherent uncertainty, those that included oval brooches seemingly *in situ*, such as in a grave excavated under modern conditions at Cumwhitton, Cumbria, can reasonably be presumed to be female (Paterson *et al.* 2014: 53–55). In addition, there are numerous other items that have been found that may indicate the presence of Viking women, in particular a large amount of female jewellery (Kershaw 2009). The latter are primarily found in rural areas and suggest that the Danelaw experienced 'a core period of female migration in the late ninth century, with further small-scale migration continuing into the early decades of the tenth century' (Kershaw 2022: 108). By wearing this Scandinavian style jewellery, along with the continued use of ON presumably passed from mothers to children, Jane Kershaw argues that women 'upheld and reaffirmed Scandinavian identities' (Kershaw 2022: 111).

Scotland has burial evidence for Viking women, including nine osteologically sexed female burials and numerous other burials that may have been women but were not scientifically tested (McLeod 2018: 15 and references therein). Indeed, Scotland has more burial evidence for Vikings, including women and children, than the other areas covered in this paper. The female burials in Scotland are also some of the richest in terms of grave goods, including the boat burial at Scar, Sanday, Orkney, where the primary occupant appears to have been a woman aged over 60, and a woman and full-term infant buried with numerous grave goods including oval brooches and an 8th century Irish brooch-pin at Westness, Roussay, Orkney (Graham-Campbell and Batey 1998: 136; Owen and Dalland 1999: 155). One interesting burial at the Broch of Gurness, Orkney Mainland, that is almost certainly female due to the presence of a pair of *in situ* oval brooches, included a Thor's hammer neck ring of a type commonly found in the eastern Mälaren region of Sweden and the Åland Islands opposite (Patterson 2021: 325–326). As their name suggests, Thor's hammers are associated with the God Thor, possibly as a reaction to Christians wearing pendant crosses, so this woman was presumably a follower of the Norse religion.

Based on the archaeological evidence discussed above, it is clear that Viking women lived, and in particular died, in Britain during the Viking Age, with all of the regions covered in this paper having Viking female burials, with the majority in Scotland and England. We not only know where they were buried and what they were buried with, but in some instances, we also know a good deal of personal information, such as their age at death, height, health issues, and in which region they spent their childhoods.

## Interpreting the evidence

There is clearly evidence for the presence of Viking women in Britain during the Viking Age. The different types of evidence provide a wealth of material about these women, especially in death, including some hints on what roles they played in Britain. What follows is an interpretation of the evidence as a whole, including surmises belonging in category 2 above.

A peculiar aspect of the burial evidence in Scotland is the relatively high number of pre-adult burials in comparison to other parts of the Viking Age world (Table 3.1). In Scotland, 30 Viking burials have been osteologically sexed and/or aged and eight of them, or approximately 27%, were pre-adults (McLeod 2018: 18). By contrast, of 13 osteologically sexed and/or aged burials from eastern England, only a single infant or juvenile was present (McLeod 2011: 345). In addition, all six of the burials found at Cumwhitton, Cumbria, are thought to have been adults (Paterson *et al.* 2014: 43). Two of eight identified Viking burials, or 25%, in flat graves on St Patrick's Isle, Isle of Man, were infants, but all five of the Manx burials under mounds were adults, dropping the percentage of pre-adults on Man to approximately 15% (Wilson 2008: 27, 47). Regardless of the differences in the numbers of pre-adult Viking burials across Britain, their existence underlines the obvious point that many Viking women would have been mothers, and probably wives. This is also attested in commemorative runic inscriptions where most of the women mentioned are done so in their capacity as a wife, daughter, mother, or foster mother, with nine of the ten female names recorded in the Manx runic corpus having such roles (Barnes 2019: 36). It is clear that such roles and family connections were considered very important within contemporary society. Whilst this conforms to gender stereotypes, it should not be thought to lessen the

*Table 3.1. Table of osteologically assessed 'Viking' burial sites that included children*

| *Modern Country* | *Area* | *Place* | *No. of Viking burials* | *No. of pre-adults* | *References* |
|---|---|---|---|---|---|
| Scotland | Sutherland | Balnakeil | 1 | 1 | Low *et al.* 2000, 28 |
| | Orkney | Westness, Rousay | 7 | 1 | Graham-Campbell and Batey 1998, 135–138 |
| | Orkney | Scar, Sanday | 3 | 1 | Owen and Dalland 1999, 52, 56, 59 |
| | Orkney | Buckquoy, Mainland | 2 | 1 | Ritchie 1976–1977 |
| | Lewis | Cnip | 7 | 3 | Dunwell *et al.* 1995 |
| | Galloway | Whithorn | 7[1] | 1 | Hill 1997, 189 |
| England | Derbyshire | Heath Wood | 3 | 1 | Richards *et al.* 2004, 76–77 |
| | Isle of Man | Peel Castle | 8 | 2 | Wilson 2008, 47 |

[1] This figure includes the minimum of four cremated probable adults whose ashes were overlaying the three inhumations.

importance of those women or the contributions and sacrifices that they made. With regards to the latter, the woman buried with a full-term infant at Westness, Orkney, is thought to have died in childbirth, a reminder of how dangerous childbearing could be in the pre-modern world (Graham-Campbell and Batey 1998: 136).

Based on the burial evidence, many of the women were buried with a fairly high number of grave goods, which may indicate that they were wealthy and/or valued in society. The women with rich burials at Scar and Westness in Scotland were mentioned above, and to these can be added other burials from Scotland, England, and the Isle of Man. The richest burial in terms of artefacts, recovered from the Cnip cemetery, Isle of Lewis, Outer Hebrides, was that of a 35–40 year old woman with numerous grave goods including a pair of oval brooches, 44 coloured glass beads, a comb, knife, needle case with two needles, and a sickle (Welander *et al.* 1987: 153–159). The woman buried at St Patrick's Isle, Isle of Man, sometimes referred to as the Pagan Lady of Peel, was the richest of the graves discovered at that site, buried with numerous household objects, with her head on a feather pillow and wearing a 73-bead necklace (Wilson 2008: 48–49). In England, one of the probable women buried at Cumwhitton was buried with a pair of oval brooches, a knife, key, and a wooden box containing more artefacts (Patterson *et al.* 2014: 54–55). While it is difficult to compare the contemporary value of different artefacts, there is no reason to think that any of the women buried with numerous objects mentioned above were valued any less than the men buried with numerous objects in the same regions.

Due to recent scientific developments, it is now sometimes possible to determine where the deceased spent their childhood and, fortunately, such tests have been done on a number of Viking Age skeletons from Britain. The research highlights that 'Viking' does not always equate with people coming directly from Scandinavia and people who spent their childhoods in Britain or elsewhere in Europe were also given Scandinavian-style burials. Many such people may have migrated from other Viking settlements, but it does not mean that they were necessarily genetically Scandinavian. With regards to women, in Scotland three female Viking burials have had isotopic testing to determine where they spent the first 15 years, approximately, of their lives, and in all cases the women had migrated from an area other than where they were buried, but none of them had grown up in Scandinavia (summarised in McLeod 2018: 21). Instead, the woman buried with multiple grave goods in the cemetery at Cnip mentioned above had grown up in either northern England or eastern or upland Scotland, and another woman buried at Cnip with fewer grave goods had probably grown up in England (Montgomery and Evans 2006: 134–137). Finally, a woman buried in an oval-shaped grave with grave goods in the Westness cemetery in Orkney had grown up in either north-eastern Ireland or eastern Scotland (Montgomery *et al.* 2014: 64). These three women were given Viking burials and all were immigrants, but not from Scandinavia. Indeed, of the 12 Viking burials from Scotland for which isotopic testing has been done, only two or possibly three,[2] at least two of whom were males, grew up in Scandinavia (Montgomery *et al.* 2014: 64;

Harris *et al.* 2017: 198–200). The others were either local to the area in which they were buried, including all three children assessed, or they had grown up elsewhere in Britain or Ireland (McLeod 2018: 21–23 and references therein). Despite this, the characteristically Scandinavian oval brooches were present in 85% of female burials, including those not osteologically sexed, with jewellery in Scotland, compared to 64% in Møre og Romsdal in Norway, 'suggesting that their use and display could have been of greater significance in a settler context' (Norstein 2022: 139). Frida Espolin Norstein (2022: 145) suggests that 'Norse women could have been imperative for the maintenance of traditions' in Scotland. If true, this is particularly interesting as this prominent display of Scandinavian culture and traditions were being undertaken by women who had not necessarily grown up in Scandinavia.

In England, in addition to isotope analysis we have some information on Viking women migrating in the *Anglo-Saxon Chronicle*. As noted above, we are informed that women were part of the Viking armies that arrived in the 890s, while some female burials belong to the earlier 'great army' of 865–878. In England, more Viking skeletons have been tested for their origins, but only two of those were women. A woman buried in the mass burial at Repton, Derbyshire, dated to the wintering of the great army in 873–874, grew up in either mid-Continental or Baltic Europe (Budd *et al.* 2004: 137–138). A woman buried wearing a pair of oval brooches at Adwick-le-Street, south Yorkshire, probably grew up in the Trondheim area of Norway, or possibly north-east Scotland (Speed and Walton Rogers 2004: 62–63). On the Isle of Man, a male 'warrior' burial plus two men and two women at the St Patrick's Isle cemetery, including the richly furnished Viking woman mentioned above, have been tested and none of them was local, although the authors of the study do not suggest where they migrated from (Symonds *et al.* 2014: 14–17). The available results from across the study area highlight the mobility of adults during the Viking Age, including women. The results from Scotland in particular encourage us to consider migration within the insular world, and how the culture in which the immigrants grew up, including the language, may have been different to that of people migrating directly from Scandinavia (McLeod 2018: 27–28).

The female burials dating to the conquests and settlements of the great army in England highlight other important roles for Viking women, including agents of acculturation and negotiation, and possibly that of warriors. Some of the female burials from Scotland have been dated to a similar late 9th century date as those in England, meaning that those women were also likely to have been part of the conquest and early settlement process (Graham-Campbell and Batey 1998: 74; Sellevold 1999: table 1). As noted above, the Viking women buried on the Isle of Man are thought to be later than the male burials in the mound, other than possibly a recently found female burial that has yet to be fully published. Until publication it cannot be certain that Viking women were present during the conquest and earliest settlement of Man. Viking settlement in Wales remains uncertain.

Fortunately, the written sources from England provide further information on where the women, and children, were: some were inside a Viking fort soon after a fleet landed in England in 893, making it almost certain that they arrived as part of that Viking army; later, those and/or different women remained in the Viking controlled kingdom of East Anglia while the rest of the army continued its attacks (Swanton 2000: 86, 88, 89). It would seem that these women were non-combatants, especially as children were reported to have been with them each time they are mentioned. Although the same written sources, the *Anglo-Saxon Chronicle* and Asser's *Life of King Alfred*, do not mention Viking women in connection with the army that had arrived in 865, burial evidence from Heath Wood and the Repton mass burial demonstrates that they were present (Swanton 2000; Keynes and Lapidge 1983; Budd *et al.* 2004: 137–138; Richards *et al.* 2004: 91). This makes the silence of the written sources on the presence of women in the earlier invasion somewhat curious. A likely explanation is that the writers, who were based in the kingdom of Wessex in southern England, were unaware of their presence. After arriving in East Anglia in 865, the great army conquered York the following year, leaving a compliant local in charge while most of the army continued to campaign (Swanton 2000: 68; McLeod 2014: 177–180). By the time that Wessex was first invaded in 870, the Viking army had also conquered the kingdom of East Anglia, again leaving a client king in charge (Swanton 2000: 70; McLeod 2014: 181). Therefore, there were two Viking controlled kingdoms in England before Wessex was invaded and the writers of our sources gained first-hand knowledge of the Viking army and, as happened in the 890s, women and children may have been amongst those Vikings who stayed in the conquered kingdoms, as reported in two later sources (McLeod 2014: 195–196). If this were the case, Viking women were ideally placed to observe local customs even before the formal Viking settlement of England began, making them an important part of the acculturation process, and raising the possibility that some were involved in negotiations between the Vikings and local leaders. Once formal Viking settlement of England began in 876 (Swanton 2000: 74), Viking women who had spent years in the conquered kingdoms living alongside Anglo-Saxons are likely to have been better suited to settling alongside Anglo-Saxon neighbours than those Vikings who had spent most of the decade fighting them.

However, Viking women who arrived as part of the great army did not necessarily spend all their time in conquered kingdoms during the campaigning period. The great army often spent the winter months in a camp that probably also acted as a trading emporium, as suggested by excavations at the site of the 872–873 winter camp near Torksey, Lincolnshire (Hadley and Richards 2016). The Torksey site has some ambiguous evidence for the presence of women in the form of textile equipment (Hadley and Richards 2016: 54–55). Another site that may be the camp of the great army under the command of Halfdan in Scotland in 874–875, located close to Loch Lomond, north of Glasgow in Scotland, has definite evidence for women in the form of burials (Swanton 2000: 72, 74; McGregor 2009; McLeod 2015: 12–13; Batey 2023). Consequently, it is likely that even if many Viking women were not travelling with the army on a regular basis, they still re-united with them periodically. As well as the emotional fulfilment of seeing friends and loved ones, this would have provided the opportunity for the women to share information on the politics and culture of the kingdoms in which they had been staying.

In Scotland, it was noted above that all the women whose childhood homes had been determined had migrated from other parts of Britain and Ireland. Along with men from those areas, this would have made the women important agents in the acculturation process in their new homes, especially in comparison to those men who had grown up in Scandinavia. Although there were great regional differences within Britain and Ireland at the time, there were still more similarities between them than there was with Scandinavia, including Christianity and, for much of the area, a Celtic language, be it Gaelic, Manx, Welsh/Cymraeg, or Pictish. People migrating from other areas of Britain and Ireland would have been more able to understand the people and culture of the area they settled into.

So far female non-combatants have been discussed but it is possible that Viking warrior women were active in Britain. Three female burials with weapons are recorded in England, all of whom were possibly members of the great army, but unfortunately all the burials are problematic. The cremation burial of a woman and unsexed child under a mound at Heath Wood, Derbyshire, contained a sword and shield, but cremation makes it more difficult to assign sex, plus the weapons may have accompanied the child (Richards *et al.* 2004: 91). At Bedale, Yorkshire, an unsexed inhumation with *in situ* oval brooches was discovered with a spear head, but although the oval brooches make it likely that the burial was of a woman, the spear head does not survive and may have been misidentified (Anon 1848; McLeod 2019: 82, 85–86). Finally, an unsexed inhumation at Santon Downham, Norfolk, was discovered with a sword and oval brooches, but it is not certain if the brooches were in the grave or nearby (Evison 1969; McLeod 2019: 82, 85–86). To these three may be added the weapons found in the mass burial of at least 264 people at Repton, Derbyshire, dated to the great army's winter camp of 873–874, with 18% of the sexed bones belonging to females, including the one mentioned above who had possibly grown up in mid-Continental or Baltic Europe (Biddle and Kjølbye-Biddle 2001: 68, 74; Budd *et al.* 2004: 137–138; Jarman 2021: 140–144). Any of these burials may be of female warriors, but none is certain, and the failure of the primary written sources to mention female warriors is surprising (McLeod 2019: 86–87). Later, the 10th or 11th century mass burial in Dorset, thought to be of a Viking raiding party, contained no women (Loe 2020). In addition to their absence in primary sources and the problematic burial record, it has recently been suggested that Viking amulets and figurines may depict ritual performances, with women with weapons representing transgression of gender roles (Deckers *et al.* 2021). If this is true of armed women shown in jewellery, it could also be true of armed women found in burials, with such women perhaps being ritual specialists rather than warriors. Although warrior women operating in Britain remains a possibility, if they did, their numbers were presumably low enough that we do not, thus far, have definitive proof for their existence (McLeod 2019).

If Deckers *et al.* (2021) are correct in their interpretation of armed women depicted on amulets and figurines being ritual specialists, it augments our evidence for the roles played by Viking women. Some of the figures discussed by the authors are found in the areas of Scandinavian settlement in eastern England following the conquests of the great army, and therefore probably date to the late 9th and early 10th centuries (Deckers *et al.* 2021: fig. 6). As the authors posit that the jewellery was worn by ritual specialists during ceremonial occasions, it suggests that some Viking women living in England were ritual specialists.[3] Such women may have been important members of the household performing domestic cult practices, or performing rituals for a community, such as the old woman presiding over a funeral on the Volga described by Ibn Fadlan (Deckers *et al.* 2021). This notion of women and cult may also relate to the woman buried with the Thor's hammer in Scotland discussed above (Patterson 2021: 325–326). Similarly, the rich mid-10th century female burial at Peel included a metre-long iron rod, considered by some scholars to be a *seiðr*-staff noted in other burials and thought to have been used in the performance of magic rituals, making it possible that the woman buried at Peel was an important ritual specialist (Gardeła 2014: 36; this volume). In addition, a Manx runestone, Kirk Michael VII, has an image of a cloaked figure interpreted as a woman holding a long, unusually shaped staff, which may represent a sorceress using a *seiðr*-staff (Gardeła 2014: 36; Barnes 2019: 197, 331). Unfortunately, the brief fragment of text preserved on the runestone does not help to explain the imagery, which also includes a tethered horse (Barnes 2019: 197–199, 331). Although the length of the iron rod at Peel may seem overly long for an implement of magic or power, the image of the figure with a similarly long staff lends credence to the notion that the woman at Peel was buried with a *seiðr*-staff. This evidence is likely to represent recent Viking arrivals to those areas (confirmed with the woman in the Manx burial) who brought their culture with them, including the role of ritual specialist. But as there is no evidence for Viking women continuing in this role over the generations after settlement, it is possible that the role disappeared during the acculturation process, or was adapted to fit into local, Christian, norms.

To the possible ritual specialists/sorceresses indicated by the figurines in eastern England and the *seiðr*-staffs found in a burial and on a runestone in the Isle of Man, can be added the written mention of a valkyrie operating in England by Archbishop Wulfstan. As noted above, the text of the sermon Wulfstan belongs to *c.* 1010–1014, the period immediately prior to the Dane Knut becoming king of England, and therefore generations later than the other pieces of evidence for Viking women acting as ritual specialists in Britain. As such, Wulfstan's mention of *wælcerian* is likely to be a re-introduction of sorceresses from Scandinavia rather than evidence for continuing practice in Britain. Although a *wælcerian*/valkyrie was a female mythological being associated with battle for pre-Christian Scandinavians, Wulfstan appears to be referring to real people when he refers to *wiccan and wælcerian* (Anderson and Williams 1963: 215) or, in Whitelock's translation (1955: 859), 'wizards and sorceresses', as they appear in a list of people despoiling the country, including robbers, murderers, and perjurers (Whitelock 1955: 858–859). Consequently, Wulfstan appears to be saying that the recently arrived Vikings attacking England included male and female magic practitioners, despite Knut and Denmark having been Christian since the time of his grandfather, Harald Bluetooth. However, Knut's army also included Vikings from Sweden and Norway, neither of which was completely Christian at the time (Lund 1997: 170–171; Meulengracht Sørensen 1997: 218–220). Although Wulfstan does not say what the Viking magicians were doing, they were clearly active in some way, and as the women are described as valkyries, their activities were presumably involved with the Viking armies that they were part of.

This paper has provided a glimpse of the activities Viking women undertook in Britain beyond the roles of mother, wife, and housekeeper. We have evidence for adults being highly mobile during the Viking Age, with most Vikings not being buried in the same region in which they grew up. For England, we have evidence for women arriving as part of armies, conquering areas before settling, and this also appears to be what happened in Scotland. Consequently, women were part of the conquests and initial land settlements, and it has been argued that they played an important role in the acculturation process, especially those women who are migrated from other parts of Britain and Ireland. Based on the grave-goods buried with women, it appears that they were wealthy and held significant status, and the esteem in which some individual women were held is apparent from the runic corpus. With regards to specific roles, we have evidence for a female rune carver, women practising forms of magic, including with armies, and contested evidence for some women warriors. It is evident that Viking women could, and did, step out of the confines of the purely domestic sphere on occasions in Britain.

**Notes**

1 'Viking' is used as it fits with the title of the book, although 'Scandinavian', 'culturally Scandinavian', or 'Norse' would be equally appropriate. The use of 'viking' is not meant to imply that all 'viking women' were pirates and went on raiding expeditions, although some may have.

2 The unsexed person in the boat burial on the Ardnamurchan peninsula may have grown up in 'eastern Ireland, north-eastern mainland Scotland, Norway and Sweden' (Harris *et al.* 2017: 200).

3 Thus far, the only part of Britain where these amulets and figurines have been found is eastern England.

## Bibliography

Alexander, M.L., 1987. A 'Viking Age' grave from Cambois, Bedlington, Northumberland. *Medieval Archaeology* 31: 101–105.

Anderson, M. and Colton Williams, B., 1963. *Old English Handbook*. Houghton Mifflin Co, Cambridge MA.

Anon., 1848. Archaeological intelligence – Anglo-Saxon period. *Archaeological Journal* 5: 220.

Barnes, M.P., 2019. *The Runic Inscriptions of the Isle of Man*. Institutionen för nordiska spark, Uppsala universitet, Uppsala.

Barnes, M.P. and Page R.I., 2006. *The Scandinavian Runic Inscriptions of Britain*. Institutionen för nordiska spark, Uppsala universitet, Uppsala.

Batey, C.E., 2023. Carrick, Mid Ross: A Viking Cemetery on Loch Lomond. In *The Viking Age in Scotland: Studies in Scottish Scandinavian archaeology*, eds T. Horne, E. Pierce and R. Barrowman. Edinburgh University Press, Edinburgh: 313–321.

Biddle, M. and Kjølbye-Biddle, B., 2001. Repton and the 'Great Heathen Army', 873–4. In *Vikings and the Danelaw*, eds J. Graham-Campbell, R. Hall, J. Jesch and D.N. Parsons. Oxbow Books, Oxford: 45–96.

Broderick, G., 1995. *The Chronicles of the Kings of Mann and the Isles*. Manx National Heritage, Douglas.

Budd, P., Millard, A., Chenery, C., Lucy, S. and Roberts, C., 2004. Investigating Population movement by stable isotope analysis: A report from Britain. *Antiquity* 78: 127–141.

Cipirska, I., 2021. Discovery of historic brooches over 1,000 years old reveal that female Vikings settled on Isle of Man. *inews.co.uk*. https://inews.co.uk/news/vikings-female-settled-isle-of-man-discovery-historic-brooches-1358498,

Clover, C.J., 1993. Regardless of sex: Men, women, and power in early Northern Europe. *Speculum* 68.2: 363–387.

Deckers, P., Croix, S. and Sinbæk, S., 2021. Assembling the full cast: Ritual performance, gender transgression and iconographic innovation in Viking-Age Ribe. *Medieval Archaeology* 65.1: 30–65.

Dunwell, A.J., Cowie, T.G., Bruce, M.F., Neighbour, T. and Rees, A.R., 1995. A Viking Age cemetery at Cnip, Uig, Isle of Lewis. *Proceedings of the Society of Antiquities of Scotland* 125: 719–752.

Evison, V.I., 1969. A Viking grave at Sonning, Berks. *Antiquaries Journal* 49: 333–335.

Gardeła, L., 2014. Viking death rituals on the Isle of Man. In *Viking Myths and Rituals on the Isle of Man*, eds L. Gardeła and C. Lamington. Centre for the Study of the Viking Age, University of Nottingham, Nottingham: 30–38.

Godden, M., 1994. Apocalypse and invasion in Late Anglo-Saxon England. In *From Anglo-Saxon to Early Middle English: Studies Presented to E.G. Stanley*, eds M. Godden, D. Grey and T. Hood. Clarendon Press, Oxford: 143–152.

Graham-Campbell, J. and Batey, C.E., 1998. *Vikings in Scotland. An Archaeological Survey*. Edinburgh University Press, Edinburgh.

Hadley, D.M., and Richards, J.D., 2016. The Winter camp of the Viking Great Army, AD 872–3, Torksey, Lincolnshire. *Antiquaries Journal* 96: 23–67.

Harris, O.J.T., Cobb, H., Batey, C.E., Montgomery, J., Beaumont, J., Gray, H., Murtagh, P. and Richardson, P., 2017. Assembling places and persons: A tenth-century Viking boat burial from Swordle Bay on the Ardnamurchan peninsula, western Scotland. *Antiquity* 91(355): 191–206. https://doi:10.15184/aqy.2016.222.

Hill, P., 1997. *Whithorn and St Ninian: The excavation of a monastic town 1984-1991*. Sutton, Stroud.

Hudson, B.T., 1998. The Scottish Chronicle. *Scottish Historical Review* 77: 129–161.

Ithel, J.W.A., 1965. *Annales Cambriae*. Kraus Reprint, Wiesbaden.

Jarman, C., 2021. *River Kings. The Vikings from Scandinavia to the Silk Roads*. William Collins, London.

Jesch, J., 1991. *Women in the Viking Age*. Boydell, Woodbridge.

Jesch, J., 2021. Women in the Viking Age. *That Jorvik Thing Podcast* 16 February: https://www.jorvikthing.com/podcasts,

Jochens, J., 1995. *Women in Old Norse Society*. Cornell University Press, Ithaca NY.

Kershaw, J.F., 2009. Culture and gender in the Danelaw: Scandinavian and Anglo-Saxon brooches. *Viking and Medieval Scandinavia* 5: 295–325.

Kershaw, J.F., 2022. Women as bearers of cultural tradition in Viking-Age England. In *Vikings Across Boundaries. Viking-Age Transformations* vol. 2, eds H.L. Aannestad, U. Pedersen, M. Moen, E.Neumann and H. Lund Berg. Routledge, London: 99–114.

Keynes, S. and Lapidge, M., 1983. *Alfred the Great. Asser's Life of King Alfred and Other Contemporary Sources*. Penguin, London.

Loe, L., 2020. Supplementary information: Ridgeway Hill Mass Grave, Dorset, for A. Margaryan, D.J. Lawson, M. Sikora, F. Racimo, S. Rasmussen, I. Miltke *et al.*: Population genomics of the Viking world. *Nature* 585: 390–396. Doi: 10.1038/s41586-020-2688-8.

Low, D.M., Batey, C.E. and Gourlay, R., 2000. A Viking burial at Balnakeil, Sutherland. In *The Province of Strathnaver*, eds J.R. Baldwin. Scottish Society for Northern Studies, Edinburgh: 24–34.
Lund, N., 1997. The Danish Empire and the end of the Viking Age. In *The Oxford Illustrated History of the Vikings*, ed. P. Sawyer. Oxford University Press, Oxford: 156–181.
McGregor, G., 2009. Changing people changing landscapes: Excavation at The Carrick, Midross, Loch Lomond. *Historic Argyll* 1: 11.
McLeod, S., 2011. Warriors and women: The sex ratio of Norse migrants to eastern England up to 900 AD. *Early Medieval Europe* 19.3: 332–353.
McLeod, S., 2014. *The Beginning of Scandinavian Settlement in England: The Viking 'Great Army' and early settlers, c. 865-900*. Brepols, Turnhout.
McLeod, S., 2015. The *dubh gall* in southern Scotland: the politics of Northumbria, Dublin and the Community of St Cuthbert in the Viking Age, *c.* 870–950 CE. *Limina* 20.3: 1–21.
McLeod, S., 2018. Gender and mobility in Viking-Age Scotland. In *Gender and Mobility in Scotland and Abroad*, eds S. Dye, E. Ewan and A. Glaze. University of Guelph, Guelph: 13–30.
McLeod, S., 2019. Shieldmaidens in Anglo-Saxon England: Historical possibility or wishful thinking? In *Vikings and the Vikings: Essays on television's History Channel series*, eds P. Hardwick and K. Lister. McFarland & Company, Jefferson: 77–92.
Meulengracht Sørensen, P., 1997. Religions old and new. In *The Oxford Illustrated History of the Vikings*, ed. P. Sawyer. Oxford University Press, Oxford: 202–224.
Montgomery, J. and Evans, J.A., 2006. Immigrants on the Isle of Lewis: Combining traditional funerary and modern isotopic evidence to investigate social differentiation, migration and dietary change in the Outer Hebrides of Scotland. In *Social Archaeology of Funerary Remains*, eds R. Gowland and C. Knüsel. Oxbow Books, Oxford: 122–42.
Montgomery, J., Grimes, V., Buckberry, J., Evans, J.A., Richards, M.P. and Barrett, J.H., 2014. Finding Vikings with isotope analysis: The view from the wet and windy islands. *Viking Settlers of the North Atlantic: An isotopic approach. Journal of the North Atlantic* Special Volume 7: 54–70.
Norstein, F.E., 2022. Displaying and (re)negotiating identities: Migration and funerary rites in Viking-Age northern Scotland. In *Vikings Across Boundaries. Viking-Age Transformations* Vol. II, eds H.L. Aannestad, U. Pedersen, M. Moen, E.Neumann and H. Lund Berg. Routledge, London: 129–150.
Owen, O. and Dalland, M., 1999. *Scar: A Viking boat burial on Sanday, Orkney*. Sutton, East Linton.
Patterson, C., 2021. Dress and dress fasteners from the Pagan Norse graves of Scotland: Origins and identity. *Scottish Historical Review* C3.254: 314–334.
Patterson, C., Parsons, A.J., Newman, R.M., Johnson, N., Howard Davis, C., 2014. *Shadows in the Sand: Excavation of a Viking-Age cemetery at Cumwhitton, Cumbria*. Oxford Archaeology North, Lancaster.
Redknap, M., 2000. *Vikings in Wales. An Archaeological Quest*. National Museums and Galleries of Wales, Cardiff.
Redknap, M., 2020. Supplementary material: Glyn, Llanbedrgoch, Anglesey: for A. Margaryan, D.J. Lawson, M. Sikora, F. Racimo, S. Rasmussen, I. Miltke *et al.*: Population genomics of the Viking world. *Nature: International weekly journal of science* 585: 390–396. Doi: 10.1038/s41586-020-2688-8.
Redmond, A.Z., 2007. *Viking burial in the north of england: a study of contact, interaction and reaction between scandinavian migrants with resident groups, and the effect of immigration on aspects of cultural continuity*. British Archaeological Report 429, Oxford.
Richards, J.D., 2011. Anglo-Scandinavian identity. In *The Oxford Handbook of Anglo-Saxon Archaeology*, eds H. Hamerow, D.A. Hinton and S. Crawford. Oxford University Press, Oxford: 46–61.
Richards, J.D., Beswick, P., Bond, J., Jecock, M., McKinley, J.I., Rowland, S. and Worley, F., 2004. Excavations at the Viking barrow cemetery at Heath Wood, Ingleby, Derbyshire. *Antiquaries Journal* 84, 23–116.
Ritchie, A., 1976–1977. Excavations of Pictish and Viking-age farmsteads at Buckquoy, Orkney. *Proceedings of the Society of Antiquaries of Scotland* 108: 174–227.

Sanmark, A., 2024. An examination of the concepts of sex and gender and their application to Viking-Age and Old Norse society. In *Women of the Past, Issues for the Present*, eds N.J. Koefoed and R. Raja. Brepols, Turnhout: 83–98.

Sellevold, B.J., 1999. *Picts and Vikings at Westness: Anthropological investigations of the skeletal material from the cemetery at Westness, Rousay, Orkney Islands.* NIKU Scientific Report 010, Oslo.

Speed, G., and Walton Rogers, P., 2004. A burial of a Viking woman at Adwick-le-Street, South Yorkshire. *Medieval Archaeology* 48: 51–90.

Swanton, M., 2000. *The Anglo-Saxon Chronicles.* Phoenix Press, London.

Symonds, L., Price, T.D., Keenleyside, A. and Burton, J., 2014. Medieval migrations: Isotope analysis of early medieval skeletons on the Isle of Man. *Medieval Archaeology* 58: 1–20.

Welander, R.D.E., Batey, C.E. and Cowie, T.G., 1987. A Viking burial from Kneep, Uig, Isle of Lewis. *Proceedings of the Society of Antiquaries of Scotland* 117: 149–174.

Whitelock, D., 1955. *English Historical Documents, c. 500–1042.* Eyre & Spottiswoode, London.

Wilson, D.M., 2008 *The Vikings in the Isle of Man.* Aarhus University Press, Aarhus.

# Chapter 4

## Women in trade and exchange

*Unn Pedersen*

In 1870–1871 a small assemblage of Viking Age objects, found at the farm Haugen in Hedrum, Vestfold, Norway, came to the University of Oslo's 'collection of old things' (*Universitetets samling af nordiske oldsager*). A weight, two silver pendants, three silver coins, and a silver arm ring were found between a pair of oval brooches, the arm ring squeezed together in order to fit into the hollow space between the brooches which were placed back to back (Ab. 1870: 81–82; C5305-6, C5357-9). In other words, the iconic brooches, worn by many Scandinavian women across the Viking world, were used as a container, holding and hiding different types of items related to trade and exchange. Viking Age weights were used in a bullion economy where cut silver, including fragments of arm rings and coins, were valued by weight (e.g. Hårdh 1996; 2008; Pedersen 2008). Oval brooches are often found in burials, where they frequently form a part of the deceased's dress. In this case, however, the short report clearly states that there were no traces of a grave, and a hoard is therefore the most likely interpretation (Ab. 1870: 81; Brøgger 1921: 84). Nevertheless, the oval brooches themselves seem to have been used in someone's life (Fig. 4.1), showing clear signs of wear and tear (Pedersen 2022). The brooches were similar, of the same type, although not identical, in line with many pairs of oval brooches found in graves (Petersen 1928; Norstein 2020). The discovery brought to light a message of a close relationship between women and economy, though this was not the story told by antiquarians or archaeologists in the late 19th century, nor indeed in larger parts of the 20th.

The objects themselves were widely publicised. They came into the collection at a time when the discipline of archaeology was being established in Norway and the museum was moving towards a more systematic way of collecting, cataloguing, and dating objects. The weight alone was depicted already in the 1870 annual report presenting the find (Ab.1870: pl. iv, fig. 21). It was then selected for illustration (Fig. 4.2), along with the oval brooches and one of the pendants, for the highly influential publication *Norske Oldsager* ('Norwegian Old Things'), still frequently used as a reference work today (Rygh 1885: figs 478; 655 and 678). The brief report described the connection between these objects. However, at the time and for many years to come, the obvious message from this hoard, visualising the close connection between female gender identity and economic activities, escaped everyone's attention. Instead, over the next century, other stories were told about economic agency, using a different vocabulary – highlighting trades*men*, as opposed to tradeswomen, foregrounding male involvement in trade as opposed to female involvement.

*Figure 4.1. The oval brooches from Haugen (photo: Ellen C. Holte © Museum of Cultural History, University of Oslo).*

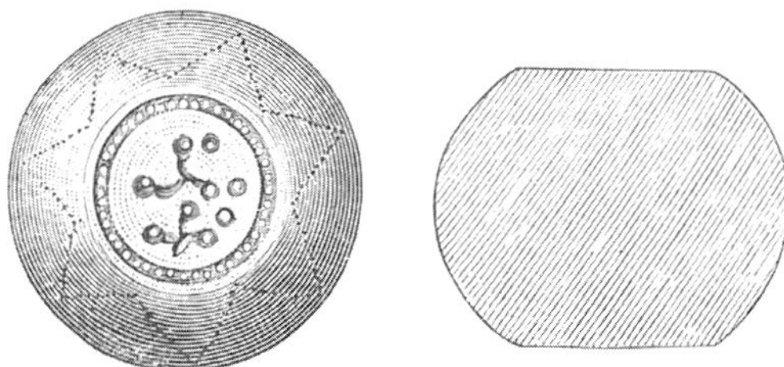

*Figure 4.2. The weight from Haugen (drawing from Rygh 1885: fig. 478).*

This paper will first look at the period when women were re-introduced into the narrative as actors in trade, continuing on to discuss what happened next. I will then assess where we stand today, returning to the hoard from Haugen, using it as a way to explore women's role in Viking Age trade and exchange, anchoring the discussion geographically to Vestfold, where the hoard was found. The terms 'woman' and 'man' as used in this chapter are social constructions, reflecting a pattern generated from objects found in the burials of wealthy people. Many persons fell outside these narrow categories, or may have moved in and out of them, and I do not take for granted that gender roles and identities necessarily equal biological sex (in itself more complex than male/female).

## 'Were they all men?'

'Tradesman' (Norw. *handelsmann* or *kjøpmann*) is a concept frequently found in scholarly and popular Scandinavian publications on the Viking Age, especially throughout the 20th century (Stalsberg 1987; 1991a; 1991b). Sometimes it is deliberately used to highlight the gender of the buried person (e.g. Brøgger 1936: 77), while in other cases, gender is taken for granted, assuming that persons involved in Viking Age trade were men (e.g. Blindheim 1971: 16). In the 1970s, following in the trend of feminist archaeology around the globe, such presumptions were being challenged in Scandinavia, as a result of a growing interest in women's roles in the past, and in research. The workshop *Var de alle menn?* held in 1979, published as *Were They All Men? An Examination of Sex Roles in Prehistoric Society* (1987) illustrates the increased gender awareness in Norwegian archaeology, even before the term 'gender' was known to the ones involved (Mandt 1992: 87). One of the aims of the workshop was to find the individual in prehistory; women, men, children, and adults. This new direction met with resistance from a more conservative branch of scholarship, and it was challenging to get the papers published. This in turn motivated the foundation of the journal (and organisation) *K.A.N. Kvinner i arkeologi i Norge* ('Women in Archaeology in Norway'). *K.A.N.* aimed at raising awareness around the working conditions of female archaeologists and producing new knowledge of women in the past (Bertelsen *et al.* 1987: 11–12; Engelstad *et al.*, 1992: 70–71; Mandt 1992: 88–89).

Anne Stalsberg (1987; 1991a; 1991b), who gave a paper at the 1979 workshop, played a key role in challenging the terminology related to trade, highlighting the discrepancy between the masculine terms of *handelsmann* and *kjøpmann* and women's graves with weights and/or balances in Russia, Norway, and the urban site of Birka. Her point of departure was that such tools were connected to trade and could be used both by traders and their customers, although also serving other functions, including the collecting of taxes (Stalsberg 1987: 98). Clarifying that most graves were gendered based on grave goods due to the lack of skeletons and adding the premise that grave goods belonged to the buried person, as frequently assumed in archaeology, she argued that it was false to explain away or neglect weighing equipment in women's graves, as several researchers had done (Stalsberg 1991a: 47–48). She further introduced the concept of *tradeswoman* to accompany tradesmen, while acknowledging that both concepts might be misleading, and that it might be more correct to envision trading households, including women, taking actively part in trade (Stalsberg 1991a; 1991b). Questioning the frequently used androcentric terminology and masculine depiction of people involved in trade, Stalsberg demonstrated that it was crude to assume that Viking Age trade was restricted to men. Inspired by her own investigation of Scandinavian graves in Russia and adding a gender perspective to earlier studies (Arbman 1943; Jondell 1974), she pinpointed that 32% of the graves with weights from Birka can be estimated as women's graves based on the artefacts, as opposed to 28% men's graves (Table 4.1). Likewise that 17% of the graves from Norway with balances were women's graves and 81% men's graves (Stalsberg 1991b: 78–79). She highlighted that such tools are also found in some children's graves, including those of girls, and graves with multiple occupants, most often a man and a woman (1991a: 47). Stalsberg consequently argued that 'trading was not a gendered role' (1991a: 45), much in line with Haakon Shetelig (1912: 175), who long before described weights and balances as something men and women had in common. Stalsberg concluded that a Scandinavian

Viking Age woman could be an important partner in an economic unit, not merely serving such a role in her husband's absence, or as a widow, as previously suggested. Her works undoubtedly provide a thought provoking context for the Haugen hoard.

## Stalsberg's impact

When reading research literature from the last 30–40 years, Stalsberg's works have had a significant impact (e.g. Pedersen 2000; 2001; Moen 2011; 2019a; Løkka 2014; Sørheim 2014), and at first sight it appears to have had an immediate effect. There is, for example, a noteworthy change of terminology in Charlotte Blindheim's influential works when comparing her publications from the '70s, in which she uses masculine terms for traders, with her work from 1981, where she questions such terms. On closer inspection, however, her line of argument is in striking contrast to Stalsberg's:

> it would be tempting to see our graves with weights as the graves of tradesmen, if we did not have the situation at Birka to take into account, where weights are not infrequently found in women's graves as we learned above. In this case one could of course have argued for a tradesman's wife, but then we are on shaky grounds.[1] (Blindheim 1981: 119, my translation)

So, instead of accepting women's involvement in trade, following Stalsberg, she dismisses even her former interpretation that men with the same objects were traders. Intriguingly her line of reasoning is quite similar to the more recent Birka warrior debate, where the sexing of a warrior as female based on DNA (Hedenstierna-Jonson *et al.* 2017) led researchers who otherwise have used artefact based gendering to question the method due to the unexpected result (Moen 2019b: 212–214; Price *et al.* 2019 with references).

On closer inspection it is actually more likely that Blindheim's insight into the Birka burials came from a different angle. She had no reference to Stalsberg's presentation at the *Were They All Men* workshop about tradeswomen,[2] but referred instead to Ola Kyhlberg's study on the weights from Birka, building on the same dataset as Stalsberg and therefore presenting roughly the same proportion of men's and women's graves with weights, without an explicit discussion on gender roles (Kyhlberg 1980: 202–203, 294–297). Moreover, Blindheim (1993: 64) was in fact quite explicit in rejecting feminism in archaeology, as stated in an article commissioned by *K.A.N.*

More generally, there has been a shift in terminology in Viking Age scholarship towards the gender neutral term 'traders'. Still, there seems to be a divide between works where the gender neutral terminology is used in order to acknowledge that both men and women were involved in trade, or that we do not always know the gender of persons involved in trade, versus those where an implicit androcentric gender perspective still materialises when looking closely at the context, with combinations such as 'craftsman or trader', 'craftsmen or traders' (Skre 2007: 451–457). One might, in these cases, wonder whether the apparent adaptation of Stalsberg's perspectives reflect the shift in research language witnessed in the last few decades: the most common words for people involved in trade have (had) a masculine connotation in Norwegian and are gender neutral in English (merchant/trader), as pointed out by Stalsberg (1991a; 1991b). However, the gender equality movement has, in recent decades, fostered a change in Norwegian terminology and today many, within and outside academia and in the public sector, avoid misleading terms and replace them with gender neutral words where appropriate, in this particular case *handelsfolk* (tradespeople) *or handlende* (traders).

## Men after all?

The fact that terms such as *kjøpmenn*, *handelsmenn*, and more rarely tradesmen, are still used in Viking Age research without further discussion of the gender implication (e.g. Jón Viðar Sigurðsson 1999: 42, 50; 2017: 159; Skre 2000; 2012), underlines that masculine undertones still linger. Strikingly enough such masculine terms even remain in use when discussing weights from Birka (Mikkelsen 2002: 106) where the link to women is unquestionable, and when referring to what has generally been acknowledged as a woman's grave with weights (Vike 2016: 113 on C30539, see below). Burials with a balance are still interpreted as men's graves by some, building on the fact that balances are most frequently found in men's graves, while neglecting women's burials with such an item. In 2011 three new graves with weighing equipment were found during the excavation of a large cemetery at Langeid, Bygland, Norway (Fig. 4.3), all dated to the late 10th–early 11th century, none of them with preserved bodies and they were gendered based on artefacts. The first, grave 6, contains two sickles and two strike-a-lights, and was on this premise interpreted as an inhumation grave for two persons. A needle-case and a pair of tweezers were taken to indicate a woman (noting that an axe could be of a type also found in women's graves). A large whetstone and trading equipment in the form of a balance, five weights, and cut coins were interpreted as the belongings of a man, a *handelsmann* (Wenn 2016: Tab. 50, 33, 35, 182, 203). Likewise grave 20 was interpreted as a man' grave, on grounds of coins, two weights, and a long whetstone (Wenn 2016: Tab. 50, 109–112, 182). Grave 18, with three weights, was interpreted as the inhumation burial of a man based on a sword, with a slightly later cremation burial containing a pair of oval brooches wrapped in textile and placed over the human bones. The sex was impossible to determine and this burial was gendered as a woman's grave due to the brooches (Wenn 2016: Tab. 50, 182). The wrapped oval

*Table 4.1. Graves with weighing equipment as presented in Stalsberg (1991b, building on Jondell 1974 and Arbman 1943), with a further calculation**

| | *Women* | *Men* | *Couples* | *Not identified* |
|---|---|---|---|---|
| Russia (37 graves) | 22% | 48% | 30% | |
| Birka (132 graves) | 32% | 28% | 3% | 37% |
| Norway (47 gendered graves with scales) | 17% | 81% | 2% | |
| Norway (63 graves with scales)* | 13% | 60% | 2% | 25% |

brooches make an interesting parallel to the Haugen hoard and I will return to this. Another two contemporary graves at the same site with coins were interpreted as for men, grave 8 based on weapons, and grave 15 merely on the coins (Wenn 2016: 183, Tab. 150). The interpretations of the latter and grave 6 and 20 are doubtful given

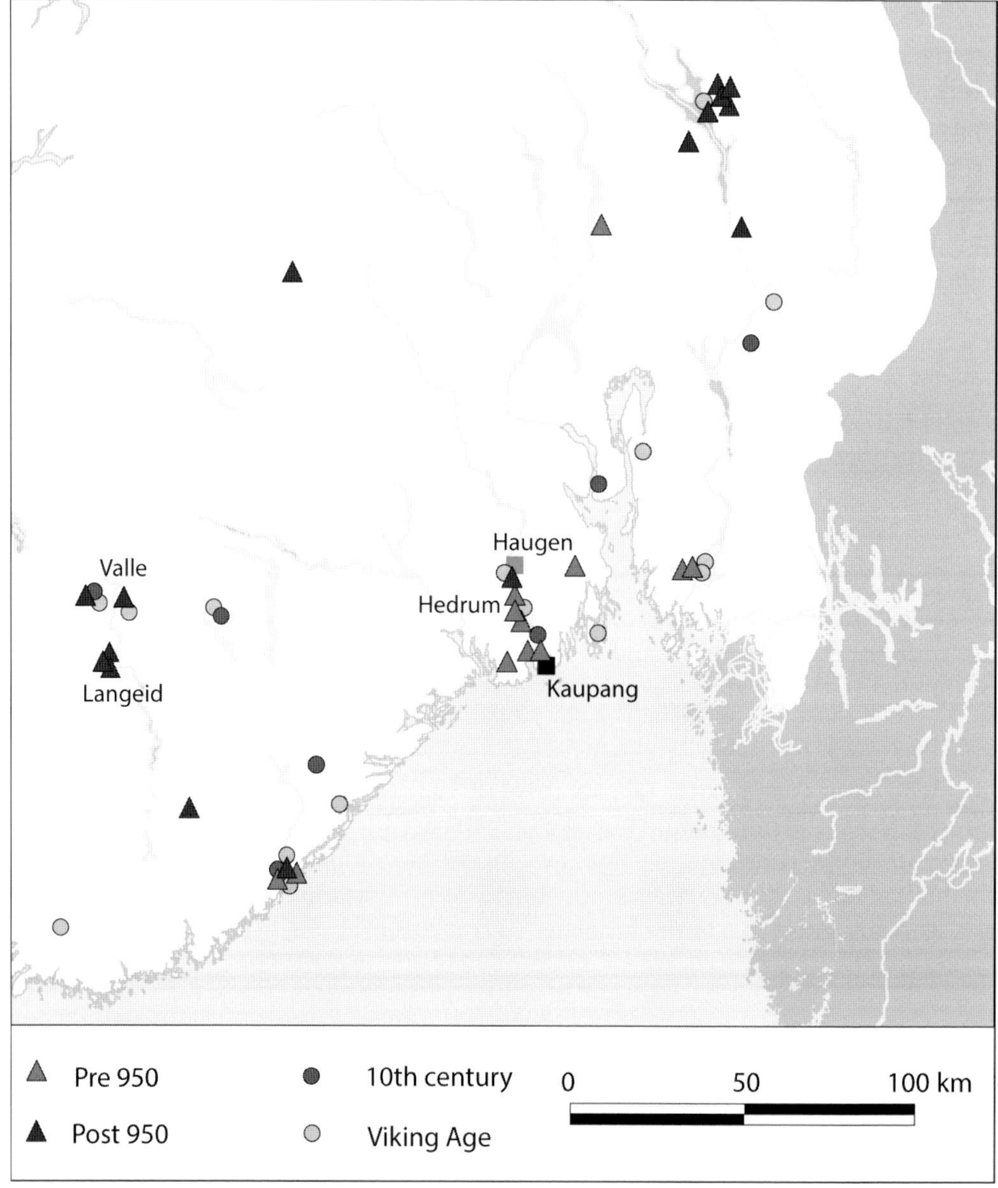


*Figure 4.3. Map of Viking Age graves in south-eastern Norway with weighing equipment (based on Pedersen 2008: fig. 6.14).*

the fact that coins, balances and weights actually occur in women's graves, while gendering based on long whetstones is unconventional, and unprecedented, as far as I know. These gendered interpretations from the open access excavation reports are nevertheless reproduced in a PhD thesis (Loftsgarden 2017: 240) and an international publication (Glørstad and Wenn 2017: Tab. 10.1), upholding a picture of trade taking place within a masculine sphere.

Applying a more generally accepted criteria for artefact based gender estimation along the man–woman model,[3] the picture of the Langeid graves with weighing equipment and/or coins gets more nuanced; one possible woman's grave (6), one man's grave (8), one burial containing a man with weights and a (slightly later?) woman's grave (18), and two graves (15, 20) neither to be classified in this way. However, the tendency of ignoring the connection between weighing equipment and women continues to impact interpretations of the site. Kjetil Loftsgarden (2017: 235–247) explicitly discusses the actors involved in trade under the headings *Bonde og handelsmann* ('farmer and tradesman') and *Handelskvinner* ('tradeswomen'). In the latter he brings in Stalsberg's works and Sæbjørg Walaker Nordeide's (2011: 186) discussion on a woman's grave along with three men's graves from Valle, close to Langeid, and states that the graves indicate a more nuanced gender distribution in late Viking Age trade than suggested by the saga literature and later descriptions. Having seemingly argued in favour of tradeswomen, he then declared: 'Still the finds show that one can hardly conclude that trade has been a female activity in Valle in this period' (Loftsgarden 2017: 240, my translation).[4] His surprising conclusion is based on his own trust in later written sources and the acceptance of the interpretations from the Langeid report (except grave 15, classified by him as indefinable and not a man's grave), while at the same time questioning a woman's grave from Valle (C30539) on the basis that it has a weapon-axe and also referring to the results from Langeid. His argument is, therefore, circular. However, the museum catalogue raises doubt on whether this specific axe belongs to the grave,[5] and I argue that it is more in line with established interpretations that a grave with a large number of beads suggest a woman (e.g. Solberg 1985: 65), rather than using weighing equipment and whetstones to assume a man. Still, his doubts surrounding the gender of this Valle grave may be relevant. Although recognised as a woman's grave for a long time, the grave contains some rather unusual copper alloy beads and I cannot exclude that they might link to three sets of straps, and fall into a different category than decorative beads worn as adornment. Nevertheless, another unquestionable woman's grave find with weights has been found in Valle (C1671–1672) and, due to some striking similarities with C30539, it has been suggested that both catalogue entries originate from the same grave, found in 1849. Accordingly, the link between women and economic agency could have been established by the research community even prior to the unearthing of the Haugen hoard.

No doubt, these uncertainties shed light on the challenges associated with grave material consisting of many 19th century accidental discoveries, but they apply equally to men's graves. In the Valle case one of them can actually be ruled out, due to the fact that what were originally interpreted as weights are in fact much later ammunition for firearms in a disturbed context, leaving us with two men's graves and one (or two) women's graves with weights. Whether one can draw conclusions on Viking Age society from much younger sources is a question under debate (for a critical discussion see Fredriksen and Amundsen 2014; Gjerpe 2014). Unlike Loftsgarden I do not find sources from the 16th and 17th century particularly relevant for making inferences on late Viking Age and early medieval social and economic relations. I will also add that I find it problematic to use late Viking Age texts uncritically when discussing the 9th century, due to the major shifts witnessed in the material record both in the 10th century (Solberg 1985) and the mid-11th century, following the official Christianisation and consolidation of royal power, which decidedly had a major and lasting impact on the identity and societal role of women (Mundal 2004). I will therefore follow up on Stalsberg's approach, using the Viking Age material record to discuss the roles of women in Viking Age trade and exchange. First, by returning to the weighing equipment in graves, and then by widening the scope, returning to the Haugen hoard and presenting its immediate and wider context in Vestfold, also bringing in settlement finds.

## Women and weighing equipment

When studying both weights and balances from south-eastern Norway two decades ago, and inspired by Stalsberg's work, I found that the overall pattern was the same as she had observed for balances from Norway (Pedersen 2000; 2001). The majority of gendered graves, 20 in total, excluding the urban site of Kaupang, could be classified as men's graves based on artefacts, while three or four could be classified as women's graves, although none of them with a balance. The find with the highest number of weights (21 or possibly 27), from Valle, could be a woman's grave, as discussed above. At the urban site of Kaupang, the two graves with balances were for men, while one out of the five graves with weighing equipment was for a woman. Although this is a higher proportion of women's graves compared to rural settings where most graves with weights belong to, it is considerably lower than the larger Viking Age town of Birka. Since my published study in 2001, a handful of graves with weighing equipment have been unearthed in south-eastern Norway, including the graves from Langeid (Gjerpe 2005: 40; Glørstad and Wenn 2017: Tab. 10.1).[6] Loftsgarden has highlighted the relatively low number of women's graves, however there are some source critical issues to take into consideration, in particular that the majority of the finds from Norway are the result of accidental discoveries or excavations carried out by non-archaeologists. It is generally acknowledged that this has led to more graves with swords and other larger weapon finds making their way to the museum storage facilities rather than grave finds with brooches or smaller textile tools (e.g. Shetelig 1912: 174; Stylegar 2007). It is not surprising then that Birka, characterised by professional excavations of high scholarly quality, stands out with a high number of women's graves – even in contrast to Kaupang. The artefact assemblages from Kaupang were undoubtedly affected by a 19th century campaign done in haste, presumably with local untrained labour, without visual documentation of individual graves or mounds (Nicolaysen 1868; Blindheim 1977). The mid-20th century campaign was a low budget excavation published many years later, of densely packed and complex cemeteries under flat ground, carried out under demanding conditions by a team who were gradually acquiring skills in excavating boat burials (Blindheim and Heyerdahl-Larsen 1995; Blindheim *et al.* 1999). While the high number of women's burials with weights at Birka may reflect urban life, the high quality excavations undoubtedly secured the high proportion of woman's graves, as compared to Kaupang and Norway (Stylegar 2007).

All in all, including women's graves with balances from elsewhere in Norway (Petersen 1940; Stalsberg 1991b), it is clear that some Scandinavian women were buried with weights and, to a lesser degree, balances, similar to some men and a few children. Moreover, women were buried with weights from the 9th to the 11th century, also compatible with men. I acknowledge that a grave is the result of a ritual, that the deceased is equipped for an afterlife and that people with social strategies and goals bury the dead (Härke 1997; Price 2008; 2010). Still, I find it likely that burials also reflect lived experiences, especially as Viking Age grave goods show traces of wear and tear, demonstrate recurring patterns over vast geographical areas, and match find assemblages from settlements. Weights and balances often seem to be personal possessions, carried as part of dress (Kyhlberg 1980: 217). Therefore, I find it likely that the graves also provide a glimpse into the use of weighing equipment in everyday life. Weights and balances are tools that reflect challenges, practices, and rhythms of daily life and, apparently, they were in some cases deemed so indispensable to women that they could not be separated from the person even, or perhaps especially, in their death. Moreover, the frequency and vast distribution of weights in graves, both for men and women, reveal a socio-political and economic practice spanning the entire Viking world which did not categorically discriminate on the basis of gender. In fact, woman:man ratios aside, the numerous weights that *are* found in women's graves across Scandinavia give testament to their active partaking in the economy of their communities and their socio-economic agency. Thus, rather than assuming that trade was a masculine domain, we should attend to and explore what these weights and balances might reveal about the nuanced role of Viking Age women.

When looking back today on research on weights from the 1980 and onwards, this undoubtedly brought attention to the fact that Viking Age women were engaged in trade and other activities involving weighing equipment, most likely extending to payment of fines, sharing spoils of war or plunder, collection of taxes, and metalworking (Kyhlberg 1980; Stalsberg 1987; 1991a; 1991b; Pedersen 2001; Gustin 2004). However, it is striking that a large proportion of graves were hardly considered when gender issues were discussed, namely the graves that could *not* be gendered as man or woman based on grave goods, making up 36–37% in Birka (Kyhlberg 1980; Stalsberg 1991b). These might be graves where gender is ambiguous today, not to those attending the funeral. What is preserved only constitutes a proportion of the physical reality at the time of burial, and it is, for example, highly likely that dress, hair style, and other bodily features could have been distinct gender markers, potentially also other items of organic material long gone (Stylegar 2007). Nevertheless, there is a growing awareness among archaeologists of the high proportion of ungendered graves of the Viking Age, suggesting that a strict binary man/woman gender model is misleading and/or that gender in terms of the categories of man and woman was irrelevant in some cases (Croix forthcoming; Moen forthcoming). The use of weights seems to be one such case, judging from the high number of ungendered graves. Stalsberg (1991a: 45) herself touched upon this when arguing that trading was not a gendered activity. This could be understood in a wider context, due to current advances in thinking around Viking Age identities (Moen 2019a; 2019b; forthcoming with references; Croix forthcoming with references). While some people involved in trade would, in a Viking Age burial setting, be staged as men with one or more weapons and/or distinct jewellery types, or as women with distinct jewellery types and/or textile tools, others were represented outside of these two gender categories. To revisit this group of graves with weighing equipment lies outside the scope of this chapter but is a promising field for further research.

## The Haugen hoard and some parallels

Returning to the hoard from Haugen, a (mid-) 10th century date is highly likely (Ab. 1870: 82; Brøgger 1921: 84; Skaare 1976: 140). The two coins that could be more precisely dated were issued in respectively AD 871–879 and 910, the weight is of a type present in Scandinavia from 870/880, while the oval brooches are of a 10th century type (P52). The brooches contain an assemblage undoubtedly related to trade and exchange. The three silver coins are Islamic dirhems, frequently found at various trading sites and in hoards where silver seems to have been deliberately hoarded, for an afterlife and also the earthly life, as indicated by easily accessible finds within houses (Östergren 1989). One of the coins, deliberately fragmented, illustrates how coins and other pieces of silver were used in a bullion economy or weight-money economy (*gewichtsgeldwirtschaft*; Steuer 1987). The arm ring and the two pendants could at first sight appear to be ornaments but are also related to the economic sphere as jewellery made to accord with standardised weight groupings (Hårdh 1996). They are all vital elements in an economy with close links between complete objects of silver and fragments of hacksilver, despite the fact that they are used in different types of exchange, including the socially laden gift giving circumstances and the more neutral trade transactions (Samson 1991; Hedeager 1993). The possibility to choose between different types of exchange is actually among the distinctive features of Viking Age economy and the Haugen hoard can be interpreted along such lines.

There is a remarkable connection between Langeid grave 6, the Haugen hoard, and the unquestionable woman's grave from Valle; they all include a silver pendant of a specific type (Figs 4.4 and 4.5), although not identical, as they are decorated

*Figure 4.4. Weights, coins, fragment of a silver pendant (C58880/7), and a silver object with granulation from Langeid grave 6 (photo: Ellen C. Holte © Museum of Cultural History, University of Oslo).*

with different punches. Maybe a further indication that this Langeid grave belongs to a woman? The pendant from Haugen is carefully packed together with the weight, the coins, and the silver arm ring, and one must question if such a pendant sent a message of an individual involved in economic transactions?

The two oval brooches placed back to back is not a unique phenomenon, it is known from elsewhere in the Viking world (Norstein 2020: 93–95), and it is worth noting that another pair of 10th century oval brooches contained a Carolingian silver mount reworked into a brooch (Norstein 2020: 93–94, 218–219). These were found in a grave from Claughton Hall in Lancashire, England, perhaps wrapped in textile, also containing two beads and a molar. The molar is noteworthy given that the wrapped in textile brooches from Langeid were placed side by side on top of cremated human bones (Wenn 2016: fig. 88). Both pairs of brooches were found in a grave with several weapons. The oval brooches from Claughton Hall, with their content, have been interpreted as the symbolic presence of a woman (Edwards 1998: 15) or referencing

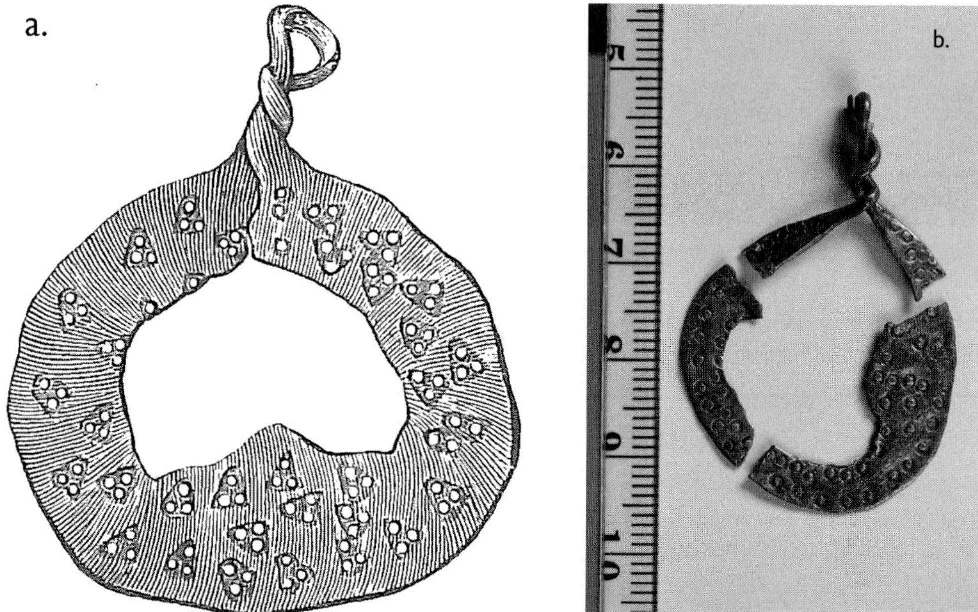


*Figure 4.5. Silver pendants: a. Haugen (C5358); b. Valle (C1672) (drawing from Rygh 1885: fig. 678; photo, Olav Heggø © Museum of Cultural History, University of Oslo).*

a specific individual (Norstein 2020: 102). Taking into account that the Langeid case most likely combined a cremation and an inhumation one might wonder whether negotiation of burial practices also played a role (inspired by Arwill-Nordbladh and Back Danielsson 2021). The Claughton Hall brooches is one of two pairs of oval brooches placed back to back found in Scandinavian Viking Age graves in Britain, Ireland, and Iceland (Norstein 2020: 93–95, 224–225), the other being a 9th century pair from Ballyholme, Ireland, found along with a bronze vessel and bronze chain. Frida Espolin Norstein demonstrates that they fit into a smaller group of graves where the oval brooches are placed in an alternate way and not in their tell-tale usage on a strapped dress. In the Haugen case, a grave is ruled out, suggesting a link between graves and hoards with oval brooches, with silver as a common denominator. Acknowledging such links between graves, hoards, and daily life, one might get a glimpse into the larger picture that the hoard belonged to.

Christoph Kilger (2008) has identified a specific type of hoard where another type of brooch within the female Viking Age dress assemblage is a key feature: the central brooch placed between the oval brooches and thought to have held a tunic, cape, or shawl together. Dress accessories of various types could fill this role, including equal armed, trefoil, and circular brooches, and Christoph Kilger has nicknamed these hoards *Mittspännedepåerna*, 'third brooch hoards'. They have a stereotyped combination of artefacts, including coins, and just like the Haugen hoard they consist of objects of various metals, as opposed to the monometallic silver hoards. Kilger even includes a possible hoard of this type with a pair of oval brooches, but adds that a grave is an equally viable interpretation in this case. Others are undoubtedly hoards, including the spectacular collection of objects from Hoen. While the 9th century third brooch hoards consist of complete objects, fragmented hack silver appear in the following centuries, increasing in amounts in the late 10th and 11th century (Kilger 2008), suggesting that the Haugen hoard fits into a pattern. Kilger demonstrates some links between these hoards and women's graves. He concludes that the combination of artefacts expresses women's roles and self-perception. Highlighting amulets and the textual elements in many of the hoards, he suggests that they contain hidden messages on the power to define what knowledge is within a society (Kilger 2008: 334). Following such a train of thought, and his premise that we should approach hoards and graves as meaningful assemblages, I will argue that female economic agency seems to be a material message both in the Haugen hoard, and the women's graves discussed above. Moreover, both the Haugen hoard and the 10th century 'third brooch hoards' seem to highlight the complex economy of the Viking Age, suggesting that women played a part, maybe even a substantial role, in economic negotiations with several modes of exchange to choose from. Further, the Haugen hoard can help us to acknowledge that Viking Age trade was only one aspect of a multi-faceted economic logic where skills to choose the right type of exchange in a given situation was crucial in maintaining social relations (Samson 1991; Hedeager 1993).

## The Haugen hoard and its wider context

The Haugen hoard was found on the farm Haugen, by the river Numedalslågen, with its outlet in the Larviksfjord, leading into Skagerak and open seas. The lower part of the river and adjacent areas (Fig. 4.3) has a concentration of graves with weighing equipment (Heyerdahl-Larsen 1999: 117; Pedersen 2000). In contrast to the Haugen hoard, the buried could be gendered as men from the artefacts, with the exception of one ungendered grave. Half of them contained a balance, making this the largest concentration of balances in present-day Norway, also outnumbering the four graves with balances in Birka (Arwidsson 1986). The location of most of these graves is along the main waterway towards inland resources, for example, bog iron, wild game, and whetstone quarries, and can be perceived as a way to control traffic on and by the river (Pedersen 2000).

Haugen is located less than 30 km from the Viking Age town of Kaupang, with the largest concentration of Viking Age weights in Norway. Kaupang is an urban settlement with up to a thousand inhabitants, characterised by trade and craft activities from around 800 until 930, and small scale trading activity around 960/970 (Pedersen 2008). The Haugen hoard could, accordingly, have been buried during the lifetime of the town, or slightly later. In addition to a total of ten weights from five graves, another 410 weights are known from Kaupang's settlement area (Pedersen 2008: 120–121), along with 101 coins (Blackburn 2008) and 115 pieces of hacksilver (Hårdh 2008). The artefact assemblage from the urban site provides another opportunity to discuss women in trade and exchange. Their presence in the settlement area is not as explicitly expressed as in the hoards, but the number of women's graves at the cemeteries encircling the small town, making up around 35–40% of the gendered graves, testifies to a substantial number of women living there (Pedersen 2014 with references). Moreover, the cemeteries and, in particular, several burial complexes with more than one individual, provide glimpses into a community where men, women, children, and animals interacted (Pedersen 2014).

One of the characteristics of Kaupang and other Viking Age towns in Scandinavia is a heterogeneous and intensive craft production, focused to a large extent on dress related items, including textiles, shoes, and various types of dress accessories (Callmer 2002: 145). The items manufactured at Kaupang were not reserved for women although a large proportion may have been, notably beads of glass and amber and many different types of metal jewellery (Wiker 2007; Resi 2011; Pedersen 2016). The production waste from non-ferrous metalworking demonstrates that the production targeted the elite, town dwellers, and the rural population, including those with more modest means (Pedersen 2016). Judging from the tools for exchange, the coins, the highly fragmented hacksilver, and the distribution of jewellery in graves, Kaupang attracted many from far and near who desired fashionable clothes and dress accessories, probably also shoes and combs, now lost due to very poor organic preservation. Given the extreme mobility of the Viking Age, where women travelled far and wide, and led their entire households to new lands, I find it unlikely that rural women in Kaupang's hinterland stayed at their farms, patiently waiting for husbands, fathers, and sons to return with things bought for them. On the contrary, I find it more likely that the high number of items produced for women in these urban sites, underlines their role as consumers and, as such, defines the economic adage of 'supply and demand' operating on the ground. Furthermore, while the term 'consumers' might have a passive ring to it and, signifying 'accepting what is offered', the power and reach of consumers to define trade and production should not be under-estimated. This interpretation fits well with the presence of a single weight attested in many graves, reflecting the situation at the time of burial (Pedersen 2000: 66–69; 2001: 26; 2008: 144). They are well suited for controlling the weights of a trading partner (Sperber 1989: 163).

Urban sites were undisputedly important loci for trade, but they were also platforms for other types of exchange (Pedersen 2017) and, as in the case of Kaupang, also formed part of a central place where political, judicial, and ritual arenas interacted with the productive and commercial aspects of their coastal environs (Brink 2007; Skre 2007). Craft production took place in the urban settlement, within and outside small urban dwellings and dedicated workshops (Pedersen 2016), and it is reasonable to assume that craftspeople were directly involved in the exchange of their own products (Pedersen 2014). With regards to the production of beads and metal jewellery it is far from straightforward to establish whether women were among the craftspeople. However, these uncertainties also extend to men, and children for that matter. Instead of merely assuming that such crafts were a male domain, based on cross-cultural guesswork (Callmer 2002: 149), we should be open to more multifaceted players with regards to age and gender (Pedersen 2015: 63). According to Ingvild Øye (2011) textile work was primarily associated with females, as suggested by the grave material and contemporary and earlier written sources from continental Europe. The textile tools from the settlement area indicates that the production in part was highly specialised and of a professional character, covering more than the needs of the inhabitants. Based on a comparison with the local graves, she convincingly argues that high status women organised and administered the work (Øye 2011: 370–372). I find it highly likely that these women also organised the exchange of textiles, including trade to locals and visitors, who judged from some lost dress items could have travelled at least as far as from the Frisian area (Wamers 2011: 90–92).

Bjarne Gaut (2011) has demonstrated that the artefact assemblage from the settlement of Kaupang also holds evidence of the social rituals connected to trade. Small fragments from glass vessels, shattered around the town, originate from a surprisingly high number of drinking vessels. Along with wine jars and containers, the glass vessel forms part of a set for drinking wine well documented in continental Europe (Gau, 2011: 255 with references). Gaut argues that the set could have been used when entering a larger trade deal, known as *kaupskál* in Old Norse. Moreover, he argues that these objects constitute an assemblage of material culture distinguishing traders, craftspeople, and other town dwellers from people in the surrounding districts. The drinking and serving equipment was brought by continental traders and craftspeople, and then adopted by locals at Kaupang, uniting the urban dwellers and creating a new social identity (Gaut 2011: 255–257). Gaut does not discuss the gender implications of his interpretation, but I find it highly likely that such a *kaupskál* was involved when major textile transactions were agreed upon, with women involved (Pedersen 2014: 175). That women took part in such a ritual, to ensure that trade was socially acceptable in a complex economic landscape that was hard to navigate, is strengthened by the re-occurring connection between female figures and drinking vessels in the material record of the Viking Age, and by their documented role in drinking rituals in the wider Germanic society (Enright 1986). Accordingly, women's role in trade could most likely come into view in other ways than we have acknowledged thus far. Being able to ritually and, therefore, effectively sanction trade, women were able to decide what costumes, customs, manners, possibly even cuisines were imported: all the 'little' things, the combs, dresses, brooches, serving, and drinking that not only structured and afforded daily life but also sustained and contested social dynamics and disputes between rural and urban, the individual and the collective, lower and upper strata of society. How to dress, what drinking and serving vessels to display, whether to serve wine or beer can all become potent signifiers and actors in the socio-political and economic drama. Those who took part in these matters, whether as consumers or adjudicators, had immense impact.

## Conclusion

The hoard from Haugen provides a condensed story of women's roles in the complex economy of the Viking Age, where skills to navigate in an intricate economic landscape was a key, and where trade and gift giving were intertwined, while separated by different rules. However, the material message from the hoard and similar finds were for long overlooked or explained away. Instead, a masculine world of trade has been upheld, far too long, despite feminist effort from the '70s onwards. Realising that androcentric thinking still has an impact on the way we portray the Viking Age should inspire new investigations of the archaeological record, not only to identify women with the items often regarded as tools for trade, but also to explore whether there are more links between women and trade that we have overlooked.

All in all, I find it likely that some Viking Age women had an essential skill and know-how within the economic sphere, knowing that certain circumstances necessitated particular types of exchange, that required decorum and tact, customs both local and foreign, having a deep familiarity of society, its issues and points of pride and the tensions of old traditions facing new ones. Perhaps it is women who mastered these skill sets and were able to assume elevated positions as arbiters, mediators, knowledgeable consumers, and traders, and were granted the power to dictate what constitutes appropriate or fair deals, which the weights attest to as they are, in effect, material reifications of 'fair', or accepted measuring standards. Moreover, how to ritually consummate the deals (*kaupskál*), what trade goods were deemed desirable either directly by mediating trade agreements or, at the very least, through their powers as consumers, materially symbolised in the Haugen and similar hoards by the inclusion of hacksilver. Following this, women can be seen as instrumental in most aspects on which a nascent market economy operates: what deals were made, what goods were imported and, as in the case of textile crafts at Kaupang, produced.

## Acknowledgements

This research was made possible with funds from UiO:Nordic to the project Gendering the Nordic Past. I am grateful for valuable input from the team members, Sveinung Utaaker, the editors and Alexa Spiwak.

### *Notes*

1 'Det vil være fristende å se våre vektgraver som kjøpmansgraver, hvis vi ikke hadde hatt forholdene på Birka å ta med i betraktning, der lå vektloddene som vi foran hørte, ikke sjelden i kvinnegraver. Her kunne man selvsagt hevde kjøpmannshustru, men da er vi ute på tynn is'.

2 The papers circulated in unpublished format (Bertelsen *et al.* 1987: 7).

3 Woman: Oval, (trefoil, equal-armed, and round) brooches; pendants; >5 or 10 beads; textile-working tools; Man: Swords; spears; shields; arrows; battle-axes; (most) penannular brooches; ring-pins (Solberg 1985; 2003: 223, 231).

4 'Likevel viser funna at ein neppe kan slutte seg til at handel har vore ein kvinneleg aktivitet i Valle i denne perioden'.

5 'Sammen med sakene b-o ble funnet en stor jernøks, muligens den betegnet som a)'.

6 In addition a grave mound in Asker was plundered by a detectorist in 1979, pulling out weighing equipment and some other items, first reported and delivered to the cultural heritage management in 2016.

## Bibliography

Ab1870., 1871. Fortegnelse over de til Universitetets samling af Nordiske oldsager i 1870 indkomne sager, ældre end reformationen. *Foreningen til norske fortidsmindesmerkers bevaring. Aarsberetning for 1870*: 66–85.

Arbman, H., 1943. *Birka I. Untersuchungen und Studien. Die Gräber. Text.* Kungl. vitterhets historie och antikvitets akademien Stockholm, Uppsala.

Arwidsson, G., 1986. Klappwagen. In *Systematische Analysen der Gräberfunde* Vol. 2.2, ed. G. Arwidsson. Birka: Untersuchungen und Studien. Kungliga vitterhets-, historie- och antikvitetsakademien, Stockholm: 163–164.

Arwill-Nordbladh, E. and Back Danielsson, I.M. 2021. Affective Interventions and 'the Hegemonic Other' in Runestones from Västergötland and Södermanland, Sweden. *Current Swedish Archaeology* 29: 155–182.

Bertelsen, R., Lillehammer, A. and Næss, J.-R., 1987. *Were They All Men? An Examination of Sex Roles in Prehistoric Society.* AmS-Varia 17, Arkeologisk museum i Stavanger, Stavanger.

Blackburn, M., 2008. The Coin-finds. In *Means of Exchange. Dealing with Silver in the Viking Age*, ed. D. Skre, Kaupang Excavation Project Publication Series 2, Norske Oldfunn 23, Aarhus University Press, Aarhus: 119–195.

Blindheim, C., 1971. 'Du mer end tusindaars gamle by'. Refleksjoner omkring byen under Slottsfjellet og Kaupangen ved Viksfjord. *Vestfoldminne* 1968: 7–22.

Blindheim, C., 1977. Den første Kaupangundersøkelse, 1867. Antikvar Nicolay Nicolaysen som feltarkeolog. En etterprøving. *Viking* 1976: 11–27.

Blindheim, C., 1981. Gravenes innhold. Sammenfatning. In *Kaupang-funnene* Bind I. Norske Oldfunn 11, Universitetets Oldsaksamling, Oslo: 115–125.

Blindheim, C., 1993. En pioner ser tilbake. *K.A.N.: Kvinner i norsk arkeologi* 15: 64–73.

Blindheim, C. and Heyerdahl-Larsen, B., 1995. *Kaupang-funnene Bind II. Gravplassene i Bikjholbergene/ Lamøya. Undersøkelsene 1950–1957. Del A. Gravskikk.* Norske Oldfunn 19, Institutt for arkeologi, kunsthistorie og numismatikk, Oldsaksamlingen, Oslo.

Blindheim, C., Heyerdahl-Larsen, B. and Stine Ingstad, A., 1999. *Kaupang-funnene Bind II. Gravplassene i Bikjholbergene/Lamøya. Undersøkelsene 1950–1957. Del B. Oldsaksformer. Kulturhistorisk tilbakeblikk. Del C. Tekstilene.* Norske Oldfunn 19, Universitetets Kulturhistoriske Museer. Oldsaksamlingen, Oslo.

Brink, S., 2007. Skiringssal, Kaupang, Tjølling – the Toponymic Evidence. In *Kaupang in Skiringssal*, ed. D. Skre. Kaupang Excavation Project Publication Series 1, Norske Oldfunn 22, Aarhus University Press, Aarhus: 53–64.

Brøgger, A.W., 1921. *Ertog og Øre. Den gamle norske vegt.* Videnskapsselskapets skrifter 2. Hist.-Filos. klasse, Kristiania.

Brøgger, A.W., 1936. Mål og vekt i forhistorisk tid i Norge. In *Mål og vekt*, Vol 30, ed. S. Aakjær. Nordisk kultur, H. Aschehough & Co, Oslo: 75–83.

Callmer, J., 2002. North-European trading centres and the early medieval craftsman. Craftsmen at Åhus, north-eastern Scania, Sweden ca. AD 750–850+. In *Central Places in the Migration and Merovingian Periods* Vol 6, eds B. Hårdh and L. Larsson. Uppåkrastudier, Almqvist & Wiksell, Stockholm: 133–158.

Croix, S., forthcoming. Gender and relationality in the Viking Age: Mortuary archaeology beyond grave-goods. In *Gendering the Nordic Past: Dialogues Between Perspectives*, eds U. Pedersen, M. Moen and L. Skogstrand. Brepols, Turnhout.

Edwards, B.J.N., 1998. *Vikings in North-West England: The Artifacts.* University of Lancaster, Lancaster.

Engelstad, E., Mandt, G. and Næss, J.R., 1992. Equity issues in Norwegian Archaeology. *K.A.N. Kvinner i arkeologi i Norge* 13–14: 67–77.

Enright, M.J., 1986. *Lady with a Mead Cup. Ritual. Prophecy and Lordship in a European Warband from La Tène to the Viking Age*. Four Courts Press, Dublin.

Fredriksen, P.D. and Amundsen, M., 2014. Når stedsbånd veves og løses opp. En sosial kronologi for bosetningen av Kalvebeitet i indre Sogn i yngre romertid og folkevandringstid. *Viking. Norsk arkeologisk* årbok 77: 79–104.

Gaut, B., 2011. Vessel glass and evidence of glassworking. In *Things from the Town. Artefacts and Inhabitants in Viking-age Kaupang*, ed. D. Skre. Kaupang Excavation Project Publication Series 3; Norske Oldfunn 24, Aarhus University Press, Aarhus: 169–279.

Gjerpe, L.E. (ed.), 2005. *Gravfeltet på Gulli. E18-prosjektet Vestfold. Bind I*. Varia. Kulturhistorisk museum, Fornminneseksjonen, Universitetet i Oslo, Oslo.

Gjerpe, L.E., 2014. Kontinuitet i jernalderens bosetning. Et utdatert postulat arvet fra 1814-generasjonen? *Viking. Norsk arkeologisk årbok* 77: 55–78.

Glørstad, A.Z.T. and Wenn, C.C., 2017. A view from the valley: Langeid in Setesdal, South Norway – a Viking-Age trade station along a mercantile highway. In *Viking-Age Transformations: Trade, craft and resources in western Scandinavia*, eds A.Z.T. Glørstad, and K. Loftsgarden. Routledge, Abingdon: 192–211.

Gustin, I., 2004. *Mellan gåva och marknad. Handel, tillit och materiell kultur under vikingatid*. Lund Studies in Medieval Archaeology 23. Almqvist & Wiksell, Stockholm.

Hedeager, L., 1993. Krigerøkonomi og handelsøkonomi i vikingtiden. In *Norden og Europa i vikingetid og tidlig middelalder*, ed. N. Lund. Museum Tusculanums Forlag, København: 44–68.

Hedenstierna-Jonson, C., Kjellström A., Zachrisson, T., Krzewinska, M., Sobrado, V., Price, N., Torsten G., Jakobsson, M. and Göotherström, A., 2017. A female Viking warrior confirmed by genomics. *American Journal of Physical Anthropology* 164: 853–860.

Heyerdahl-Larsen, B., 1999. Kapittel 16. Mannsredskapene. In *Kaupang-funnene. Bind II. Gravplassene i Bikjholbergene/Lamøya. Undersøkelsene 1950–1957. Del B. Oldsaksformer. Kulturhistorisk tilbakeblikk. Del C. Tekstilene*, eds C. Blindheim, B. Heyerdahl-Larsen, and A. Stine Ingstad. Norske Oldfunn 29, Universitetets Kulturhistoriske Museer. Oldsaksamlingen, Oslo: 109–120.

Härke, H., 1997. The nature of burial data. In *Burial and Society. The Chronological and Social Analysis of Archaeological Burial Data*, eds C. Kjeld Jensen and K. Høilund Nielsen. Aarhus University Press, Aarhus: 19–27.

Hårdh, B., 1996. *Silver in the Viking Age. A Regional-Economic Study*. Acta Archaeologica Lundensia. Series in 8°, 25, Almquist & Wiksell, Stockholm.

Hårdh, B., 2008. Hacksilver and Ingots. In *Means of Exchange. Dealing with Silver in the Viking Age*, ed. D. Skre. Kaupang Excavation Project Publication Series 2; Norske Oldfunn 23, Aarhus University Press, Aarhus: 95–118.

Jondell, E., 1974. *Vikingatidens balansvågor i Norge C1-uppsats i arkeologi, särskilt nordeuropeisk*. Uppsala University, Uppsala.

Jón Viðar Sigurðsson., 1999. *Norsk historie 800–1300: Frå høvdingmakt til konge- og kyrkjemakt*. Det Norske Samlaget, Oslo.

Jón Viðar Sigurðsson., 2017. *Skandinavia i vikingtiden*. Pax, Oslo.

Kilger, C., 2008. Kombinationer av föremål. De vikingatida mittspännedepåerna. In *Facets of Archeology. Essays in Honour of Lotte Hedeager on her 60th Birthday* 10, eds K. Chilidis, J. Lund, and C. Prescott. Oslo Archaeological Series. Unipub, Oslo: 323–338.

Kyhlberg, O., 1980. *Vikt och värde. Arkeologiska studier i värdemätning, betalningsmedel och metrologi under yngre järnålder. I Helgö. II Birka*. Stockholm Studies in Archaeology. Akademilitteratur, Stockholm.

Loftsgarden, K., 2017 Marknadsplassar omkring Hardangervidda: ein arkeologisk og historisk analyse av innlandets økonomi og nettverk i vikingtid og mellomalder.Unpublished Ph.D. Thesis, University of Bergen.

Løkka, N., 2014. Vikingtidskvinnen i ettertidens lys. In *Kvinner i vikingtid*, eds N.L.Coleman and N. Løkka. Scandinavian Academic Press, Oslo: 11–37.

Mandt, G., 1992. Hva styrer våre valg av tolkningsmodeller? Om fremveksten av et nytt perspektiv i arkeologisk forskning. *K.A.N. Kvinner i arkeologi i Norge* 13–14: 78–113.

Mikkelsen, E., 2002. Handel – misjon .– religionsmøter. Impulser fra buddhisme, islam og kristendom i Norden 500–1000 e.Kr. *Viking* 65: 91–136.
Moen, M., 2011. *The Gendered Landscape: A discussion on gender, status and power in the Norwegian Viking Age landscape*. British Archaeological Report S2207, Oxford.
Moen, M., 2019a. *Challenging Gender – a reconsideration of gender in the Viking Age using the mortuary landscape.* University of Oslo, Oslo.
Moen, M., 2019b. Gender and archaeology: Where are we now? *Archaeologies: Journal of the World Archaeological Congress*: 206–226.
Moen, M. forthcoming. The spaces in between: Exploring the Interpretative potential of ungendered graves. In *Gendering the Nordic Past: Dialogues Between Perspectives*, eds U. Pedersen, M. Moen and L. Skogstrand. Brepols, Turnhout:
Mundal, E., 2004. Female impurity and cultic incapability: The influence of Christianisation on Nordic gender models. In *Christian and Islamic Gender Models*, ed. K.E. Børresen. Herder, Rome: 203–218.
Nicolaysen, N., 1868. Tillæg til 'Norske Fornlevninger'. *Foreningen til norske fortidsmindesmerkers bevaring. Aarsberetning for 1867*, 72–115.
Nordeide, S.W., 2011. *The Viking Age as a Period of Religious Transformation: The Christianization of Norway from AD 560 to 1150/1200.* Studies in Viking and Medieval Scandinavia, Brepols, Turnhout.
Norstein, F.E., 2020. *Processing Death: Oval brooches and Viking graves in Britain, Ireland, and Iceland.* GOTARC series B 73. University of Gothenburg, Gothenburg.
Östergren, M., 1989. *Mellan stengrund och stenhus. Gotlands vikingatida silverskatter som boplatsindikation.* Theses and Papers in Archaeology, Stockholm.
Øye, I., 2011. Textile-production Equipment. In *Things from the Town. Artefacts and Inhabitants in Viking-age Kaupang*, ed. D. Skre. Kaupang Excavation Project Publication Series 3; Norske Oldfunn 24, Aarhus University Press, Aarhus: 339–372.
Pedersen, U., 2000. *Vektlodd – sikre vitnesbyrd om handelsvirksomhet? Vektloddenes funksjoner i vikingtid. En analyse av vektloddsmaterialet fra Kaupang og sørøst-Norge Mangfoldiggjort hovedfagsoppgave i nordisk arkeologi.* Institutt for arkeologi, kunsthistorie og konservering, University of Oslo, Oslo.
Pedersen, U., 2001. Vektlodd – sikre vitnesbyrd om handelsvirksomhet? *Primitive tider* 4: 19–36.
Pedersen, U., 2008. Weights and balances. In *Means of Exchange. Dealing with Silver in the Viking Age*, ed. D. Skre. Kaupang Excavation Project Publication Series 2, Norske Oldfunn 23, Aarhus University Press, Aarhus: 119–195.
Pedersen, U., 2014. Kaupangs kvinner. In *Kvinner i vikingtid*, eds N.L. Coleman, and N. Løkka. Scandinavian Academic Press, Oslo: 167–185.
Pedersen, U., 2015. Urban craftspeople at Viking-age Kaupang. In *Everyday Products in the Middle Ages: Crafts, consumption and the individual in Northern Europe* c *AD 800–1600*, eds G. Hansen, S.P. Ashby, and I. Baug. Oxbow Books, Oxford, 51–68.
Pedersen, U., 2016. *Into the Melting Pot: Non-ferrous metalworkers in Viking-period Kaupang*. Kaupang Excavation Project Publication Series 4, Norske Oldfunn, 25, Aarhus University Press, Aarhus.
Pedersen, U., 2017. Viking-period non-ferrous metalworking and urban commodity production. In *Viking-Age Transformations: Trade, craft and resources in western Scandinavia*, eds A.Z.T. Glørstad, and K. Loftsgarden. Routledge, Abingdon: 124–138.
Pedersen, U., 2022. Early medieval metalwork in the Viking world. In *The Medieval Scandinavian Art Reader*, eds M.C. Stang and L. Tillery. Scandinavian Academic Press, Oslo: 75–96.
Petersen, J., 1928. *Vikingetidens smykker*. Stavanger Museum, Stavanger.
Petersen, J., 1940. *British Antiquities of the Viking Period, found in Norway*. Viking Antiquities in Great Britain and Ireland. Part 5. H. Aschehoug & Co., Oslo.
Price, N., 2008. Dying and the dead: Viking Age mortuary behaviour. In *The Viking World*, eds S. Brink and N. Price. Routledge, London: 257–273.
Price, N. 2010. Passing into poetry: Viking-Age mortuary drama and the origins of Norse mythology. *Medieval Archaeology* 54: 123–156.

Price, N., Hedenstierna-Jonson, C., Zachrisson, T., Kjellström, A., Storå, J., Krzewińska, M., Günther, T., Sobrado, V., Jakobsson, M. and Götherström, A., 2019. Viking warrior women? Reassessing Birka chamber grave Bj.581. *Antiquity* 93(367): 181–198.

Resi, H.G., 2011. Amber and Jet. In *Things from the Town. Artefacts and Inhabitants in Viking-age Kaupang*, ed. D. Skre. Kaupang Excavation Project Publication Series 3; Norske Oldfunn 24, Aarhus University press, Aarhus: 107–128.

Rygh, O., 1885. *Norske Oldsager*. Alb. Cammermeyer, Christiania.

Samson, R., 1991. Fighting with silver: Rethinking trading, raiding and hoarding. In *Social Approaches to Viking Studies*, ed. R. Samson. Cruithne Press, Glasgow: 123–133.

Shetelig, H., 1912. *Vestlandske graver fra jernalderen*. Bergens museums skrifter, Grieg, Bergen.

Skaare, K. 1976. *Coins and Coinage in Viking-Age Norway. The establishment of a national coinage in Norway in the XI century, with a survey of the preceding currency history*. Universitetsforlaget, Oslo.

Skre, D., 2000. Kaupang – et handelssted? Om handel og annen vareutveksling i vikingtid. *Collegium Medievale* 13: 165–176.

Skre, D., 2007. Towns and markets, kings and central places in south-western Scandinavia *c.* AD 800–950. In *Kaupang in Skiringssal*, ed. D. Skre. Kaupang Excavation Project Publication Series 1; Norske Oldfunn 22, Aarhus University Press, Aarhus: 445–469.

Skre, D., 2012. Markets, towns and currencies in Scandinavia ca. AD 200-1000. In *From One sea to Another. Trading Places in the European and Mediterranean Early Middle Ages*, eds S. Gelichi, and R. Hodges. Breipols, Turnhout: 47–63.

Solberg, B., 1985. Social status in the Merovingian and Viking periods in Norway from archaeological and historical sources. *Norwegian Archaeological Review* 18: 61–76.

Solberg, B., 2003. *Jernalderen i Norge. 500 før Kristus til 1030 etter Kristus*. Cappelen Akademisk, Oslo.

Sperber, E., 1989. How accurate was Viking Age weighing in Sweden. *Fornvännen* 83: 156–166.

Stalsberg, A., 1987. The interpretation of women's objects of Scandinavian origin from the Viking period found in Russia. In Bertelsen *et al.* (eds): 89–100.

Stalsberg, A., 1991a. Tradeswomen during the Viking Age. In *Nordic Tag. Report from the 2nd Nordic Tag conference Umeå 1987*, ed. E. Baudou. University of Umeå, Umeå: 45–52.

Stalsberg, A., 1991b. Women as actors in north European Viking Age trade. In *Social Approaches to Viking Studies*, ed. R. Samson. Cruithne Press, Glasgow: 75–83.

Steuer, H., 1987. Gewichtsgeldwirtschaften im frühgeschichtlichen Europa – Feinwaagen und Gewichte als Quellen zur Währungsgeschichte. In *Der Handel der Karolinger- und Wikingerzeit*, Vol 4, eds K. Düwel, H. Jankuhn, H. Siems and D. Tiempe. Untersuchungen zu Handel und Verkehr der vor- und frühgeschichtlichen Zeit in Mittel- und Nordeuropa, Vandenhoeck & Ruprecht, Göttingen: 405–527.

Stylegar, F.-A., 2007. The Kaupang cemeteries revisited. In *Kaupang in Skiringssal*, ed. D. Skre. Kaupang Excavation Project Publication Series 1; Norske Oldfunn 22, Aarhus University Press, Aarhus: 65–128.

Sørheim, H., 2014. Female traders and sorceresses. In *Kvinner i vikingtid*, eds N.L. Coleman and N. Løkka. Scandinavian Academic Press, Oslo: 107–119.

Vike, V., 2016. 'Det er ikke gull alt som glimrer' – bredøkser med messingbeslått skaft fra sen vikingtid. *Viking* 79: 95–116.

Wamers, E., 2011. Continental and insular metalwork. In *Things from the Town. Artefacts and Inhabitants in Viking-age Kaupang*, Vol. 3, ed. D. Skre. Kaupang Excavation Project Publication Series 3; Norske Oldfunn 24, Aarhus University Press, Aarhus: 65–97.

Wenn, C.C., 2016. *RV. 9 Kroká-Langeid del II: Gravfelt fra vikingtid, Langeid Øvre, 2/1, Bygland k., Aust-Agder.* Kulturhistorisk Museum, Universitetet i Oslo, Oslo.

Wiker, G., 2007. Monocrome blue Kaupang-beads: Local manufacture or import. In *Innere Strukturen von Siedlungen und Gräberfeldern als Spiegel gesellschaftlicher Wirklichkeit?*, eds C. Grünewald, and T. Capelle. Veröffentlichungen der Altertumskommission für Westfalen. Landschaftsverband Westfalen-Lippe 17. Aschendorff, Münster: 137–143.

# Chapter 5

## Women as partners – gender balance and co-operation in the Viking Age household

*Alexandra Sanmark and Tara Athanasiou*

### Introduction

This chapter investigates the concepts of gendered work and gendered space in the Viking Age and Norse period (*c.* AD 750–1300). These two concepts, which are often used to reconstruct gender roles of the past, will be critically examined in the light of subsistence farming households in Scandinavia and Iceland. It is argued that scholars have placed too much reliance on idealised gender roles, often derived from written sources, ethnology, and studies of 'traditional' farming practices, without proper consideration of the limited choice open to subsistence farmers available in terms of daily tasks. Practical needs for survival, rather than ideology, must be considered as a main driver of work undertaken in the Viking Age and Norse period (cf. Löfgren 1982: 7; Croix 2012: 114). This is likely to have applied to most or all households, although the top elite would have been less susceptible to fluctuations in production as they presumably had many different sources of income and food supply. However, effects of, for example, consecutive poor harvests would have been difficult to escape also for these households. In terms of gendered space, the tendency by researchers to treat women and men as two homogeneous and separate groups, with different aims and priorities, is challenged. As part of such arguments, women have frequently been placed in the 'passive', 'private', and 'domestic' sphere relating to the home and family, while men have been seen to belong in a sphere that is 'active' and 'public' (Clover 1993: 363–387; Ney 2002: 26; Moen 2020: 622, 625; cf. Sanmark forthcoming). This separation of public and private is applied generally to the sort of responsibilities, tasks, and roles men and women undertake and also the places and spaces in which they enact these. There has been some acknowledgement that this division was an ideal rather than a 'literal' principle (Jochens 1995: 117–118), but there is still room for further examination of this, especially in the context of everyday work for subsistence farmers.[1]

This chapter moreover argues that the whole household must be treated as an important concept, with husbands ('householders', ON *húsbóndi*) and wives ('housewives', ON *húsfreyja*), as well as other members such as relatives by blood and marriage, hired hands, and slaves frequently working together for their joint survival (cf. Jochens 1995: 116; Croix 2012: 114). From a legal perspective, the authority of the male head of the household was a feature of Scandinavian and Icelandic households but, in reality, many households may have been run through a partnership between a male and a female head of the household (Mundal 2001: 243). The members of the household were bound together by common consumption and (frequently) common production (Brink 2008: 21; Jón Viðar Sigurðsson 2017: 109–110). This is likely to have created a rather cohesive approach, naturally to varying degrees and with varied results. Moreover, in terms of work, other household members, such as children, slaves, and servants, most likely performed other tasks than the 'householders' and the 'housewives'. This links in with the hierarchical nature of society and the model set up by Carol Clover, which suggests that status was an important determinant in the Norse period (Clover 1993). This model too is, of course, based on ideal circumstances and such norms and rules are unlikely to have been followed at all times (cf. Löfgren 1982: 8–11). The Icelandic sagas provide evidence that the division of labour was stratified along the lines of status, especially in the elite households that were the focus of the saga authors. Not only do the sagas provide evidence of complex intra-household partnerships, but also that hierarchical relationships existed between the women of the household. An example of this, which focuses on the role of the female household head in managing the work of lower status and hired workers, can be seen in chapter one of the 13th century *Valla-Ljóts saga*:

> *Einn dag at konur váru í dyngju sinni ok Halli var þar kominn. Móðir hans mælti: 'Ek á at greiða málagjöld í dag griðkonum várum.'* (Valdimar Ásmundarson 1898: 8)

> One day the women were in their *dyngja* (female workroom) and Halli came in there. His mother said 'I have to pay the wages to our hired household women today'. (our translation)

This scene provides interesting insights into the role of the housewife within the household, with Halli's mother taking direct responsibility for the payment of the hired women. Her personal control of at least part of the household finances is clear, suggesting that there may have been a gendered split of responsibilities in the management and payment of hired workers, as she only refers to the payment of the female workers. It is also notable that the *griðkonur*, 'the hired household workers', are described as receiving their own wages. This short scene suggests that the stratification of the women within the household was complex and multi-layered. The saga author does not elaborate on the identities of the women who were in the *dyngja* with Halli's mother, although we can speculate that they were female relatives, dependants, or permanent servants. Whatever their identities, these women are differentiated from the *griðkonur*, who took contracts for work and household residence on the annual *fardagar* ('moving days') (Dennis *et al.* 1980: 159; Miller 1988: 330).

## Sources

The source materials used in this study include written and archaeological evidence from Scandinavia and Iceland, with some consideration of material from other Norse North Atlantic settlements. The written sources are wide ranging, including Icelandic sagas, Eddic poetry, and laws. These texts are all preserved in manuscripts dating from the 13th and the 14th centuries onwards. For this reason, and the nature of each different type of text, the reliability and value of their descriptions of daily life and gender roles at the farms may be debated, but it is likely that they to some extent capture the realities of life in earlier periods (see e.g. Lönnroth 2008: 309–310). It is moreover important to note that the sagas are very masculine and are generally seen to have been written down by men, so their validity concerning gender roles, and perhaps above all women and their lives, is uncertain (cf. Ney 2002: 31; Phelpstead 2020: 72). The Icelandic sagas put the lives and stories of social elites at centre stage, although fleeting glimpses into the interactions with lower status characters, such as household workers, slaves, or less well-off households, provide useful insights into the ways in which social relationships were formed and navigated. Whilst settlement patterns and social organisation in Iceland were different to Scandinavia (for example, Miller 1988: 324; Byock 2001: 31), the Icelandic sagas provide a useful point of comparison to the archaeological and legal sources from Scandinavia in terms of the requirement for collaboration and partnership to ensure survival. The social, physical, economic, and production challenges experienced in the newly settled diasporic setting of Iceland meant that basic subsistence would have been a challenge even for higher status families, particularly in the earlier years of settlement (Miller 1988: 336). Some insight also comes from Eddic poems, such as *Rigsþula*. These are anonymous mythological poems, found in manuscripts dating from the 13th century, but which are seen to reflect longstanding myths (for a thorough overview, see Meulengracht Sørensen 1991; Fidjestøl 1999).

The Norse laws, such as the Icelandic *Grágás*, the Norwegian *Gulaþingslög*, the Swedish *Äldre Västgötalagen*, and the Danish *Eriks sjællandske lov*, share some of the same problems since they too are preserved in later manuscripts. The earliest manuscripts date above all from the 13th to the 14th centuries, but there is no doubt that all these laws contain a mix of regulations from different time periods, many of which are a lot older than the surviving manuscripts. For example, the use of mnemonic device within the laws, around the classification of heirs into counted categories, points to these laws being memorised, used, and reproduced orally before they were captured in written form (Vestergaard 1988: 163; Brink 2018: 185). No court records have, however, been preserved from this period and it is therefore not known if, or to what extent, these laws were enforced (for an overview, see Sanmark 2004: 133–146 with references). The laws can nevertheless give an indication of perceived threats to the social balance of society (Ney 2002: 26). It is possible that the laws may have been more applicable and relevant to the lives of both men and women than the rather masculine sagas. Many regulations refer to *maðr* in the sense of 'human' or 'person' (although this has often been translated as 'man'), and when needed the terms *karlmaðr* ('man') and *kona* or *kvennmaðr* ('woman') were used (Venås 1989; Mundal 1994: 600–601).

The archaeological material used in this chapter is above all derived from excavated farms and shielings, with some examination of grave goods from furnished Viking Age burials. With the growing numbers of modern and well-published excavations, such as Hofstaðir (Iceland) (Lucas 2009), Borg in Lofoten (Norway) (Munch *et al.* 2003), Bornais on South Uist (Scotland) (Sharples 2020; 2023), and Aggersborg (Denmark) (Roesdahl 2014) our knowledge of Viking Age and Norse settlements has greatly increased over the last 20 years. Another positive development is the expanding interest in non-elite settlements, which has widened our understanding of various farming traditions as well as everyday life (Croix 2011: 113). Shielings, which played an important role in seasonal farming practices, form a central part of this evidence. Some such 'summer farms' have been excavated, for example Skarðsvík on Fugloy in the Faroe Islands (Matras *et al.* 2004), Pálstóftir (Lucas 2008) and Þorvaldsstaðasel, both in Iceland (Kupiec *et al.* 2016).

Archaeological studies of social and gendered space, focusing on both landscape and architecture, have been produced since the 1980s. Many of these are based on the premise that space is 'an active medium of social importance' (Emanuelsson *et al.* 2003: 59; cf. Delle 1998: 9). More detailed studies of gendered space, investigating for example flexible social practices and the public/private distinction, started appearing in the late 1990s (Parker Pearson and Richards 1996; Arwill-Nordbladh 1998; Sørensen 2000: 148). Through the use of modern excavation techniques, such as detailed recording of contexts and artefacts, and advanced scientific analyses, increasingly detailed examinations of excavated materials have been carried out, providing further insight into daily life (Emanuelsson *et al.* 2003: 59–60). In terms of the Viking Age, important studies that have contributed to the discussion of gendered space have been completed e.g. by Sarah Croix (2011; 2012), Karen Milek, and Patrycja Kupiec (Milek 2012; Kupiec and Milek 2015; Kupiec *et al.* 2016). The study of gendered space and tasks on the basis of artefacts is naturally challenging. One issue is that interpretations are often informed by modern assumptions and biases about which objects were predominately used by men and women respectively. These difficulties have been long debated in relation to grave goods. From the 19th century onwards particular artefacts have been argued to indicate the sex, and later gender, of the buried person. Weapons and certain tools have for example been seen to signify male sex or gender, while jewellery, specifically more than three beads, or two or more brooches, and textile implements have been argued to indicate female sex or gender (see e.g. Petré 1993; Sørensen 2000: 27–28, 51–52; Emanuelsson *et al.* 2003: 59–60, 64–65; Johnson 2011: 125–127; Moen 2021; Moilanen *et al.* 2022). This issue will be returned to below.

Due to the sparse nature of the source materials, studies of gendered tasks and spaces are often based on historical analogies with 'traditional' farming practices derived from late written sources. This approach has been useful to some extent, but there are a number of drawbacks. A major issue is that farming societies have frequently been viewed as homogeneous, and therefore local, regional, and social differences as well as changes over time have been ignored (Löfgren 1982; Emanuelsson *et al.* 2003: 60–62). Another problem for this particular study is that most extant documents with information about life on farms derive from the 18th and 19th centuries, a time far removed from the Viking Age and Norse period, and when agricultural processes and mentalities had already been changed by industrialisation. By this time, the aim for upper and middle class women was to be free from manual work and spend time indoors and oversee the home, while many men, for the first time, gained desk-based work (Löfgren 1982: 11; Arwill-Nordbladh 1998: 39; Emanuelsson *et al.* 2003: 60–61; Abrams 2010). By using this model of comparison it is suggested that people of the Viking Age and Norse period could select which tasks to perform at the farm, and indeed choose to avoid manual labour altogether if they so wished. In view of the struggle for survival among subsistence farmers, this comparison therefore clouds the waters rather than benefits our understanding of the past.

Another common problem with the late documents as well as the works of ethnographers of the 20th century, which constitute another frequently used source material, is that they tend to emphasise gendered tasks, rather than examine the practical aspects of farming life (Emanuelsson *et al.* 2003: 60–62). The same applies to folklore and folktales, which have also been used in the study of traditional farming practices, but which may instead represent idealised behaviours (Löfgren 1982: 6–9). After thorough study of subsistence farming, Orvar Löfgren queried these sources and argued that many tasks were in fact not gendered and that those gender rules that were in place were often overridden by daily needs at the farm. In Löfgren's view, female work has often been poorly understood by ethnographers, who were above all male. This has contributed to the rather vivid descriptions of male farm work in contrast to little known female 'chores', the value of which have often been under-estimated especially in economic terms and for the overall survival of the family (Löfgren 1982: 6–9).

In order to overcome such problems in the study of the excavated farms and shielings of the hamlet of Backa, Värmland, Sweden a list of tasks, sorted according to gender and to some extent age, was created. This list drew on an initial study of farming practices (Löndahl *et al.* 2002), 'recent studies of the "old farming society"', but also medieval sources, such as the early laws (Emanuelsson *et al.* 2003: 12–14, 59–63, table 8). The results, presented in Table 5.1, suggest that while there were some shared jobs, women were tasked with e.g. textile production, skin/leather work, collection of fuel and animal fodder, caring for the sick etc, while men were assigned fencing, lumber work, ploughing, and sowing crops. The table further suggests that both women and men carried out work both at the farmstead and in the outlands.

This list was used in the interpretation of the excavated settlements at Backa in order to determine if there were any gendered tasks or spaces (Emanuelsson *et al.* 2003: 12–14, 59–63). For such a retrospective method to be successfully applied it was argued that the societies being studied should be in the same local area and have the same modes of production. This was seen to be more important than the use of medieval documents from different geographical areas, even though these may be closer in time to the society being studied (Emanuelsson *et al.* 2003: 60–62). The results of this study will be returned to below.

*Table 5.1. Suggested reconstruction of labour division according to gender from Emanuelsson* et al. *(2003: 63, table 8) and building on previous work by e.g. Löndahl* et al. *(2002)*

| *Women* | *Men* | *Both* | *Location* |
|---|---|---|---|
| Animal husbandry (excl. horses) | (Animal husbandry (excl. horses)) | | Farmstead |
| Berry picking | | | Outland |
| Brewing | | | Farmstead/indoor |
| | Building | | Farmstead/outland |
| (Charcoal production) | Charcoal production | | Outland |
| Child rearing | | | Farmstead |
| Cleaning | | | Farmstead/indoor |
| Collection of fuel | | | Outland |
| Collection of leaves (animal fodder) | (Collection of leaves (animal fodder)) | | Infield/outland |
| | | Collection of moss (animal fodder) | Infield/outland |
| Collection of twigs, sticks and bark (raw material) | | | Outland |
| | Ditch digging | | Infield/outland |
| | Fencing | | Infield/outland |
| Fetching water | | | Farmstead |
| | Fishing | | Outland |
| Food conservation | | | Farmstead/indoor |
| Food preparation | | | Farmstead/indoor |
| Handling of slaughter products | | | Farmstead |
| | | Harrowing | Infield/outland |
| | Harvesting with scythe | | Infield/outland |
| Harvesting with sickle | | | Infield/outland |
| | | Haymaking with scythe | Infield/outland |

(*Continued*)

*Table 5.1. (Continued)*

| *Women* | *Men* | *Both* | *Location* |
|---|---|---|---|
| Herding | | | Outland |
| (Horse rearing) | Horse rearing | | Farmstead |
| | Hunting | | Outland |
| Laundry | | | Farmstead/outland |
| | Lumber work | | Farmstead/outland |
| Maintenance of implements and buildings | | | Farmstead/outland |
| | Metalwork (excl. smithing) | | Farmstead |
| Milking | | | |
| | Ploughing | | Infield/outland |
| Preparation of raw materials (other than food) | | | Farmstead/indoor |
| Raking at harvest | | | Infield/outland |
| Raking at haymaking | | | Infield/outland |
| | Sharpening weapons | | Farmstead |
| Shieling-related activities | | | Outland |
| | Skin/leather work | | Farmstead |
| (Slaughter of large animals) | Slaughter of large animals | | Farmstead |
| Slaughter of small animals | | | Farmstead |
| | Smithing | | Farmstead |
| | Soapstone handicraft (incl. quarrying) | | Outland/farmstead |
| | Sowing (excl. peas, beans, and flax) | | Infield/outland |
| Sowing and harvesting of flax | | | Infield |
| | | Sowing and harvesting of hemp, peas, and beans | Infield |
| | | Spreading of manure | Infield |
| Taking care of the sick and dead, and midwifery | | | Indoor |
| | Tar production | | Outland |
| Textile production | | | Indoor/outland |
| | | Threshing | Farmstead |
| | | Transport of hay, etc. | Infield/farmstead/outland |

## Gendered roles and tasks

The discussion will now move on to gendered roles and tasks at Viking Age and Norse farms. In order to move away from late traditions and documentation, a detailed examination of the archaeological record, sagas, and medieval laws has been conducted. Our intention is not to provide an exhaustive list of the tasks seen to have been undertaken by women and men respectively but, instead, to discuss and critically examine the source materials in order to provide new insight into gendered work.

Certain tasks in Viking and Norse society have been seen as strictly gendered. Textile production for example seems to have been almost exclusively carried out by women. This is supported by archaeological evidence, such as female Viking Age burials equipped with artefacts relating to textile production including spindle whorls, weaving swords, needle cases, and weaving tablets (Andersson Strand 2007; Moen 2019: 126; Hayeur Smith 2020: 17, 21–22). Written evidence also commonly refers to women occupied with textiles; *Eyrbyggja saga* for example states that *Þórgunna vann váðverk hvern dag* ('Þórgunna spent every day weaving') (*Einar Ól.* Sveinsson and Mattías Þórðarson 1935: ch. 50, 139; Hermann Pálsson and Edwards 1989: 132) while in *Rigsþula, Sat þar kona, sveigði rokk* ('there sat a woman, spinning a distaff') (Guðni Jónsson 1949; our translation). Milking too is a job most commonly associated with women and it is has been argued that this 'was an exclusively female occupation' (Lindkvist 2021: 67; cf. Löfgren 1982: 10). Such assertions are supported by *Äldre Västgötalagen* which stated that *Þen barn a vid ambut han skal varþæ hanni til þæs* ær *hun gitær kuærn draghit ok ko molkæt* ('A man who has children with a thrall woman shall be responsible for her *until she can grind a mill and milk a cow*') (Delsing 2017; Lindkvist 2021: 45, our emphasis). *Grágás* is more specific and lists as women's work the milking of animals, making of dairy products and carrying milk for storage and processing (Dennis *et al.* 1980: 51; 2000: 66). In terms of male gendered labour, metalworking is commonly mentioned, although this notion seems to be based on assumption and parallels, rather than direct evidence (see e.g. Croix 2011; 2012; Kupiec and Milek 2015: 113). Unn Pedersen and Marianne Moen have both expressed scepticism and stressed the sparsity of the evidence. Moen also drew attention to three Norwegian female gendered burials with metalworking tools, which can be seen to contest the claim for 'male only metalworkers' (Pedersen 2014: 177; Moen 2019: 98, 127).

The evidence thus suggests that there were some gendered restrictions in terms of labour, even if they were not always strictly followed. It is, however, important to note that an individual's work was also determined by their personal status. The reference in *Äldre Västgötalagen* to the female thrall being responsible for milking, suggests that in sufficiently wealthy, large, and stratified households at least it may have been women of lower status who were responsible for some of the more laborious tasks connected to milk production. Stratification in terms of work is also suggested by *Grágás* which specifies that a *griðmaðr* (a 'houseman, servant, lodger, labourer') (Cleasby and Vigfusson 1874: 215) should do what the householder wants of him, except shepherding. This is followed by listing a *griðmaðr*'s tasks which include slaughtering, spreading dung in spring, looking after cattle, and repairing the home field walling (Vilhjálmur Finsen 1974: 129; Dennis *et al.* 1980: 159). Archaeological evidence provides further support that certain activities, such as those relating to textile and metal production, were organised for the spatial demonstration of power and status as much as for more practical purposes (Croix 2011; 2012). These considerations will be developed later in this chapter.

There is also a range of evidence that suggests that work, including certain agricultural tasks, was often shared by men and women, thus at times overriding idealised gender roles. Tools and agricultural implements, such as sickles, are found in the graves of both men and women, although ratios vary between geographical areas and possibly due to methods of sex/gender determination (Owen and Dalland 1999: 89–91). In Scotland, sickles have, for example, been found in the boat burial from Swordle Bay in Ardnamurchan, a male grave with an 'exceptional' assemblage including a sword and an axe (Batey 2016: 44; 2023: 310); among the grave goods belonging to the woman in the Scar boat burial on Sanday, Orkney; and in a male grave at Westness, Rousay, Orkney (Graham-Campbell and Batey 1998: figs 7.10 and 7.11; Owen and Dalland 1999: 89–91). This is interesting as saga evidence too supports the idea that tasks for which sickles were used, such as haymaking, were shared. A major reason for this is the short window of opportunity for such tasks which necessitated a collaborative effort between men and women, and presumably also children. *Eyrbyggja saga* tells us how the Hebridean woman Þórgunna undertook work to cover her board, describing the tasks that she undertook:

> *Þórgunna vann váðverk hvern dag, er eigi var heyverk. En þá er þerrar váru, vann hon at þurru heyvi í töðunni ok lét gera sér hrífu, þá er hon vildi ein með fara.* (Einar Ól.Sveinsson and Matthías Þórðarson 1935: ch. 50, 139)

> Þórgunna spent every day weaving, unless there was haymaking to do, and when the weather was good, she used to work drying the hay in the home meadow. She had a special rake made for her which she let no one else touch. (Hermann Pálsson and Edwards 1989: 132)

This is not to say that there was no division of labour within the haymaking process. The same saga suggests that these tasks could at times be allocated according to both status and gender. For example, we are told that whilst the farmhands were ordered to start the haymaking using scythes, the heavy work of stacking the hay and then transporting it by cart was, in one case, undertaken by slaves. However, although Þórulfr, the householder, pressed these slaves to work harder he also worked alongside them, testament to the urgency of finishing the task before the weather turned (Hermann Pálsson and Edwards 1989: 83–84). *Eyrbyggja saga* therefore stresses the primacy of practicality when it came to task allocation, especially when tasks needed to be performed within a short space of time. This can be seen in the following example, where the task of carting the hay home was in this case undertaken by farmhands rather than slaves:

> *Kom þá góði þerridagr ok var veðir kyrrt ok þunnt svá at hvergi sá ský á himni. Þóroddr bóndi stóð upp snemma um morguninn ok skipaði til verks. Tóku þá sumir til ekju en sumir hlóðu heyvinu en bóndi skipaði konum til at þurrka heyit ok var skipt verkum með þeim ok var Þórgunnu ætlat nautsfóðr til atverknaðar.* (Einar Ól.Sveinsson and Matthías Þórðarson 1935: ch. 51, 139–140)
>
> One day was ideal for drying, calm and clear, with not a cloud in site. Þórroddr was up early that morning and arranged the work for the day. Some of the farmhands were to cart the hay home others to stack it. He told the women to help with the drying of the hay and shared out the work between them. Þórgunna was given as much hay to dry as would have been winter fodder for an ox. (Hermann Pálsson and Edwards 1989: 131)

Hence, after what the saga author tells us was a wet summer, the assignment of tasks was determined by the demands of getting the work completed quickly, rather than adhering to strictly demarcated roles. Although tasks appear to have been allocated according to gender, with the women leading on the drying rather that the stacking or transportation, this division of labour appears to have been practical, with the emphasis always on collaboration and partnership to get the overall job completed in order to ensure the survival of the farm animals and in extension the family.

Cookery and food production is another everyday task that is often assumed to have been undertaken by women. This seems to have been based on assumed gender roles and a small number of written references to women cooking, rather than firm evidence based on thorough analysis of grave goods (Jesch 1991; Jochens 1995: 131; Roesdahl 1998: 60; Øye 2006: 47; Jón Viðar Sigurðsson 2008: 44). Further evidence suggests that although this may have been an ideal there were times when practical considerations meant that men would have been involved in food production. Both the *Gulaþingslög* and *Eriks sjællandske lov* make specific reference to the ability of householders to send a man or boy as cook in order to meet their household obligations when called up for military service to the *leiðangr* ('naval levy') (Tamm and Vog 2016: 207–208; Simensen 2021: 201). The provision in *Gulaþingslög* states that:

> *Sa scal matgerðar mann fa. er sveina a i skipreiðu. oc luta sin i mellom. Matgerðar menn skolo fararkaup taca sem hasetar. Skal bonde sa heima væra er matgerðar mann fær. nema skip se eigi skipat. Böndr scolo skylldir til stemnu at fara. þvi at eins drengmenn. ef styrimaðr vill. Nu scal styrimaðr gera stemnu ollom monnom til er skip scal skipa æða útdraga.* (Keyser and Munch 1846)
>
> Those who have slaves (ON *sveinn*) in the warship district should provide the cook (ON *matgerðr maðr*), and they have to draw lots among them (to assign the duty). Cooks shall have the same wages as sailors. The householder who provides the cook must stay at home, unless the ship is not fully manned. (Simensen 2021: 201)

Although this provision is somewhat ambiguous, suggesting that the *sveinn* and the *matgerðr maðr* may have been two separate people, it clearly indicates the gender of the cook as male, even if his exact status is perhaps unclear (Jòhanna Katrin

Friðriksdóttir: pers. comm.) *Eriks sjællandske lov* is more explicit in its stipulation of a young male slave as a suitable cook: *Æn cumær swa at nokær lething warthær buthæn. tha ma ængin man sin thræl ut for sic sændæ. thys enæ at han far styris manz lof til. at han ma han til mat swen hauæ* (Anon. 2015) (Now if it happens that if military duty is called for, no man may then send his slave in his place, unless he has the permission of the steersman that he can have him as a cook; Tamm and Vogt 2016: 207–208). The use of boys as cooks on board ships can also be found in sagas, for example in *Ragnars saga loðbrókar* when the *matsveinnar* ('meat boys' who cook, especially on board ships (Cleasby and Vigfusson 1874: 414) left the ship to go to land in order to *baka brauð* ('bake bread') in the morning (Olsen 1906–1908: ch. 5, 122). If one presumes that any boy (whether as a servant or slave) being sent to serve as a cook as part of military service would need to have some previous knowledge and experience of cooking, this indicates that within the household this task would have been undertaken by male as well as female servants or slaves. The use of the term *sveinn* within the laws, a word that is usually translated as boy, lad, or servant (Cleasby and Vigfusson 1874: 608) also suggests that cooking was perhaps a task deemed most appropriate for younger male slaves, perhaps until they gained the size and strength necessary to undertake heavier labour. Moreover, cooking implements, which are usually seen as female grave goods, have been shown to be 'almost as common in male graves as in female' ones (Arwill-Nordbladh 1998: 84–122; Moen 2019, 127). The Swordle Bay burial, for example, contained an impressive iron cooking ladle or pan, and a similar example is known from a male burial at Kiloran Bay, Colonsay (Scotland) (Graham Campbell and Batey 1998: 119, 122; Batey 2016: 43–44; 2023: 310; cf. Petersen 1951: 375, figs 200 and 201). Altogether, this implies that cooking and food handling was not solely a female domain, which may also link into the role of food and feasting in social organisation, power relations, and ally formation (see e.g. Sundqvist 2007: 13–14; Jón Viðar Sigurðsson 2008: 58–60; Moen 2019: 98).

An examination of recent research into ceramic production exemplifies how assumption and bias can influence how evidence is interpreted. In his research into the rapid change of pottery style around the end of the 10th century in Skåne in modern Sweden, Mats Roslund argued that this can be explained by a shift from local pottery production to one undertaken by female Slavic slaves from the Polabian region along the Elbe river of modern-day eastern Germany (Roslund 2021: 81). A closer examination of the evidence behind this claim reveals how some very plausible interpretations of historical and archaeological evidence can be skewed by the application of unsubstantiated assumptions about the gendered division of labour. As Roslund shows, the archaeological record does indicate a shift in ceramic style in both rural and town settings in late 10th century Skåne, with a swift change from rather simple and squat pots to higher quality ones in the style of pottery produced in the Western Slavic Polabian region. The timing of this shift coincided with a high level of conflict, with seasonal raiding of the Polabian territory from eastern Denmark, and political upheaval in the western Slavic region (Roslund 2021:

81, 87). It is highly plausible that in this period of turmoil, many people from the Polabian region were captured and became slaves on the farms of Skåne. Roslund then takes his hypothesis a step further, arguing that the Polabian-style pottery, which became dominant within the space of a generation, was produced by female Slavic slaves. However, no archaeological or contemporary written evidence is provided to substantiate this claim. Indeed, the hypothesis appears to rest on a traditionalist assumption seen in some 20th century research (for example, Arnold 1985: 100) that pottery in pre-industrial societies was a low value task undertaken by women, whose tasks were largely confined to the household sphere because of the need to fit their work around pregnancy and child rearing (Bolger 2012: 161; Roslund 2022: 220). More recent studies of pottery production in pre-industrial societies across different geographies and time periods, however, suggest a more nuanced picture. For example, excavations of pottery produced by Ancient Puebloan societies in Central America show that there were both male and female fingerprints on the pots, which calls into question the validity of assuming strictly gendered task differentiation (Kantner *et al.* 2019: 12220). Comparative studies of ceramic production moreover suggest not only that there was significant variation between different geographical areas and time periods in terms of gendered responsibilities, but also importantly that the production of pottery was a drawn-out process. This included collecting and preparing clay, producing and decorating the vessel, and firing the pots, and therefore required co-operative labour between men, women, and children (Bolger 2012: 175). If we return to the example of the Polabian pottery from late 10th century Skåne, it is impossible to arrive at a firm answer regarding who produced it, but we must be open to the idea that it may have been produced through collective labour of both men and women of Slavic origin.

Most research into female roles in the Viking Age focuses on the role of housewives, perhaps because they are easier to find in the sources. But the stereotype of the Viking Age housewife with the keys at her belt (Berg 2015: 30) distracts from both the variety of different roles that women could have on a household farm and the hierarchies that existed within it. A woman's status, her age, whether or not she had a kinship relationship with the householder or housewife, her marital status, and whether her membership of the household was temporary or permanent all influenced her position, the roles that she did, and what agency she had (cf. Clover 1993; Ricketts 2010: 297). Within a household there could be the 'lady of the house' who was married to the householder, any female children, a mother or mother-in-law, and also perhaps one or more concubines, in addition to female workers, servants, and slaves. Therefore, the hierarchical nature of households and society was not limited to the position and status of men, but also included women.

## Gendered space – indoor women and outdoor men?

We will now shift our attention to the places in which certain tasks were undertaken in order to examine the application of gendered binaries, such as public/private and outside/inside that have been traditionally layered onto male and female work. The concept of social space and, by extension, gendered space, has been much debated by scholars of both history and archaeology. The notion of a separation between the 'public' and 'private' spheres that was originally developed by Friedrich Engels in 1884 has underpinned traditional scholarly arguments for the gendered division of labour and existence of gendered spaces (Gilchrist 1999: 6; Engels 2010: 199). The idea behind the public/private divide was rooted in the belief that the increasing division of labour after the development of agriculture led to the emergence of private property and a differentiated private sphere, concerned with the family, reproduction, and domestic work. It was in this sphere, which both related to physical space and the type of tasks that were undertaken within it, where women were seen to have been placed. This was in contrast to men, who through their assumed control over agriculture and the domestication of animals were seen to have had dominance and power within the public and political sphere (Landes 2003: 28; Engels 2010: 199). Within this model, women are associated with the private domestic space whilst men are seen to operate in the higher value public, political sphere. This assumed binary is simplistic and reductive and therefore problematic on many levels. Perhaps the most obvious issue is that concepts of 'public' and 'private' held very different meanings in the Viking Age and Norse period, with much of what we may today consider to be public activity, like religion, ritual, and economic production, taking place within the bounds of the household (e.g. Moen 2010: 78; Athanasiou 2020; Sanmark forthcoming). The use of binary oppositions also imply that 'women' and 'men' were homogeneous groups, when in reality the situation was far more complex and nuanced, as already demonstrated. The tasks that people did and the places and spaces that they undertook them in were influenced not just by their gender but by many other cross-cutting factors, such as the size and structure of their household and a person's status, age, and whether or not they were married.

Despite the shortcomings of the public/private and by extension outside/inside binaries, and the sparse evidence supporting this, these ideas have shaped research on gendered work and space in Viking Age and Norse society (Jochens 1995; Ney 2002: 26; Moen 2010: 70–73). This is particularly clearly seen in the discussions around the term *innanstokks* ('within the threshold'), the area that has often been understood to be the sphere of women's responsibilities and work, revolving around childcare, cooking, and textiles. These tasks are seen to be of lower social, political, and economic value than the tasks undertaken by men outside of the house (Clover 1993: 365; Jochens 1995: 117, 169). There is a small number of references to women's responsibilities inside the house both in sagas and laws, which have been over-interpreted as evidence for the public/private and outdoor/indoor binaries for men and women (Clover 1993: 363–387; Jochens 1995: 117; Roesdahl 1998: 59; Ney 2002: 26; Raffield *et al.* 2017: 165–167; Sharples 2020; 2023; Moen 2021: 622, 625).

An example from the sagas that supports the idea that indoor sphere is the responsibility of women, particularly upon their marriage, is found in *Fljótsdæla saga*. In the saga Þórdís is described as *skapstór og skörungur mikill, skafinn drengur og líkleg til góðs forgangs* (a 'proud and notable woman, strong, and well-fitted to manage a house' who *tók hún þar við búi og öllum forgangi* ('took over the house and all the management of it') after her marriage to Helgi (Young and Haworth 1990: 22; Sveinbjorn Thordarson 2017: ch.10). Regulations in *Grágás* are also cited as evidence that the female sphere was inside the threshold of the house, although an examination of the legal clause shows that situation was rather more nuanced:

> *Þar er samfarar hiona ero oc scal hann raða fyrir fe þeirra oc cavpom. Eigi er kono scyllt at eiga ibue nema hon vile. en ef hon á ibve með honom. þa a hon at raða bv ráðom fyrir inan stocc. ef hon vill oc smala nyt.* (Vilhjálmur Finsen 1974: 44)
>
> Where a man and wife are in wedlock, then he shall have charge of their property and buying and selling. It is not required of the wife that she should own a share in the household, but *if she has a share in the household with him, then she is to run the indoor household as she wishes and the dairying.* (Dennis *et al.* 2000: 66, our emphasis)

The wording of this clause, as well as *Fljótsdæla saga* quoted above, casts doubt on the overall principle that the women's sphere was indoors with men as a result having the rest of the space to themselves. The most obvious challenge is that *Grágás* plainly gives wives authority inside the house, rather than restricting her movements or tasks outside. Jenny Jochens has rightly pointed out that this was an ideal rather than an 'architectural' or 'literal' principle and moreover that it was not legally enforced (Jochens 1995: 117–118). The law furthermore refers specifically to wives, and only those who owned a share of the household. Indeed, the many other types of women, such as servants, slaves, salaried workers, unmarried women, widows, and itinerant women who made up society are not included. The reference to the wife as having responsibility for dairying is also problematic in this context, as clearly, dairying is a task that does not take place within the threshold of the house, which further challenges the assumption of a simplistic inside/outside boundary of responsibility.

An examination of medieval laws from Scandinavia also illustrates how gendered responsibilities were contextual and variable in different places and times. *Äldre Västgötalagen* is more explicit than *Grágás* in giving the wife responsibility for running the home, but also outlines alternatives if she is not able to do this:

> *Kona giftiss bort fræ barnum sinum eghu barn ambut ællær þræll þa ma þem firi bo sætiæ [...] Faþur broþir barnæ mæli mælæ ok fostræ skal firi bo sitiæ. Moþer skal raþæ arkær lyklum ok lætæ skyldir takæ ok skyldir lukæ.* (Delsing 2017)
>
> If a wife remarries and moves away from her children and the children own a thrall woman or a thrall, they take care of the home [...] The father's brother speaks for the children and a home-born thrall woman run the home. The mother has control over the keys of the coffer and she collects debts and pays debts. (Lindkvist 2021: 39)

The provisions made within *Äldre Västgötalagen* clearly indicate the social expectation and convention for a woman to run the household but are also underpinned by a vein of pragmatism. In the absence of the wife, a *fóstra* ('home-born female slave') to run the home is clearly the preference. This indicates both the association of this work with women and also provides insight into the structure of the household and the *fóstra*'s trusted position within family. However, the law also refers to a male *þræl* ('slave') taking responsibility for running the household where needed, suggesting that the demarcation of gendered roles was an ideal rather than an absolute. The distinction between the responsibilities of the *fóstra* in running the home and the widowed wife of a householder in taking responsibility for the household finances also indicates the multi-faceted nature of household management and suggests that tasks and responsibilities were structured according to status as well as gender.

Altogether, there is little evidence of strict gendering of space at Viking Age farms. Rather the mixed gender, indoor spaces seem to have been an important social feature (Emanuelsson *et al.* 2003: 79–80). Bearing in mind the overlap and sharing of space by women and men, the suggested division between the public and the private spheres does not hold up. Instead it is important to stress that the household must have been run in co-operation between man and wife. The importance of the household is reflected in the Old Norse terms for husband (*húsbóndi*) and housewife (*húsfreyja*) which both include the word for house (*hús*). The term 'housewife' is problematic in that it is difficult to move away from the modern usage of the term which means 'woman whose occupation is looking after her family, cleaning the house', both in terms of what the 'job' involves and the social value attributed to it (Hornby and Cowie 1989: 605; Sanmark forthcoming). The term *húsbóndi* has been treated very differently to *húsfreyja*. Although the title of the male householder is defined by his role in the *hús* this has not led to the relegation of his role, either practically or symbolically, to the 'private' and domestic sphere. In contrast, the inclusion of *hús* in the female role seems to have fitted in with assumptions about the lives of women. In view of the farm work discussed above, these two roles could instead be seen as complementing each other, with two people making sure that all the work needed for the survival of the family, was carried out.

## Beyond the farm boundary

As a parallel to the *innanstokks* and *utanstokks* discussion, the outfields and infields have been brought into the discussion. This goes back to arguments by Kirsten Hastrup that 'the enclosed farm' 'in the Late Iron Age reflected the cosmos of Old Norse religion and was therefore divided into the two spheres of 'the social' and 'the wild', which equated *útangarðs* and *innangarðs. Innangarðs,* 'the social sphere' was seen to be the equivalent of *Miðgarðr*, the cosmological world of the humans. *Útangarðs,* 'the wild' was labelled the equivalent of *Útgarðr*, the dwelling place of giants and other non-humans in Old Norse myths. As a consequence, the enclosed farm was seen as safe, and everything outside was part of 'the wild' and thus potentially dangerous and outside social control (Hastrup 1985 136, 137, 143).

Hastrup's structuralist analysis has been criticised by numerous scholars. Gro Steinsland viewed it as too simplistic, criticising Hastrup's notion that the ideas of cosmos applied also to the real human world (Steinsland 2005: 138–139) and Stefan Brink argued that the landscape outside the farm was not seen as dangerous by the people of the Viking Age (Brink 2001: 81–82). An important point to consider is that areas both inside and outside the enclosed farm were useful in economic terms. The outfields could be particularly rich in resources, such as forests and wild animals, and use of these areas formed an integral part of subsistence farming, as established by archaeological investigations. It has moreover been established that people went further away from the farms for hunting, fishing, sources of wood and charcoal, for food, farm, and also trade. The outlands at Backa have been seen as a 'mixed gender landscape' (Emanuelsson *et al.* 2003: 138, 140). Another recent study has argued that Viking Age hunting was not necessarily a male activity and that, by acknowledging this, conceptions of gendered space can also be challenged (Lund and Moen 2019). In this context the inclusion of animal images or hunting scenes on runic crosses that were raised only to women on the Isle of Man are interesting. These include a hunting scene depicted on MM131 Andreas IIa (by a husband for a wife with a Norse name) and a horse and rider in MM132 Kirk Michael Va (by a son for a mother with a Norse name) (Barnes 2019: 96–98, 185–191; Athanasiou 2020: 44). In view of all these points, it is not clear why these areas would have been seen as wild and dangerous. It is also possible that the various types of source materials relate to different aspects of life; the written sources have many motivations and biases, while that the archaeological evidence arguably shows people's routine activities (Emanuelsson *et al.* 2003: 138).

This brings us to the shielings. An examination of the activity that took place in shielings, which served as an important extension of the social and economic world of the farm, provides interesting insights into how spaces and places beyond the farm were used and understood along gendered lines. Transhumance, the seasonal movement of livestock from the main farm to upland pastures (shielings) in the summer, was an integral part of the medieval Scandinavian and Icelandic economy (Kupiec and Milek 2015: 106). So important was the shieling economy to Iceland that one of the names for the third month of summer (mid-June to mid-July) was *selmánuðr* 'shieling month' during which 'milk cattle are removed to the shieling (*sel*)' and temporary occupation was taken in habitations that were outside of the usual farm boundaries (Cleasby and Vigfusson 1874: 521; Hastrup 1985: 31–33; Kupiec and Milek 2015: 106). The importance of the shieling economy in medieval Iceland is also seen in *Grágás*. As well as specifying the freedom of people to drive their livestock across other people's land to reach the uplands, fines were incurred if these rights of way were blocked (Dennis *et al.* 1980: 51; Kupiec and Milek 2015: 222). The shielings were part of the 'mental map' of the farm, its extended area, and the surrounding locality (Kupiec and Milek 2015: 106). Archaeological, place name, documentary, and field survey data indicate that shielings were on average

2–5 km from the main farm, though this was variable; in most cases this meant that daily travel between the shieling and the home farm was possible, although even these small distances would have meant they were out of sight (Kupiec and Milek 2015: 107–108, 110).

Some scholars have argued that the archaeological record and sagas suggest that shielings were a domain that was primarily female, a place where they stayed during the summer and undertook tasks such as dairying (Jochens 1995: 122; Svensson 2005: 165; Kupiec and Milek 2015: 102; Kupiec *et al.* 2016: 337). One such example is the shieling at Backa hamlet which has been interpreted as a 'predominantly a female sphere' (Emanuelsson *et al.* 2003: 140). The sagas also provide some evidence that shielings were a site of female activity and work. An example of this can be seen in *Egils saga Skallagrímssonar,* which tells us that *At Mosfelli var höfð selfor, ok var Þórdís í seli um þingit* ('the cattle at Mosfell were kept in a shieling and Þórdís stayed there while the Þing took place') (Bjarni Einarsson 2003: ch.87, 182; Scudder 2002: 203). Whilst the gendered division of labour and roles is interesting to note, with Þórdís staying at the shieling during the summer to focus on dairying while others, at least some of the men of the household, were presumably at the assembly, the evidence does not suggest that shielings were distinctive female spaces. Indeed, more saga, legal, and archaeological evidence instead suggests that they can best be understood as an important seasonal space, utilised in the summer months for a variety of different purposes, by different members of the household. Investigation of the site at Pálstóftir shows occupation of the shieling between 950 and 1070, with microscopic investigation of floor surfaces indicating periods of abandonment. Evidence of various different activities, most of which are non-gendered, including gaming pieces (five sheep astragali in a cluster), hunting, portable crafts, harvesting, plus a thimble and clay pipe, showing sewing and smoking, indicate that this was a place of relaxation, not just work (Kupiec and Milek 2015: 113–114; Kupiec *et al.* 2016: 332). This is also suggested by recent archaeological excavations showing that the tasks carried out at the summer farms were more varied than those concerned with dairying and tending livestock and included activities such as hay gathering, hunting, charcoal making, and iron extraction (Kupiec and Milek 2015: 110).

Kupiec and Milek question whether the gender-ambiguous nature of the many tasks undertaken in shielings may have reflected a relaxing of normal gender roles and tasks, with either men or women taking on tasks more normally done by the opposite gender, but perhaps it's more likely that the shieling was a place used by both genders according to need during the busy summer period (Kupiec and Milek 2015: 115). This interpretation is supported by evidence from both the saga corpus and medieval Scandinavian and Icelandic laws. In *Laxdœla saga,* a shepherd boy sent to find out who is staying at the Laugar shieling, reports that Guðrún is there, whilst her husband Þórðr is working hard on house building at the main farm (Magnus Magnusson and Herman Pálsson 1969: ch. 35, 127). But although husband and wife are clearly working and staying in separate places, she on the shieling and he on the main farm, there is no indication that the shieling is only occupied at this time by women. Rather, according to the shepherd boy, only Þórðr and Osvif are staying at the home farm, suggesting the rest of the Laugar household (*Laugamenn*) were at the shieling (Magnus Magnusson and Herman Pálsson 1969: ch. 35, 127). Similarly, in *Vatnsdæla saga* we are told that Guðbrandr moved his household to the shieling when summer was approaching (Wawn 1997: 253). The presence of both women and men at the shielings is further supported by *Laxdæla saga* when Hallþórr reports that *Bolli sé at seli í Sælingsdal, ok sé þar ekki fleira manna en húskarlar þeir, er þar vinna heyverk* ('Bolli is at the shieling at Sælingsdale with only farmhands who are doing the haymaking there') (Kristian Kåland 1889–1891: ch. 54, 203; Magnus Magnusson and Herman Pálsson 1969: ch. 54, 184). *Gunnlaugs saga ormstungu* moreover describes Gunnlaugr riding to Þórsteinn's shielings at *Thorgilsstadir* where Þórsteinn had a stud of four chestnut horses (Finnur Jónsson 1916: ch. 5, 15; Attwood 1997: 568).

The argument that shielings should be understood as an important seasonal habitation for production purposes for the entire household is supported by the laws. The *Gulaþingslög*, for example, stipulated that when a message stick was used to summon an assembly *Nu scal þat fara með vetrhusum. en eigi með sætrum* ('It must go to the winter houses and not to the shielings') (Keyser and Munch 1846: Simensen 2021: 133) which suggests the seasonal nature of shieling occupation as opposed to the farm. The seasonality rather than gender specific nature of shielings is suggested by *Grágás* in another regulation; this one concerns the delivery of dependents to those with a legal responsibility for them: *Ef men ero iseliurn oc er þar bu allt. Þa er rett at fora þar omagan með eið* ('If men [people] are at shielings and the whole household is there, then it is lawful to deliver the dependent there') (Vilhjálmur Finsen 1974: 7; Dennis *et al.* 2000: 33). Taken together, the legal sources and sagas suggest fluid and necessity-driven movement between the shieling and home farm by both men and women during the summer months.

## Conclusion

As the primary social unit within the Viking Age and Norse period, the household provides a useful platform from which to examine the everyday tasks that women and men undertook and where their work took place. The sagas, medieval laws, and archaeological record provide insights into the work that men and women actually did on the farm, and although patterns emerge around what can be seen as women's and men's work, there was also a practical cross-over and a sense that exigencies of the season, weather, and day to day real life led to a blurring of the boundaries.

In this chapter, we have sought to demonstrate that the assumptions made by some scholars about gendered roles can be challenged based on a broader examination of the evidence, thus suggesting that strict gendered division may have been rarer than envisaged in previous research. The examination of cooking, for example, based on evidence from the sagas, medieval laws, and archaeological record, suggests a nuanced picture where cooking may have been a task for servants or slaves, at least in larger and wealthier households. Although some work seems to have been limited to one gender, the collective evidence also suggests that many tasks were shared by women and men; and importantly in some circumstances status could be a stronger stratifying line than gender in determining what jobs and responsibilities an individual had.

The roles of the householder and housewife were interconnected and symbiotic, and the central importance of the provision of food to their household provides useful insights into the foundations of authority within the household and the intertwining of the roles of the householder and housewife as the male and female heads of the household. However, as shown above, for both men and women the association with the house did not limit their role to either the house as a geographic space or as a site of private domestic life. The theme of partnership and co-operation in the Viking Age and Norse household was pervasive, going beyond the householder and housewife to influence the day to day roles and activities of other members of the household. This is not to say that there was no division of labour within the tasks carried out. Rather, the evidence suggests teamwork, with tasks allocated according to characteristics, such as age, sex/gender, and status.

This chapter has demonstrated that the dividing line between 'male' and 'female' tasks in the Viking Age and Norse household was blurred and porous. We have also challenged the assumption that male and female work took place in specifically gendered spaces. Although we have shown that there is some evidence that the indoor/outdoor dichotomy reflected the idealised spheres of influence of the housewife and householder respectively, this was not always practical, feasible, or desired. Moreover, it is important to differentiate between spheres of activity and spheres of influence. It is clear that both women and men went beyond the farm boundary, thus further illustrating the problem with the indoor/outdoor dichotomy. Women, and also men, spent time at the shielings and also spent time in the outlands hunting, gathering firewood, and food stuffs, as well as for other activities. An examination of written sources and archaeological excavations also suggests that the space within the house itself was multi-functional, with no restrictions on the movement of women and men. Where there is evidence that a particular space was used predominantly by women (usually due to evidence of textile production) the use of these spaces was likely determined as much by status as gender. This provides a particularly salutary reminder of the danger of viewing 'women' and 'men' as homogeneous groups.

## Acknowledgments

We would like to express our gratitude to the two anonymous peer reviewers, whose comments helped us refine the arguments in this chapter. We would also like to thank Vigdis Sanmark for lending a hand with the typography.

### *Note*

1 The work of Anne Stalsberg is important as she argued already in the 1980s and '90s that women took an active role in both travel and trade (see e.g. Stalsberg 1988; 1991; 2001).

## Bibliography

Abrams, L., 2010. *Myth and Materiality in a Woman's World. Shetland 1800–2000.* Manchester University Press, Manchester.

Andersson Strand, E., 2007. Engendering central places. Some aspects of the organisation of textile production during the Viking Age. In *Archäologische Textilfunde, NESAT IX. Nordeuropäisches Symposium für archäologische Textilien*, eds A. Rast-Eicher and R. Windler. ArcheoTex: Ennenda: 148–153.

Anon., 2015. *Eriks Lov (AM 455, 12mo).* Danish Language and Literature Society: Copenhagen. https://tekstnet.dk/books/anon_eriks-lov/003/accessed 04.09.24.

Arnold, D.E., 1985. *Ceramic Theory and Cultural Process.* Cambridge University Press, Cambridge.

Arwill-Nordbladh, E., 1998. *Genuskonstruktioner i nordisk vikingatid: förr och nu.* Göteborgs universitet, Göteborg.

Athanasiou, T., 2020. Private women and public men? A critique of the gendered dichotomy of the Viking Age. *Northern Studies* 51: 34–49.

Attwood, K.C. (trans.), 1997. Gunnlaugs saga ormstungu. In *The Sagas of Icelanders*, ed. J. Smiley. Penguin: London: 558–594.

Barnes, M.P., 2019. *The Runic Inscriptions of the Isle of Man.* Viking Society for Northern Research: University College London, London.

Batey, C., 2016. Viking burials in Scotland: Two 'new' boat burial finds. In *Shetland and the Viking World.* eds V.E. Turner, O.A. Owen and D.J. Waugh. Shetland Heritage Publications, Lerwick: 39–45.

Batey, C., 2023. Swordle Bay, Ardnamurchan: A Viking boat burial. In *The Viking Age in Scotland: Studies in Scottish Scandinavian Archaeology*, eds H. Tom, E. Pierce and R.C. Barrowman. Edinburgh University Press, Edinburgh: 308–312.

Berg, H.L., 2015. 'Truth' and reproduction of knowledge. Critical thoughts on the interpretation and understanding of iron-age keys. In *Viking Worlds: Things, spaces and movement*, eds M.H. Eriksen, U. Petersen, B. Rundberget, I. Axelsen and H.L. Berg. Oxbow Books, Oxford: 124–142.

Bjarni Einarsson (ed.), 2003. *Egils saga Skalla-Grímssonar.* Viking Society for Northern Research, London.

Bolger, D., 2012. Gender, labor, and pottery production in prehistory. In *A Companion to Gender Prehistory*, ed. D. Bolger. Wiley-Blackwell, Hoboken NJ: 161–179.

Brink, S., 2001. Mytologiska rum och eskatologiska föreställningar i det vikingatida Norden. In *Ordning mot kaos. Studier av nordisk förkristen kosmologi*, eds A. Andrén, K. Jennbert and C. Raudvere. Nordic Academic Press: Lund: 291–317.

Brink, S., 2008. *Lord and Lady – Bryti and Deigja. Some historical and etymological aspects of family, patronage and slavery in early Scandinavia and Anglo-Saxon England.* Viking Society for Northern Research: London.

Brink, S., 2018. Law. In *Handbook of Pre-Modern Nordic Memory Studies: Interdisciplinary Approaches*, Volume 1,eds J. Glauser, P. Hermann and S.A. Mitchell. De Gruyter: Berlin: 185–197.

Byock, J., 2001. *Viking Age Iceland.* Penguin, London.

Cleasby, R. and Vigfusson, G., 1874. *An Icelandic-English Dictionary. Enlarged and completed by Gudbrand Vigfusson.* Clarendon Press, Oxford.

Clover, C.J., 1993. Regardless of sex: Men, women, and power in early Northern Europe. *Speculum: A Journal of Medieval Studies* 68.2: 363–387.

Croix, S., 2011. Status, gender and space on high status settlement sites from the Viking Age. In *Archäologie in Schleswig,* eds L. Boye, P. Ethelberg, L. Heidemann Lutz, P. Kruse and A.B. Sørensen. Wachholtz, Neumünster: 113–122.

Croix, S., 2012. *Work and Ritual Space in Rural Settlements in Viking-Age Scandinavia – Gender Perspectives.* Unpubished Ph.D. thesis, Aarhus University.

Delle, J.A., 1998. *An Archaeology of Social Space: Analyzing coffee plantations in Jamaica's Blue Mountains.* Plenum Press, New York.

Delsing, L.-O., 2017. *Äldre Västgötalagen.* https://project2.sol.lu.se/fornsvenska/.

Dennis, A., Foote, P. and Perkins, R. (ed. and trans.), 1980. *Laws of Early Iceland, Grágás I.* University of Manitoba Press, Winnipeg.

Dennis, A., Foote, P. and Perkins, R. (ed. and trans.), 2000. *Laws of Early Iceland, Grágás II.* University of Manitoba Press, Winnipeg.

Einar Ól. Sveinsson and Matthías Þórðarson (eds), 1935. *Eyrbyggja saga.* Hið íslenzka fornritafélag, Reykjavík.

Emanuelsson, M., Johansson, A. and Nilsson, S., 2003. *Settlement, Shieling and Landscape: The local history of a forest hamlet.* Lund Studies in Medieval Archaeology 32, Stockholm.

Engels, F., 2010. *The Origin of Family, Private Property and the State.* Penguin, London.

Fidjestøl, B., 1999. *The Dating of Eddic Poetry: A historical survey and methodological investigation* (ed. O.E. Haugen). Reitzels, Copenhagen.

Finnur Jónsson, F. (ed.), 1916. *Gunnlaugs saga ormstungu.* https://onp.ku.dk/onp/onp.php?c548872

Gilchrist, R., 1999. *Gender and Archaeology: Contesting the past.* Routledge, London.

Graham-Campbell, J. and Batey, C.E., 1998. *Vikings in Scotland: An archaeological survey.* Edinburgh University Press, Edinburgh.

Guðni Jónsson., 1949. *Rígsþula Eddukvæði.* Reykjavík. Íslendingasagnaútgáfan. https://heimskringla.no/wiki/R%C3%ADgs%C3%BEula

Hastrup, K., 1985. *Culture and History in Medieval Iceland. An Anthropological Analysis of Structure and Change.* Oxford University Press, Oxford.

Hayeur Smith, M., 2020. *The Valkyries' Loom: The archaeology of cloth production and female power in the North Atlantic.* University Press of Florida, Gainesville FL.

Hermann Pálsson and Edwards, P. (eds and trans.), 1989. *Eyrbyggja Saga.* Penguin, London.

Hornby, A.S. and Cowie, A.P., 1989. *Oxford Advanced Learner's Dictionary.* Oxford University Press, Oxford.

Jesch, J., 1991. *Women in the Viking Age.* Boydell Press, Suffolk.

Jochens, J., 1995. *Women in Old Norse Society.* Cornell University Press, London.

Johnson, M., 2011. *Archaeological Theory: An introduction* (2nd edn). Wiley: Hoboken NJ.

Jón Viðar Sigurðsson., 2008. *Det norrøne samfunnet: vikingen, kongen, erkebiskopen og bonden.* Pax, Oslo.

Jón Viðar Sigurðsson., 2017. *Viking Friendship. The Social Bond in Iceland and Norway, c. 900–1300.* Cornell University Press, London.

Kålund, K., (ed.). Laxdæla saga. København, STUAGNL 19.

Kantner, J., McKinney, D., Pierson, M. and Wester, S., 2019. Reconstructing sexual divisions of labor from fingerprints on ancestral Puebloan pottery. *Proceedings of the National Academy of Sciences* 116: 12220–12225.

Keyser, R. and Munch, P.A. (eds), 1846. *Gulaþingslǫg* https://onp.ku.dk/onp/onp.php?b1467-98.

Kupiec, P. and Milek, K., 2015. Roles and perceptions of shielings and the mediation of gender identities in Viking and medieval Iceland. In *Viking Worlds: Things, spaces and movement*, eds M.H. Eriksen, U. Petersen, B. Rundberget, I. Axelsen and H.L. Berg. Oxbow Books, Oxford: 102–123.

Kupiec, P., Milek, K., Gisladóttir, G.A. and Woollett, J., 2016. Elusive *sel* sites: The geoarchaeological quest for Icelandic shielings and the case of Þorvaldsstaðasel, in northeast Iceland. In *Summer Farms, Seasonal Exploitation of the Uplands from Prehistory to the Present Day*, eds J. Collis, M. Pearce, and F. Nicolis. J.R. Collis and Equinox: Bristol: 221–236.

Landes, J.B., 2003. Further thoughts on the public/private distinction. *Journal of Women's History* 15.2: 28–39

Lindqvist, T. (ed. and trans.), 2021. *The Västgöta Laws.* Routledge: London.

Löfgren, O., 1982. Kvinnfolksgöra: om arbetsdelning i bondesamhället. *Kvinnovetenskaplig tidskrift* 3.3: 6–14.

Löndahl, V., Nilars, M. and Svensson, E., 2002. Who did what – and where? An attempt to visualise the social space at Skramle during the late 13th and early 14th centuries. In *Skramle – The True Story of a Deserted Medieval Farmstead*, eds S. Andersson and E. Svensson. Lund Studies in Medieval Archaeology 27, Lund and Stockholm.

Lönnroth, L., 2008. The Icelandic Sagas. In *The Viking World*, eds S. Brink and N. Price. Routledge, Abingdon: 304–322.

Lucas, G., 2008. Pálstóftir: A Viking Age shieling in Iceland. *Norwegian Archaeological Review* 41.1: 85–100.

Lucas, G., 2009. *Hofstaðir: Excavations of a Viking Age feasting hall in north-eastern Iceland*. Institute of Archaeology Monograph Series 1, Reykjavik.

Lund, J. and Moen, M., 2019. Hunting identities: Intersectional pPerspectives on Viking Age mortuary expressions. *Fennoscandia Archaeologica* 36: 142–155.

Magnus Magnusson and Herman Pálsson (eds and trans.), 1969. *Laxdœla Saga*. Penguin, London.

Matras, A.K., Andreasen, H. and Hansen, S.S., 2004. A Viking Age shieling in Skarðsvík, Fugloy, Faroe Islands. *Fróðskaparrit* 51: 200–211.

Meulengracht Sørensen, P., 1991. Om Eddadigtenes Alder. In *Nordisk hedendom. Et symposium*, ed. G. SteinslandOdense Universitet forlag, Odense: 217–228.

Milek, K., 2012. The roles of pit houses and gendered spaces on Viking-Age farmsteads in Iceland. *Medieval Archaeology* 56: 85–129.

Miller, W.I., 1988. Some aspects of householding in the medieval Icelandic Commonwealth. *Continuity & Change* 3: 321–355.

Moen, M., 2010. The Gendered Landscape: A Discussion on Gender, Status and Power Expressed in the Viking Age Mortuary Landscape. Unpublished Master's dissertation, University of Oslo.

Moen, M., 2019. Challenging Gender. A Reconsideration of Gender in the Viking Age Using the Mortuary Landscape. Unpublished PhD thesis, University of Oslo.

Moen, M., 2020. Ideas of continuity: Gender and the illusion of the Viking Age as familiar. In *Viking Encounters*, eds A. Pedersen and S.M. Sindbæk. Aarhus Universitetsforlag, Aarhus: 621–632.

Moen, M., 2021. No man's land or neutral ground: Perceived gendered differences in ideologies of war. *Viking* 84(1): 43–62.

Moilanen, U., Kirkinen, T., Saari, N.J., Rohrlach, A.B., Krause, J., Onkamo, P. and Salmela, E., 2022. A woman with a sword? Weapon grave at Suontaka Vesitorninmäki, Finland. *European Journal of Archaeology* 25.1: 42–60.

Munch, G.S., Johansen, O.S. and Roesdahl, E., 2003. *Borg in Lofoten: A chieftain's farm in north Norway*. Tapir Academic Press: Trondheim.

Mundal, E., 1994. The position of women in Old Norse society and the basis for their power. *NORA: Nordic Journal of Feminist and Gender Research*, 2.1: 3–11.

Mundal, E., 2001. The double impact of Christianisation in Old Norse culture. In *Gender and Religion: European studies*, eds K.E.Børresen, S. Cabibbo and E. Spech. Carocci, Rome: 237–253.

Ney, A., 2002. Myter, ideologi och ogifta kvinnor: Mö-traditionen i fornnordisk myt och verklighet. In *Makalösa kvinnor: Könsöverskridare i myt och verklighet*, ed. E. Borgström. Alfabeta/Anamma, Stockholm: 25–61.

Olsen, M. (ed.), 1906–1908. *Vǫlsunga saga ok Ragnars saga loðbrókar*. Møller Bogtrykkeri, Copenhagen.

Owen, O. and Magnar, D., 1999. *Scar: a Viking boat burial on Sanday Orkney*. Sutton, East Linton.

Øye, I., 2006. Kvinner, kjønn og samfunn; fra vikingtid til reformasjon. In *Med kjønnsperspektiv på norsk historie: fra vikingtid til 200-årsskiftet*, eds I. Blom and S. Frogner. Cappelen Akademiske Forlag: Oslo: 27–144.

Parker Pearson, M. and Richards, C., 1996. *Architecture and Order: Approaches to social space*. Routledge: London.

Pedersen, U., 2014. Kaupangs kvinner. In *Kvinner i vikingtid*, eds N. Coleman and N.L. Løkka. Scandinavian Academic Press, Oslo: 163–180.

Petersen, J. 1951. *Vikingetidens redskaper*. Skrifter utgitt av Det Norske Videnskaps-Akademi i Oslo 1951.4. Det Norske Videnskaps-Akademi, Oslo.

Petré, B., 1993. Male and female finds and symbols in Germanic Iron Age graves. *Current Swedish Archaeology* 1.1:149–154.

Phelpstead, C., 2020. *An Introduction to the Sagas of Icelanders*. University Press of Florida, Gainesville, FL.

Raffield, B., Price, N. and Collard, M., 2017. Polygyny, concubinage, and the social lives of women in Viking-Age Scandinavia. *Viking and Medieval Scandinavia* 13: 165–209.

Ricketts, P., 2010. *High-Ranking Widows in Medieval Iceland and Yorkshire. Property, Power, Marriage and Identity in the Twelfth and Thirteenth Centuries*. Brill, Leiden.

Roesdahl, E., 1998. *The Vikings*. Penguin, London.

Roesdahl, E., 2014. *Aggersborg: The Viking-Age settlement and fortress*. National Museum of Denmark, Copenhagen.

Roslund, M., 2021. Legacy of the disowned. Finding *ambátts* in High Medieval Scania and Östergötland through ceramic production. In *The Archaeology of Slavery in Early Medieval Northern Europe. Themes in Contemporary Archaeology*, eds F. Biermann and M. Jankowiak8. Springer, Cham: 81–89.

Roslund, M., 2022. Tacit knowing of thralls – style negotiation among the unfree in 11th and 12th century Sweden. In *Archaeologies of Contact and Hybridity*, ed M. Brittain and T. Clack. Oxford University Press, Oxford: 211–236.

Sanmark, A., 2004. *Power and Conversion. A Comparative Study of Christianization in Scandinavia*. OPIA, Uppsala University, Uppsala.

Sanmark, A., forthcoming. The role of women in Viking Age society: An evaluation of previous research. In *Viking Women*, eds J. Morawiec, A.I. Riisøy and C. Hedenstierna-Jonson. Turnhout, Brepols.

Scudder, B. (trans.), 2002. *Egil's Saga*. Penguin, London.

Sharples, N., 2020. *A Norse Settlement in the Outer Hebrides: Excavations on Mounds 2 and 2A, Bornais, South Uist*. Oxbow Books, Oxford.

Sharples, N., 2023. The use of space in Norse houses: Some observations from the Hebrides. In *The Viking Age in Scotland: Studies in Scottish Scandinavian Archaeology*, ed. T. Horne, E. Pierce and R.C. Barrowman. Edinburgh University Press, Edinburgh: 75–84.

Simensen, E. (ed. and trans.), 2021. *The Older Gulathing Law*. Routledge, London.

Sørensen, M.-L.S., 2000. *Gender Archaeology*. Polity Press, Cambridge.

Stalsberg, A., 1988. The Scandinavian Viking Age finds in Rus. *Berichte der Römisch-Germanischen-Kommission* 69: 448–471.

Stalsberg, A., 1991. Women as actors in North European Viking age trade. In *Social Approaches to Viking Studies*, ed. R. Samson. Boydell & Brewer, Woodbridge: 75–87.

Stalsberg, A., 2001. Visible women made invisible. Interpreting Varangian women in Old Russia. In *Gender and the Archaeology of Death*, eds B. Arnold and N.L. Wicker. Altamira Press, Walnut Creek CA: 65–80.

Steinsland, G., 2005. The late Iron Age worldview and the concept of 'Utmark'. *UBAS. International* 1.1: 137–146.

Sundqvist, O., 2007. *Kultledare i fornskandinavisk religion*. University of Uppsala, Uppsala.

Sveinbjorn Thordarson (ed.), 2017. *Fljótsdæla saga. Icelandic Saga Database*. http://www.sagadb.org/fljotsdaela_saga.is.

Svensson, E., 2005. Gender and spatial patterns in the Scandinavian farmstead and outland. In *'Utmark' The Outfield as Industry and Ideology in the Iron Age and the Middle Ages*, eds I. Holm. S. Innselset and I. Øye. University of Bergen, Bergen: 157–170.

Tamm, D. and Vogt, H., 2016. *The Danish Medieval Laws. The Laws of Scania, Zealand and Jutland*. Routledge, Abingdon.

Valdimar Ásmundarson 1898. Valla-Ljóts saga.Sigurðr Kristjánsson: Reyjavík.
Venås, K., 1989. Kvinne og mann i Gulatingslova. Etter ein idé av Lis Jacobsen. In *Festskrift til Finn Hødnebø 29. Desember 1989*, eds B. Eithun, E. Fjell Halvorsen, M. Rindal and E. Simensen. Novus, Oslo: 258–303.
Vestergaard, T.A., 1988. The system of kinship in early Norwegian law. *Mediaeval Scandinavia* 12: 160–193.
Vilhjálmur Finsen., 1974. *Grágás: Konungsbók.* Odense Universitetsforlag, Odense.
Wawn, A., 1997. Vatnsdæla saga. In *The Sagas of Icelanders*, ed. J. Smiley. Penguin, London: 185–269.
Young, J. and Haworth, E., 1990. *The Fljotsdale Saga and The Droplaugarsons.* Everyman, London.

# Chapter 6

## Choosing the hero: Drink and the institutionalisation of heroism

*Karen Bek-Pedersen*

The notion of special drinks offered by extraordinary women to exceptional men constitutes a repeated theme in Old Norse heroic and mythological tradition. Such drinks are always alcoholic, the women powerful, and the men invariably heroes. In some texts, but by no means all, these women are called *valkyrjur*, valkyries, and in the relevant iconographic material, scholars frequently interpret the female figures as valkyries. This, however, is not really justified, since other women feature prominently in the narrative motif. Old Norse valkyries partake in battle, personify good luck and protection, and they possess numinous wisdom, but it is the drink that is of interest here.[1] The drink and the offering of it symbolise a singling out of a man by a woman, so valkyries, ostensibly choosers of heroic men, are the obvious starting point for the discussion.

In everyday life, all sorts of unremarkable serving must have existed – slaves serving drink for their masters regardless of gender, men fetching their own drink, women serving other women.[2] This, however, does not detract from the fact that the motif just outlined is persistent in Norse mythic-heroic tradition. I intend here to offer an interpretation of what happens at the symbolic moment when the heroic man accepts the drink from the powerful woman.

### Valkyries in Valhǫll

Three texts in particular paint a consistent picture of valkyries as barmaids in the beyond: *Grímnismál* 36, *Eiríksmál* 1, and *Gylfaginning* 36.

*Grímnismál* is a mythological poem from the anonymous collection of Old Norse mythological and heroic poems known as the *Poetic Edda*. Written *c.* 1270, the narratives recounted in this manuscript are rooted in pre-Christian Norse tradition, probably going back to around the 9th century. In *Grímnismál*, Óðinn recounts much mythical lore, including a mention of the valkyries. Stanza 36 reads:

> *Hrist ok Mist / vil ek at mér horn beri, / Skeggjǫld ok Skǫgul, / Hildr ok Þrúðr, / Hlǫkk ok Herfjǫtur, / Gǫll ok Geirǫmul, / Randgríðr ok Ráðgríðr / ok Reginleif, / þær bera einherjum ǫl.* (Neckel and Kuhn 1962: 64)

> Hrist and Mist, I want them to bring me a horn, Skeggjǫld and Skǫgul, Hildr and Þrúðr, Hlǫkk and Herfjǫtur, Gǫll ok Geirǫmul, Randgríðr ok Ráðgríðr and Reginleif, they serve ale for the einherjar.[3]

The stanza shows 13 valkyries who serve ale for Óðinn's chosen warriors in Valhǫll, the *einherjar*, and Óðinn also wants them to bring him a drinking horn. Although the names indicate affairs of the battlefield, the focus in this stanza is on serving drink. The term *valkyrjur* is not used, but there can be no doubt that this is what the named women are. It is interesting that Óðinn asks them to give him a drink, too. In other words, he seems to be requesting a drink, rather than being in charge of who is served. This is significant.

A comparable description occurs in stanza 1 of the anonymous skaldic poem *Eiríksmál*, composed around 950 in honour of the Norwegian king Eiríkr blóðøx. The stanza is preserved in *Skáldskaparmál* 2, v. 20, which is part of the medieval Christian scholar Snorri Sturluson's work on Norse myth and poetry, written *c.* 1220 and known as *Edda*:

> *'Hvat er þat drauma?' kvað Óðinn. / 'Ek hugðumk fyrir dag rísa / Valhǫll ryðja / fyrir vegnu fólki, / vekða ek einherja, / bæða ek upp rísa / bekki at stráa, / bjórker at leyðra, / valkyjur vín bera, / sem vísi komi.'*[4] (Faulkes 1998: 10)

> 'What sort of dream is this', said Óðinn. 'I thought that just before dawn I was tidying up Valhǫll for slain men, I woke up the einherjar, asked them to get up and strew the benches, rinse the beer cups, [I asked] the valkyries to serve wine as though a prince were coming'.

Here, Óðinn prepares Valhǫll for the arrival of dead men, ordering the *einherjar* to tidy up and the valkyries to serve. Óðinn is clearly in charge; he gives the orders and *einherjar* and valkyries alike obey. The serving of alcoholic drink again appears to be the high point, this time beer and wine.

The third description of valkyries is *Gylfaginning* 36, which is also part of Snorri's *Edda*. Following his cursory portraits of individual goddesses, Snorri says:

> *Enn eru þær aðrar er þjóna skulu í Valhǫll, bera drykkju ok gæta borðbúnaðar ok ǫlgagna. (...) Þessar heita valkyrjur. Þær sendir Óðinn til hverrar orrostu. Þær kjósa feigð á men ok ráða sigri.* (Faulkes 2005: 300)

> There are still others, whose function it is to wait in Valhǫll, serve drink and look after the tableware and drinking vessels. (...) These are called valkyries. Óðinn sends them to every battle. They allot death to men and govern victory. (Faulkes 1987: 31).

This is similar to, yet different from, the two older sources. In *Eiríksmál*, the *einherjar* tidy up while valkyries serve wine; but in Snorri's description, valkyries do the cleaning too. They thus look more like maids who do household chores, although their placement together with a long line of goddesses suggests they are powerful supernatural forces who influence human lives. Snorri has no doubts, however, that they act (or should act) on the orders of Óðinn.

Together, *Grímnismál* 36, *Eiríksmál* 1, and *Gylfaginning* 36 present a coherent view of how valkyries serve alcoholic beverages in Valhǫll – with the slight discrepancy that *Eiríksmál* and *Gylfaginning* have Óðinn in charge, while *Grímnismál* shows him requesting a drink. This little difference in Óðinn's role is significant.

## Romantic valkyries

The Eddic heroic poem *Sigrdrífumál* gives another image (Neckel and Kuhn 1962: 189–197). In the prose introduction, the hero Sigurðr, after slaying the dragon Fáfnir, comes to a shield-fortress so bright it looks like fire. Inside, he finds a sleeping woman wearing helmet and armour, which he cuts open, thus waking her. The actual poetry begins here. In stanza 1, the woman asks who Sigurðr is and he answers; in stanza 2, she says Óðinn caused her to sleep. In the following prose, Sigurðr asks her name, and she offers him a drink of mead called *minnisveig*, 'memory drink'. In stanzas 3 and 4, she calls on cosmic powers to look benignly upon her and Sigurðr and, in the subsequent prose, she says her name is Sigrdrífa and describes herself as a *valkyrja*, although this term is never used in the poetry. The prose preceding stanza 5 says Óðinn made her sleep because she allotted victory to the wrong man and he also declared she must marry. Sigrdrífa swore she would only marry a fearless man. Sigurðr asks her for wisdom from other worlds. Her response follows in stanza 5:

> *Bjór fœri ek þér, / brynþings apaldr, / magni blandinn / ok megintíri; / fullr er hann ljóða / ok líknstafa, / góðra galdra / ok gamanrúna.* (Neckel and Kuhn 1962: 190).
>
> I bring you beer, apple-tree of battle, mixed with strength and great glory; it is full of songs and helping-staves, good charms and joy-runes.

Stanzas 6–19 constitute a catalogue of runic lore that she teaches him; then follows a mythical section, stanzas 14–19, about the origins of runes. In stanzas 20–21, she asks him to make a choice and he chooses her *ástráð*, 'loving advice'. In the last section, stanzas 22–37, she imparts more pragmatic pieces of advice (cf. Weber Pedersen 2012: 93–113).[5]

In the case of *Sigrdrífumál*, the woman offers the hero a drink twice over – in the prose she offers him mead right after he wakens her; in the poetry she offers him beer mixed with songs, staves, charms and runes as a preamble to the catalogue of runic lore. Stanza 18 mentions *heilagr miǫðr*, 'holy mead', mixed with various runes, but this seems to refer to a mythical beverage, not the concrete drink given to Sigurðr. Even so, the three drinks in this poem should likely be seen as separate manifestations of the same thing.[6]

In the prose, the drink is called *minnisveig*, 'memory-drink', which suggests a link to the *speki*, 'knowledge', that Sigrdrífa reveals to Sigurðr. But the drink simultaneously conjures the notion of a marriage between Sigrdrífa and Sigurðr. When Óðinn put her to sleep, she stipulated that she would only marry a fearless man, and that man must presumably prove his fearlessness. Sigrdrífa seems to expect the man who rouses her from her sleep to be that fearless hero. When she offers him the drink, she could therefore be seen to offer herself in marriage, too.

*Sigrdrífumál* possibly conflates two different manifestations of the present theme: 'special woman offers special drink to a special man' – in one, the drink represents knowledge, in the other marriage. Significantly, Sigurðr, in the prose, accepts the drink before he knows Sigrdrífa's identity.[7]

Unlike the three examples discussed above, this is a personal interaction between one man and one woman. *Grímnismál*, *Eiríksmál*, and *Gylfaginning* speak of *valkyrjur* and *einherjar* as collective entities, with only Óðinn standing out as an individual; *Sigrdrífumál* shows two named individuals and suggests a marriage between them. This makes Sigrdrífa different from the valkyries considered hitherto. Her name, 'Victory-driver', fully resembles other valkyrie names, such as those of *Grímnismál* 36, but she only offers drink to the man who is her intended groom. This groups her with Eddic valkyries, who usually enter into romantic relationships with a chosen hero and have human lineages, while valkyries in skaldic poetry are typically decidedly unemotional (Bek-Pedersen 2011: 48–56).

The collective aspect in *Grímnismál* 36, *Eiríksmál* 1, and *Gylfaginning* 36 may point in a specific direction. These valkyries interact with large groups of men, possibly providing a link to the drinks served by Wealþeo, Hygd, and Freawaru in the Old English poem *Beowulf*, where an important part of the motif is the establishment and/or maintenance of a hierarchy within the warband, the highest ranking men being served first (*Beowulf* 611–630 (Fulk *et al.* 2008: 23), 1980–1983 (*ibid.*: 67), 2020–2024 (*ibid.*: 68–69)).[8] Whether the women have a say in who is served first is unclear; they may well be following conventions and so the notion of choosing becomes less relevant. Were a woman to offer drink to 'the wrong man' in an act of volition, this would likely upset expectations. Sigrdrífa was punished for something like this when Óðinn put her to sleep and declared that she must marry. Anyhow, the collective affair is different from the instances where only one man is offered – and accepts – the drink.

## Goddesses and jǫtunn-women

Another three Eddic mythological poems, *Hávamál* 104–110, *Hyndluljóð*, and *Fǫr Skírnis*, portray yet other drink-serving women.

*Hávamál* is likely a compilation of five separate narrative strands, only one of which is of interest here, namely the myth of how Óðinn acquires the mead of poetry from Gunnlǫð in stanzas 104–110 (Neckel and Kuhn 1962: 33–34). A prose version is told in *Skáldskaparmál* G58 (Faulkes 1998: 4–5), which is part of Snorri's *Edda*, but these two versions differ so much from one another that they must be considered separately (Svava Jakobsdóttir 2002: 30–34). The poetic one is clearly more relevant in the present context.

Stanzas 104–110 recount the events as follows: Óðinn is visiting the *jǫtunn* Suttungr's hall where he 'speaks to his own advantage', *mælta ek í minn frama*. Gunnlǫð,

Suttungr's daughter, then gives Óðinn a drink of mead for which he rewards her poorly. In stanzas 106–107, Óðinn leaves the hall abruptly and in disguise, thus apparently bringing the mead, called Óðrerir, to human beings. Óðinn acknowledges that he deceived Gunnlǫð – the impression is that his intentions were never the same as hers, or Suttungr's. In stanza 109, the *jǫtnar* are pursuing him. In stanza 110, Óðinn describes his own untrustworthiness: He swore a sacred oath which he then proceeded to break, and 'he stole the mead from Suttungr and left Gunnlǫð weeping', *Suttung svikinn / hann lét sumbli frá / ok grœtta Gunnlǫðo.*

This situation recalls *Sigrdrífumál* in that the woman offers drink to a particular man, but it changes Óðinn's role radically because, in *Hávamál*, he is merely the recipient, in charge of neither woman nor drink. Although her name sounds valkyrie-like – *gunnr* means 'battle', *lǫð* means 'invitation' – Gunnlǫð, daughter of Suttungr, is not a woman over whom Óðinn has any authority, and the drink clearly does not belong to him. In *Hávamál*, the drink represents something that Óðinn cannot just take; he can only obtain it by receiving it from Gunnlǫð.

This myth – as preserved in *Hávamál* – has been interpreted as a ritual whereby the protagonist (Óðinn) becomes king when he accepts a special drink from the goddess of sovereignty (Gunnlǫð) (Svava Jakobsdóttir 2002; *cf.* Enright 1996: 264–265; Bek-Pedersen 2018). That the context in *Hávamál* 104–110 is ritual can hardly be doubted, nor can the fact that the ritual goes wrong because Óðinn breaks the rules and makes away with the drink. From the Norse material alone, however, kingship may not be the obvious interpretation, but the man who is offered the drink is clearly singled out as special.

In *Hávamál*, too, a kind of marriage is enacted, since Óðinn has sex with Gunnlǫð after accepting the drink from her; he says in stanza 108 that 'I put my arms around her', *lǫgðomk arm yfir*. In this respect, the *Hávamál* sequence resembles that of *Sigrdrífumál*: The man proves himself 'the right one', the woman offers him drink – this act signifies his status as 'the right one' – then follows (the promise of) a marriage between the two of them. In *Hávamál*, Óðinn sleeps with Gunnlǫð; in *Sigrdrífumál*, Sigrdrífa vows to marry only 'the right one' and Sigurðr proves to be that man.

This is one of several points where the prose version of the myth about Óðinn and Gunnlǫð differs markedly (Svava Jakobsdóttir 2002: 30–34, 52–53). In *Skáldskaparmál* G58, Óðinn sneaks in to have sex with Gunnlǫð, and the sex is his way of bargaining with her to get the drink – yet, even in this case, it seems important that she give him the drink. In the poetic version, Óðinn is an honoured guest in Suttungr's hall, and it is only after Gunnlǫð gives him drink that he sleeps with her – so the drink is the doorway to the sex. The drink, in this case, seems to represent the (intended) marriage, but it also carries connotations of wisdom and knowledge. The link to knowledge is implied in stanza 107, which calls the mead *Óðrerir*, 'Mind-Stirrer'. The poem likely represents an older pattern for the myth than the prose.

Also *Hyndluljóð* is relevant to the theme of drink offered to certain men by certain women (Neckel and Kuhn 1962: 288–296). In this poem, Freyja ensures that her protégé, Óttar, acquires the knowledge that allows him to outdo his opponent, Angantýr, by strengthening Óttar's claim to the inheritance that both men seek to obtain. The knowledge is grudgingly imparted by the *jǫtunn*-woman Hyndla, and Freyja moreover ensures that Hyndla gives Óttar a 'memory-drink', *minnisǫl*, to help him remember. Knowledge is clearly the central issue here, the woman is definitely no valkyrie, and she does not (intend to) marry the man who gets the drink. *Hyndluljóð* differs from the other cases discussed hitherto in that the woman in charge of the drink gives it to the man unwillingly; she even poisons it as she hands it to him.

This 'memory-drink' serves primarily as a magical potion that enables the protagonist to recall the information given to him, as in *Sigrdrífumál*. Looking beyond this layer for more latent messages in the scene in *Hyndluljóð* may be stretching things too far, but the poem clearly incorporates the idea of the hero being singled out at the point when he is offered the drink. Óttar is chosen above Angantýr because he is offered the special drink – or is offered it first.

Hyndla is anything but willing to part with her knowledge and the drink. At the beginning of the poem (stanzas 1–8), Freyja has to coax Hyndla out of her cave to a place on the road to Valhǫll where the two of them sit down and talk about the lineages, and she also disguises Óttar as her boar, Hildisvíni, although Hyndla sees through that. Then follows the genealogical and mythical knowledge (stanzas 9–44). After this, Freyja requests a 'memory-drink' for her boar in stanza 45: *Ber þú minnisǫl / mínum gelti, / svát hann ǫll muni / orð at tína*, 'Give memory-ale to my boar, so that he may recall all these words'. Hyndla refuses, insults Freyja, and threatens to raise a 'troll-woman's fire', *eldr of íviðio*, so that Freyja and Óttar cannot get away. When she finally does give Óttar a drink of beer in stanza 49, it is mixed with poison. She says to Freyja: *ber þú Óttari / biór at hendi, / eitri blandinn miǫk, / illo heili*, 'Give this beer into Óttar's hand, mixed with much poison and ill fortune'. Freyja, however, seems able to avert Hyndla's bad intentions so that Óttar can drink unscathed.[9]

As mentioned, this is no direct counterpart to Sigrdrífa, yet important similarities exist: Óttar is singled out by a powerful goddess, Freyja, as the one who deserves the drink and thus also the contested inheritance; the drink is a key step for Óttar to attain the status he seeks; the words spoken over the drink as it is served matter. Sigrdrífa speaks very positively as she offers Sigurðr the drink; in Óttar's case, Hyndla speaks with great animosity, but this is then apparently changed into a blessing by Freyja's intervention. In *Hyndluljóð*, the drink symbolises knowledge and high social status – as Óttar receives it, he becomes able to claim his inheritance – but neither sex nor marriage is involved.

Marriage and/or sex, however, is clearly the issue in *Fǫr Skírnis* where Freyr's servant Skírnir persuades Gerðr to enter into a relationship with Freyr (Neckel and Kuhn 1962: 69–77). In this myth, Freyr becomes obsessed with Gerðr after seeing her from a distance and he sends Skírnir off to convince her to enter into a union with Freyr. On arriving at her father's house, Skírnir overcomes various obstacles and holds a conversation with Gerðr during which he first offers her gold, then threatens to kill her if she declines. She declines nonetheless, but when he threatens her mental, physical, social, and sexual health, she consents. At the point where Skírnir has threatened her with an extremely harsh curse, Gerðr says (in stanza 37):

> *Heill verðu nú heldr, sveinn, / ok tak við hrímkalki, / fullom forns mjaðar; / þó hafða ek þat ætlað, / at myndak aldregi / unna vaningia vel.* (Neckel and Kuhn 1962: 76).
>
> Be welcome now, young man, and receive the cup full of ancient mead, though I had never intended that I should love one of the Vanir well.

This resembles *Hyndluljóð* in that very persuasive means are used to force the woman to give in to her visitor's request; it recalls *Hávamál* in that a sexual union is (one of) the main objective(s); and, as in these two poems, the woman is of *jǫtunn*-kin. Interpreting the drink-serving scene in *Fǫr Skírnis* 37 is, however, complicated by the fact that Gerðr says already in stanza 16 – when her servant girl sees Skírnir arriving outside the house – that she should 'Invite him to come into our hall and drink from the renowned mead', *Inn biddu hann ganga / í okkarn sal / ok drekka inn mæra mjǫð*. So, the drink is actually offered twice over – first when Skírnir arrives and again after he has uttered the curse to which Gerðr succumbs.

The exact nature of the obstacles overcome by Skírnir in order to get through to Gerðr is not clear. In stanzas 8–9, Freyr equips him with a horse that will carry him through darkness and a sword that will fight by itself in the hands of a wise man; in stanza 10, Skírnir crosses mountains, and the subsequent prose passage mentions *hundar ólmir*, 'savage dogs'; in stanzas 11–12, a herdsman tells him he will never get to speak to Gerðr; and in stanza 16, Gerðr says she fears that the man outside has slain her brother. Given this, Skírnir looks rather like the hero who proves himself by passing all the tests, and the fact that Gerðr offers him mead already at this point recalls *Sigrdrífumál*, where Sigrdrífa offers Sigurðr mead when he enters the shield-fortress and wakens her. In both cases, the man who manages to make his way through to the woman arguably proves himself 'the right one' simply by doing so. In *Fǫr Skírnis*, Gerðr's reluctance perhaps indicates that she is obliged to offer the drink to the successful candidate, whether she likes him or not. Here, the hero who gets through to the woman with the drink gets his reward, despite her deep-felt averseness.

It is possible that also *Fǫr Skírnis* conflates separate manifestations of the motif. At least, it seems odd that Skírnir is offered the drink twice and that Gerðr expresses similar reluctance both times. An unusual detail is that, in *Fǫr Skírnis*, the man who is offered the drink is only stand-in for the 'groom'. Likewise, Freyja in *Hyndluljóð* is the one who overcomes Hyndla, though she does it on behalf of Óttar who receives the drink. It is odd that Skírnir receives the drink, while Freyr is the one who sleeps with Gerðr, but whatever causes this duplication, *Fǫr Skírnis* does contain a version of the present theme.

## A very old drink

It is clear that Norse tradition knew the motif of an extraordinary woman who offers a special drink to an exceptional man and at the same time chooses him. This is not necessarily an act of volition, but sometimes a reluctant singling out. My suggestion is that the act of offering the drink *is* the choice. The man is not offered the drink because he has been chosen; instead, he is chosen at the point when the drink is offered to him – handing him the drinking vessel *is* the act of choosing. If this is correct, the motif involves a performative act featuring female agency. This idea fits with the scenes in *Sigrdrífumál, Hávamál, Hyndluljóð*, and *Fǫr Skírnis*. It also suggests that when the valkyries in *Grímnismál*, *Eiríksmál*, and *Gylfaginning* serve drink in Valhǫll, the two notions of choosing the slain and offering drink to 'the right one' merge, and the establishment and/or maintenance of a hierarchy among the men is likely also involved. It moreover fits my interpretation of Óðinn's words in *Grímnismál* 36 as his desire to receive a drink rather than an order to be served one. Furthermore, it suggests that the prose version of the myth about Óðinn and Gunnlǫð (in *Skáldskaparmál* G58) presents an alteration of the motif wherein the drink no longer symbolises the act of choosing the hero, although the idea that he must be given the drink by the woman is retained.

One reason why I see the pattern wherein the drink *is* a symbol of choosing 'the right one' as the older one is that it exists in a very old manifestation. It surfaces in what is probably a continental Celtic tradition regarding the founding of Marseilles. The Greek scholar Athenaeus refers in his *Deipnosophistae* (Book 13.576a b; the title means 'The Learned Banqueters') from the early 3rd century AD to a now lost work by Aristotle called 'The Constitution of Massilia'. From this, he cites the following story:

> The Phocaeans who inhabit Ionia were traders and founded Massilia. Euxenes of Phocaea was a guest-friend of King Nanos – which was actually his name.[10] Euxenes happened to be visiting when this Nanos was celebrating his daughter's wedding, and he was invited to the feast. The wedding was organised as follows: After the meal, the girl had to come in and offer a bowl full of wine mixed with water to whichever suitor there she wanted, and whoever she gave it to would be her bridegroom. When the girl entered the room, she gave the bowl, either by accident or for some reason, to Euxenes; her name was Petta. After this happened, and her father decided that the gift had been made in accord with the god's will, so that he ought to have her, Euxenes married and set up housekeeping with her, although he changed her name to Aristoxene. There is still a family in Massilia today descended from her and known as the Protiadae; because Protis was the son of Euxenes and Aristoxene.[11] (Olson 2010: 332–335).

Aristotle, to whom Athenaeus attributes this legend, lived in the 4th century BC, and the founding of Marseilles is historically dated to around 600 BC (Chadwick 1970: 35).[12] The story about Petta who chooses her husband from several suitors on the day of her wedding, and chooses the stranger, involves a marriage as well as a change of status on the part of the chosen man, who becomes the king's son-in-law *and* is accepted into a new society. Offering the drink is a deeply symbolic act: this is how Petta chooses her husband. She is clearly expected to offer the drink to someone and her choice apparently expresses a divine will. She chooses Euxenes by giving him a drink and he practically becomes her husband at the point when he accepts it. There is no reason to imagine that this was the only drink served on the occasion of Petta's wedding but this one merits a mention because it stands out as ritually significant. Petta probably does not have the option of refusing to offer it to anyone, and one may wonder what would have happened if her choice had been deemed to go against the will of the god – something her father determines. The extent to which she expresses her own personal will thus appears limited. As in the Norse narratives, the man is a stranger, an outsider, or a newcomer – yet he is 'the right man'.

Petta's story resembles *Sigrdrífumál*, *Hávamál*, and *Fọr Skírnis* in that the drink is a pre-amble to a marriage or sex; it resembles *Sigrdrífumál*, *Hávamál*, *Hyndluljóð*, and *Fọr Skírnis* – potentially also Óðinn in *Grímnismál* – in that the man is singled out as he is offered the drink; it resembles all of the Norse cases discussed above in that the man's status or abilities change (for the better) when he accepts the drink. In all instances, it is crucial that the drink be offered by the woman; the man cannot take it himself. Athenaeus's account – and even more so Aristotle's, if we accept this reference – adds significant time depth to the motif. It moreover shows that the motif was current in probably both Greek and Celtic tradition and so it is likely to have existed across various European cultures (*cf.* Bek-Pedersen 2018).

Incidentally, having considered the Norse mythical-heroic material, it is noteworthy that the link between a ritual drink and marriage is nowhere to be seen in the saga literature, which is supposedly set during the Viking Age and the centuries preceding it (Guerrero Rodríguez 2007: 232–233). This in itself does not mean that no such ritual existed, but it cannot be verified, which provides grounds for pondering how the mythical-heroic symbolism related to the actual lives of human beings. All the more interesting that the symbolism implied in the mythic-heroic narratives is so clear, a situation which suggests that the symbolism was understood.

*Figure 6.1. The drink-bearing woman featured on the longer of the two Golden Horns from Gallehus, dated to c. 400 and found in 1639. The original was lost and only copies based on 17th century drawings exist (drawing by Nora Bek-Pedersen ©).*

## Iconographic drinks

Scandinavian tradition contains expressions of the motif that pre-date the written accounts by several centuries, including one that rivals Athenaeus's story for age. This is found on the longer of the two Golden Horns of Gallehus, dating from the 5th century AD and found in 1639 (Jensen 2004: 113, 118).[13] This horn carries seven bands of images and the second one features a woman holding a large drinking horn in her hand; she is placed between a riderless horse and another horse with a male rider, and she is facing the horse-riding man (Fig. 6.1). The remaining two figures in this band are a man holding two knives and a man with bow and arrow. It is uncertain whether or how these five images link up and likewise how they relate to the images in the other bands. Still, the woman on the Gallehus horn evokes the story of Petta, as well as the Norse narratives. She is, moreover, strikingly similar to later iconographic representations from Scandinavia – even ones from the Christian Middle Ages.

The Lewis Chessmen, which were found in Scotland but made in Norway around 1200, include two queens holding drinking horns in their left hand while cradling their chin in their right hand (Caldwell *et al.* 2009: 157 fig. 2 b and c, 173; Fig. 6.2). Without any context it is hard to tell how the chess queen's drinking horn is to be understood, although her status as queen likely points in the direction of Wealþeo who maintains a hierarchy, rather than the women who single out a man for marriage, status, or knowledge. Obviously, the survival of the motif over an extensive period does not in itself mean that it was understood in the same way throughout the centuries; yet, the many versions from the period in between suggest iconographic continuity.

*Figure 6.2. One of the two Lewis chess queens who are portrayed holding a drinking horn in their left hand, carved from walrus ivory and dating from c. 1200. The piece measures just over 9 cm in height (Caldwell* et al. *2009: 182) (drawing by Nora Bek-Pedersen ©).*

Several of the Gotland picture stones depict images evoking the present theme: a woman offers a drinking horn to a man.[14] A virtually consistent feature of these images is that the man is riding a horse, which distinguishes the Gotland iconography from some of the textual sources discussed above. There could be many reasons for the discrepancy – the iconography may be stylised, there could be regional differences or the like. The relevant stones date from the 8th, 9th, and 11th centuries (Ney 2012: 73–74, 81). I cannot here go into detail with them all, but one of the best-known such images is found on Klinte Hunninge I (Fig. 6.3).[15] In the top panel – on stones displaying the image, it is always placed in the top panel – a warrior on horseback, carrying a shield and a spear, is riding towards the right; above him two men are fighting with drawn swords, and a flying (?) person holds out a ring; a dog runs in front, and a woman standing on the righthand side holds out a horn. The woman and horseman are recognisable, but the other elements are hard to decode on the basis of the known narratives.

These stone images, sometimes called 'the welcome/welcoming scene' (e.g. Nylén and Lamm 1988; Ney 2012), have been interpreted variously as the meeting between Sigurðr and Sigrdrífa; as Óðinn, because some of the images show an eight-legged horse; and as a valkyrie welcoming a deceased warrior to Valhǫll (Raudvere 2003: 66–67, 78–79, 82– 83; Ney 2008: 144–145; cf. Murphy 2013: 121–123). All of these are valid interpretations – they all fit, but this broad validity also means that none of them is *per se* more valid than the others. The general applicability suggests a stock image that may describe a whole range of situations in which a well-dressed woman serves a drink to a horse-riding man.

*Figure 6.3. Uppermost panel of the picture stone Hunninge I, Klinte parish in Gotland, dating from the 8th century and measuring c. 295 cm above ground (Nylén and Lamm 1988: 99) (drawing by Nora Bek-Pedersen ©).*

Archaeology also provides five small Viking Age figurines depicting well-dressed women carrying drinking horns, often grouped with other female figurines of similar size and provenance that do *not* feature drinking horns (Wihlborg 2019: 25, 31–44). An example is the 9th or 10th century silver figurine from Klinta in Öland, Sweden (Fig. 6.4).[16] These figurines are commonly interpreted as valkyries simply on the basis of the drinking horn, but they are, in fact, equally widely applicable (Watt 2019: 200). They may just as well portray Gunnlǫð, Gerðr, Wealhþeo, or none of them, or they could have multiple meanings. The fact that the figurines occur in high status female graves could

*Figure 6.4. Silver figurine found in 1775 as part of a silver hoard at Klinta, Köping parish in Öland, dating from the 9th or 10th century and measuring 3 cm (Helmbrecht 2011: 122; Wihlborg 2019: 81) (drawing by Nora Bek-Pedersen ©).*

well indicate that they are intended to convey something about the human women thus buried rather than represent supernatural creatures (Plochov 2007: 61–62).

Likewise, a few of the many *guldgubber* or gold foil figures from the Vendel Period, c. AD 500 to 800 A, feature women holding drinking vessels (Fig. 6.5). These have recently been interpreted as seeresses or *vǫlur* (*völur*) (Watt 2019: 200–202). The purpose and meaning of *guldgubber* have been much discussed, but their motifs – fairly easily divided into separate groups (Ratke 2009: 151) – differ so widely that they must convey quite different meanings. Again, the drink-carrying woman is only one of several manifestations within this category of artefact. Distinguishing rigidly between *guldgubber* depicting single women with drinking horns and those without may ultimately be irrelevant, but we cannot know for sure.

This extensive relevance of the image evokes Snorri's description of kennings for men and women, respectively, in *Skáldskaparmál* 31 (Faulkes 1998: 40). Here, men are kenned by their achievements, property, genealogy, killings, voyages, hunts, or by mentioning their weapons or ships; women are kenned by their dress, jewellery, gold, and by the beer, wine, or other drink that they serve, and by all things that is proper for them to do or provide. This corresponds neatly to the Gotlandic images, where carrying weapons (and riding horses) is typical of men, while serving drink is typical of women. The kennings must refer to aspects that are either characteristic of or ideals for men and women, and the range of poetic images may well be reflected in the diverse iconographic images.

*Figure 6.5. The 'Melle I'* guldgubbe *found in a location called* Guldhullet *('the gold hole') in Bornholm in 1725, it measures about 2 cm (Watt 2019: 201) (drawing by Nora Bek-Pedersen ©).*

Snorri presents the kennings as if they are descriptions of men and women as such, but this does not guarantee that they present everyday pictures of men and women, all and sundry. Since kennings are directly associated with poetry, might they instead correspond to the poetically minded woman telling her beloved that he is the most marvellous man who ever walked on earth? It amounts to a stock image, while also suggesting that he *is* special – the description, trite and formulaic though it is, renders him anything but ordinary. If this is the sort of image that the poetic kenning material creates, then such stereotypical kennings *are* used to denote women and men as such, while *also* describing them as outstanding and exceptional.

The Gallehus image dates from *c.* AD 400, the Melle I *guldgubbe* from *c.* 600, the age of the Gotland images cover the Scandinavian Viking Age from *c.* 700 to *c.* 1000, as do the female figurines, and the Lewis chess queens date from *c.* 1200. The Norse narrative material was recorded *c.* 1220–1270. This yields a remarkable longevity, although, as mentioned, the motif was not necessarily understood in the same way at all times; indeed, it may always have had multiple meanings. In terms of the ideas presented here, the image may be referred to as 'the singling-out scene', 'the knowledge-bestowing scene', or 'the status-conferring scene', as much as 'the welcoming scene'.

## Real women

As already noted, the motif in focus here is well established in Norse mythical-heroic tradition, and it has deep historical roots, as both the Iron Age iconographic material and Athenaeus's account show. But what does it say about real women in Norse society?

The woman's role in the narrative sources suggest agency on her part – she has the power to give the drink to the man of her choice. Yet, her choice is often curbed, sometimes by convention – warriors who enter Valhǫll are by definition, it seems, greeted by drink-serving valkyries; sometimes by formulaic rule – the man able to pass the test must be offered the drink in recognition of the fact that he is 'the right one'; sometimes by the authority of a more powerful male figure – when Sigrdrífa went against Óðinn's will in battle he punished her. It is likely that the mythical-heroic motif does reflect social reality, but possibly only in ritualised forms of behaviour rather than expressions of volition on the part of individual women. Since the saga literature, whose descriptions of Norse society are more socially realistic, does not contain traces of the motif it may have lost currency by the time of writing the sagas down in the Christian Middle Ages. Whether or not Viking Age women serving drinks to men saw themselves, or were regarded by anyone else, as reflections of powerful supernatural figures is thus a moot point. If so, the mythical-heroic narratives also constitute the oldest evidence for the social reality reflected in them, and the argument thus becomes circular. If not, the many manifestations of the motif, narrative as well as iconographic, convey purely abstract ideas anchored in conceptual spheres, but not attached to concrete social circumstances. This is perhaps not so likely.

Regarding marriage, the sagas do at times suggest that going against a woman's wishes leads to trouble, but such cases are relatively rare in comparison to how often girls simply yield to their fathers' wishes when it comes to choosing a husband (Jochens 1995: 24–48, esp. 47). This makes it hard to argue in favour of female agency as a stable and serious social reality. Yet, the mythical-heroic motif must stem from at least the idea that the woman's opinion mattered – not least because the women in the narratives are anything but meek and compliant. The persistence of the motif combined with the fact that the females it involves are creatures of consequence implies that power over men's lives was – at least at one time – regarded as residing within the feminine principle (cf. Bek-Pedersen 2011).

That exactly a drink constitutes the symbolic choosing of the hero must relate to the fact that alcoholic drink was high status in Norse society, rated above drinks such as milk or water (Guerrero Rodríguez 2007: 99). Moreover, in Norse mythical-heroic tradition, alcoholic drink often symbolises knowledge, insight, memory, and wisdom, as is evident in *Sigrdrífumál* and *Hyndluljóð* and implied in Óðinn's quest for the mead in *Hávamál* 104–110 (cf. Guerrero Rodríguez, 2007: 160–161). Intellectual capacity and social status are thus aspects easily encoded as drink and so these are the things bestowed upon the man who accepts drink from the woman.

## Conclusions

Considering the amount of drinking that must have taken place in Scandinavia throughout the Iron Age and the Viking Age, and thus the inordinate number of times ordinary women must have served ordinary drink to ordinary men, this cannot possibly have been a significant act every time. Yet, the narrative and iconographic material suggests that this act *did* in certain circumstances hold symbolic significance.

In Valhǫll, as described in *Grímnismál*, *Eiríksmál*, and *Gylfaginning*, the serving act seems to have become institutionalised because the singling out happens to all who enter: *valkyrjur* (who choose) serve drink to *einherjar* (who are chosen), and yet both parties remain anonymous collectives. This differs from the notion of one special woman choosing one special man, but at the same time it underlines the idea that only the chosen ones enter Valhǫll and that the valkyries do, or manifest, the choosing. Looking more broadly at the narrative material, the woman in question is not a 'chooser of the slain' but a 'chooser' as such. By offering him drink, she bestows upon the man a prestigious status – as hero, husband, champion, fearless, worthy of attaining insight and wisdom. The motif has multiple meanings and thus multiple purposes.

The narrative material discussed here reveals that it is a crucial feature that the drink – and whatever it symbolises in the given context – comes from the woman. The man cannot simply take it, she has to give it to him. This suggests that she possesses agency and is able through singling out one man to exercise her own individual will; yet, the extent to which it should be seen as an act of volition on her part or as a performance required of her by convention is unclear.

The symbolism entailed in the drink involves a change in social status for the man who accepts it – a marriage, the acquisition of special knowledge, acceptance by a god. And the woman who offers this drink holds some sort of power; she is able by means of her choice to transform the life and status of the man she singles out. Within the realm of myth and legend, female agency is thus prominently conveyed. Although the socially realistic saga literature never shows human women who conform to this motif, it is hard not to see it as the expression of a deep-rooted traditional view of the power of the feminine principle, whose role and function was still remembered and retained in old mythical-heroic imagery. Within the human world, this imagery would only be able to surface through actions performed by ordinary mortal women.

### Notes

1 For general explorations of *valkyrjur*, see Egeler (2011); Murphy (2013).

2 The mythical-heroic tradition also has men serving special drinks to other men, e.g. the prose introduction to *Grímnismál* where Agnarr offers drink to the disguised Óðinn, upon which the god divulges knowledge (Neckel and Kuhn 1962: 57); another instance is *Beowulf* 494–496 where a *þegn*, high ranking retainer of King Hroðgar, *scencte scir wered*, 'poured bright mead', for a band of warriors (Fulk *et al.* 2008: 19).

3 Unless otherwise stated, translations are my own.

4 See also Skaldic Project online: https://skaldic.org/m.php?p=text&i=1009

5 In *Vǫlsunga saga* 21, the corresponding scene has Brynhildr inviting Sigurðr to drink with her after he wakes her. She also offers him drink in chapter 25 when she predicts they will never marry (Grimstad 2000: 146–153). See also note 9.

6 Especially mead was regarded as imbued with poetic qualities (Guerrero Rodríguez 2007: 124–125).

7 In some Irish mythical tales, the hero is offered a drink and/or sex by an old hag who, upon his acceptance, turns out to be a beautiful, young personification of sovereignty (Bek-Pedersen 2018: 10–13).

8 *Beowulf* 611–630 (Fulk *et al.* 2008: 23); lines 1162–1232 show Wealhþeo in a similar scene, lines 1980–1983 show Hygd, Hygelac's queen, serving mead for all the Geats, and lines 2020–2024 show Hroðgar's daughter, Freawaru, serving ale to the men in the hall. Enright (1996: 1–37) explores the aristocratic woman's role within the ruler's group of retainers.

9 In *Vǫlsunga saga* 28, Grimhildr concocts a drink for Sigurðr to make him forget his promise to Brynhildr and marry Guðrún instead (Grimstad 2000: 166–171). Sigurðr falls in love with Guðrún as she serves him drink, possibly an echo of the present theme.

10 *Nanos* means 'dwarf', hence the comment (Olson 2010: 333).

11 Cf. Enright (1996: 82); ÓhÓgáin (2002: 27); Bek-Pedersen (2018: 22–23).

12 At that time, the area was inhabited by Ligurians rather than Celts, but the story probably made sense in Aristotle's time, because by the 4th century BC the area was under the control of Celtic tribes (Chadwick 1970: 54–56; ÓhÓgáin 2002: 27).

13 Both horns were later stolen; today, only copies survive (Jensen 2004: 115–118). This yields reservations about the exact look of the images on the original horns.

14 Ney (2012: 81) lists 14 stones depicting (elements of) the scene: Klinte Hunninge I, Lärbro Tängelgårda I, Lärbro Stora Hammars III, Lärbro Stora Hammars IV, Halla Broa II, Halla Broa III, Halla Broa IV, Stenkyrkja Lillbjärs III, Klinte socken, Alskog Tjängvide I, Garda Bote, När Bosarve, Hablingbo kyrka, and Ekeby kyrka (Ney 2012: 73–74). It is, however, a sobering thought to note how different people's drawings of the same stones deviate from one another (Ney 2012: 72, 74).

15 Nylén and Lamm (1988: 175) contains a visual overview of ten different manifestations of the image.

16 Hitherto, all examples of this type have been found in Swedish and Danish areas; see Helmbrecht (2011: 121–123, Abb. 23f, no.803); *cf.* Wihlborg (2019: 20–21, 32–33, 78–82).

## Bibliography


Bek-Pedersen, K., 2011. *The Nornir in Old Norse Mythology*. Dunedin Academic Press, Edinburgh.

Bek-Pedersen, K., 2018. Gefjun, Gylfi and Skjöldr: Kingship and land. *Queastiones Medii Aevi Novae* 23: 7–25.

Caldwell, D.H., Hall, M.A. and Wilkinson, C.M., 2009. The Lewis Hoard of gaming pieces: A re-examination of their context, meanings, discovery and manufacture. *Medieval Archaeology* 53: 155–203.

Chadwick, N., 1970. *The Celts*. Penguin, London.

Egeler, M., 2011. *Walküren, Bodbs, Sirenen: Gedanken zur religionsgeschichtlichen Anbindung Nordwesteuropas an den mediterranean Raum*. Ergänzungsbände zum Reallexikon der Germanischen Altertumskunde 71, Berlin.

Enright, M.J., 1996. *Lady with a Mead Cup. Ritual, Prophecy and Lordship in the European Warband from la Tène to the Viking Age*. Four Courts Press, Dublin.

Faulkes, A. (ed. and trans.), 1987. *Edda - Snorri Sturluson*. Everyman, London.

Faulkes, A. (ed.), 1998. *Snorri Sturluson - Edda: Skáldskaparmál 1: Introduction, text and notes*. Viking Society for Northern Research, University College London, London.

Faulkes, A. (ed.), 2005. *Snorri Sturluson - Edda: Prologue and Gylfaginning*. Viking Society for Northern Research, University College London, London.

Fulk, R.D., Bjork, R.E. and Niles, J.D. (eds), 2008. *Klaeber's Beowulf* (4th edn). University of Toronto Press, Toronto.

Grimstad, K. (ed.), 2000. *Vǫlsunga Saga - The Saga of the Volsungs*. AQ-Verlag, Saarbrücken.

Guerrero Rodríguez, J.F., 2007. *Old Norse Drinking Culture*. Unpublished PhD thesis, University of York. https://etheses.whiterose.ac.uk/14217/1/542807.pdf.

Helmbrecht, M., 2011. *Wirkmächtige Kommunikationsmedien: Menschenbilder der Vendel- und Wikingerzeit und ihre Kontexte*. Acta Archaeologica Lundensia Series in 4° 30, University of Lund, Lund. https://lup.lub.lu.se/record/1936472.

Jensen, J., 2004. *Danmarks Oldtid: Yngre Jernalder og Vikingetid 400-1050 e.Kr*. Gyldendal, København.

Jochens, J., 1995. *Women in Old Norse Society*. Cornell University Press, Ithaca NY.

Murphy, L.J., 2013. Herjans Dísir: Valkyrjur, Supernatural femininities, and elite warrior culture in the late pre-Christian Iron Age. Unpublished Master's Thesis, University of Iceland, Reykjavík. https://skemman.is/handle/1946/15652.

Neckel, G. (ed.) and Kuhn, H. (rev.), 1962 [1914]. *Edda: Die Lieder des Codex Regius nebst verwandten Denkmälern*. Carl Winter Universitätsverlag, Heidelberg.

Ney, A., 2008. Sigurdtraditionens välkomstmotiv i text och bild. In *Fornaldarsagaerne - Myter og virkelighed*, eds A. Ney, Á. Jakobsson and A. Lassen. Museum Tusculanum, København: 143–152.

Ney, A., 2012. The welcoming scene on gotlandic picture stones, in comparison with Viking period and medieval literary sources. In *Gotland's Picture Stones - Bearers of an Enigmatic Legacy*, ed. M.H. Karnell. Gotland Museum, Visby: 73–82.

Nylén, E. and Lamm, J.P., 1988. *Stones, Ships and Symbols. The Picture Stones of Gotland from the Viking Age and Before*. Gidlunds Bokförlag, Stockholm.

Olson, S.D. (ed. and trans.), 2010. *Athenaeus: The Learned Banqueters VI, Books 12–13.594b*. Loeb Classical Library 327, Cambridge MA.

ÓhÓgáin, D., 2002. *The Celts: A history*. Collins Press, Cork.

Plochov, A.V., 2007. An interesting find from Staraja Ladoga: A representation of Freyja? In *Cultural Interaction Between East and West. Archaeology, Artefacts and Human Contacts in Northern Europe*, eds U. Fransson, M. Svedin, S. Bergerbrant and F. Androshchuk. Stockholm Studies in Archaeology 44, Stockholm: 61–65.

Raudvere, C., 2003. *Kunskap och insikt i norrön tradition - mytologi, ritualer och trolldomsanklagelser*. Nordic Academic Press, Lund.

Ratke, S., 2009. Guldgubber – a glimpse into the Vendel Period. *Lund Archaeological Review* 15: 149–159.

Skaldic Project online (Skaldic Poetry of the Scandinavian Middle Ages). https://skaldic.org/m.php?p=skaldic.

Svava Jakobsdóttir., 2002. Gunnlǫð and the precious mead. In *The Poetic Edda: Essays on Old Norse mythology*, eds P. Acker and C. Larrington. Routledge, New York: 27–57.

Watt, M. 2019. Gold foil figures and Norse mythology: Fact and fiction? In *Myth, Materiality, and Lived Religion: In Merovingian and Viking Scandinavia*, eds K. Wikström af Edholm, P.J. Rova, A. Nordberg, O. Sundqvist and T. Zachrisson. Stockholm University Press, Stockholm: 191–221.

Weber Pedersen, B., 2012. De mytiske runer som viden og magt. Unpublished kandidatspeciale, Religionsstudier, Syddansk Universitet, Odense.

Wihlborg, J., 2019. Mer än valkyrior: En omtolkning av vikingatidens feminine figuriner. Unpublished Master's Dissertation, University of Lund, https://www.diva-portal.org/smash/get/diva2:1366723/FULLTEXT01.pdf.

# Chapter 7

# The housewife and cult leader Friðgerðr Þorðardóttir in Viking Age Iceland[1]

*Olof Sundqvist*

## Introduction

Old Norse sources report that women could be in charge of religious and ritual practices in Viking Age Scandinavia. Several scholars have in previous research produced the impression that these female leaders belonged to a social and religious periphery (see e.g. Olsen 1926: 254; Steinsland and Vogt 1981; Ström 1985: 87–88, 223–28; and nuanced in Murphy 2018). The males, on the other hand, they state, appeared in the public cult at the aristocratic halls located at central places. There, they devoted themselves to worshipping the war-like Æsir deities, such as Óðinn and Þórr. The female leaders, however, performed rites in considerably more limited social environments; that is, in the household and local cult of simpler sanctuaries. If they sacrificed publicly, it was exclusively in a fertility cult devoted to the Vanir deities, especially Freyr and Freyja (on the background of the term/name *vanir* in pre-Christian mythology, see the debate between e.g. Simek 2010; Frog and Roper 2011; Lindow 2020). The main cult activity for women, researchers argued, was the ritual called *seiðr* (see below). These kinds of rites were often questioned by the elite and considered ill-fitting for men (e.g. Ström 1985: 224). If pushed, one could say thus that previous scholars sometimes construed a kind of stereotypic dichotomy in their description of cult leaders and religious specialists (see Table 7.1).

The present writer has in several studies opposed this view (see Sundqvist 2005; 2007; 2016; 2020a). There are several problems with this binary model when read against the Viking source material, not least regarding the social categories of private and public. Probably, these spheres were much more intertwined, and some activities that took place at an individual farm, especially in the magnate's hall, belonged also to public life. There was a sliding scale between the private and public, and leadership roles related to gender could cross the boundary between them.

*Table 7.1. Former stereotypic dichotomy in descriptions of cult leaders and religious specialists*

| *Female cult leaders* | *Male cult leaders* |
|---|---|
| Private/household religion | Public religion |
| Local cult (periphery) | Central cult at halls |
| Vanir | Æsir |
| Cult related to Freyr & Freyja | Cult related to Óðinn & Þórr |
| Fertility cult | Ruler, warrior & death cult |
| Witchcraft & magic (*seiðr*) | Blót & public sacrifices |

The statement that women had religious authority only within the house could also be questioned (see e.g. Arwill-Nordbladh 1998; cf. Jesch 1991; Sawyer 1992; Gräslund 2011; Back Danielsson *et al.* 2012; Hedenstierna-Jonson *et al.* 2017; Hållans Stenholm 2019). The same is true of the belief that female leaders and specialists exclusively devoted themselves to fertility and witchcraft. There are clear signs that women could also include ritual roles at aristocratic halls in contexts that concerned war lords with warrior bands, in Latin sources called *comitatus* (cf. Enright 1996). Their cult was centred on Óðinn, the god of war, death, and knowledge (cf. Nordberg 2004; Price 2019). Sources also indicate that females were involved in sacrificial rituals (see below).

The present writer has previous argued that one reason why researchers have adopted the binary model maybe their choice of sources (Sundqvist 2020a). Often, they based their reasoning on the Sagas of the Icelanders, all of which were written by Christian hands. In the medieval Church, religious leadership in public contexts was purely a male business. Females could, however, play religious roles in the private sphere (cf. Gräslund 2001: 65–69). These Christian gender roles could thus have had an impact and been projected onto the descriptions of pre-Christian religious leadership in the medieval sagas. Within a public and legal sphere, perceived as male, Christianity was adopted first while, within a domestic sphere, perceived as female, the pagan cult was maintained in the lived religion (Grønlie 2006a; cf. Murphy 2018: 81). The description of the cultic role of the *húsfreyja* 'housewife' in *Vǫlsa þáttr* could be an example of this (Þorleifur Hauksson and Marteinn Helgi Sigurðsson 2018: 271–79; *Flateyjarbók* II (Guðbrandur Vigfússon and Unger 1860–1868): 331–335). She performs obscure fertility rites still during St Óláfr's reign (r. 1015–1028, 30), when most Norwegians had already converted to Christianity. By means of highlighting completely different source categories and re-interpreting the sagas, we may also find female cultic leaders and religious specialists in public contexts, also appearing in 'Odinic discourses' involving war, death, and funerals. The present writer concluded in the previous article (Sundqvist 2020a) that some *húsfrúr* indeed functioned as cult leaders on individual farms in more limited social contexts, but some ladies, such as the chieftain's wife or the queen, probably appeared publicly in ritual roles at the halls of central settlements. The rites led by these women were probably not limited to fertility and the cult of Freyr or Freyja, but included also military aspects, death, and the worship of the male Æsir deities. These rites performed in sovereign contexts probably concerned society as a whole, for instance when a chieftain died and power had to be renegotiated. The female ritual specialists called *vǫlur*, moreover, probably had some kind of connections with Óðinn. The archaeological evidence indicates that they not only performed rites in a social periphery but also played important roles publicly in aristocratic milieus and places related to a social centre (see below).

In the present study, I will take my point of departure from an Old Norse prose text called *Kristni saga* ('The Story of Conversion') and a narrative about a *gyðja* and *húsfreyja* called Friðgerðr and her son Skeggi. In this text they appear in a clear cultic context on their farm, at Hvammr, in western Iceland, in the end of the 10th century. Most scholars argue that *Kristni saga* (Grønlie 2006b) should be dated to the middle or second half of the 13th century. The narratives in it are affected by a medieval ecclesiastic tendency, however, the saga also includes contemporary skaldic stanzas. These verses are usually considered to have a significantly higher historical source value than the prose. In what follows, the role, social significance and the function of the *gyðja* Friðgerðr will be discussed. In this discussion, I will broaden the perspective and put the light on some other female ritual performers who, in the sources, appear on different levels of the Viking Age society. But before that, the native concepts focused on as well as the analytic terminology and a classification system used in this chapter will be presented.

### Old Norse terms of female cult leaders

There are several native terms denoting female cult leaders in the Old Norse sources. The most common terms are *húsfreyja* (*húsfrú*), *gyðja*, and *vǫlva*. In dictionaries the term *húsfreyja* (f.) has the meaning 'a house-wife, lady, mistress of the house' but also 'a wife' (Zoëga 2004 [1910]; *Ordbog over det norrøne prosasprog* (ONP); see also Heggstad *et al.* 2012: *kone i huset, husfru, husmor; matmor; ektekone*). This term's etymology does not testify to a religious function (*hús* 'house' + *freyja* (*frú*) 'wife, lady'). However, the sources indicate that the women who were designated *húsfreyja* (*húsfrú*) were involved in the cult which was performed more privately within the household (cf. Murphy 2018). Some of these *húsfreyjur* (*húsfrúr*) have also been called *gyðjur* and may have had a role in a more public cult at a *hof*-shrine. There is no indication that these women performed the ritual known as *seiðr*, however.

The term *gyðja* (f.) designates a female equivalent of a male titled *goði*. The Old Norse appellative *goði* (m.sg) is derived from the noun *goð* (n.pl) 'gods'. According to Jan de Vries (1956–1957 I: 400), the concept *goði* should be understood as '[a man] who belongs to, or is in the service of, a god' ([*ein Mann*], *der zu einem Gott gehört, oder in dessen Dienst steht*), thus indicating an original cultic function of these leaders. The etymology of the term *gyðja* shows thus an original relation to the gods, that is, a female cult leader or religious specialist (or less likely 'goddess'). As will be seen below, a *gyðja* could be in charge of a *hof*-sanctuary in the Old Norse sources, where she performed sacrificial rituals.

The females designated *vǫlur* (f.pl.) (*vǫlva* sg.) appear mostly in the medieval prose texts, where they travelled from farm to farm and performed a ritual called Old Norse *seiðr*.[2] The word *vǫlva* is linked with the term *vǫlr*, meaning 'staff', referring to a ritual object, also called Old Norse *stafr*, *seiðstafr*, *gandr*, and *gambanteinn*. The term *vǫlva* means thus 'a female bearer of a staff' (*Stabträgerin*) (de Vries 1961). Recently, Leszek Gardeła (2016) has made a thorough and critical assessment of all such known staffs from the Viking Age North including archaeological, iconographic, and textual sources leading to an interpretation of these staffs as 'multivalent objects', but often with magical purposes (cf. Tolley 2009 1: 536–544). Eldar Heide (2006) made an interesting interpretation where he suggested that these staffs actually were distaffs, including a symbolic meaning and used in connection to the *seiðr* ritual. The question whether the *vǫlva* included the same functions as a *húsfrú* or a *gyðja*, will be discussed below.

***Analytic terms for classification of religious leadership***

In previous research it has been argued that common features of priests or priesthood are vague or completely lack in sources related to early Scandinavian conditions (see e.g. Ström 1985: 72–73; cf. Sundqvist 1998; 2020a; 2020b). Because of these circumstances, it has been argued that the use of the concept 'priest' could be misleading in treatments on Old Norse religion, and especially when the survey is about women's religious leadership. Since the concept of 'priest' (from Greek *presbyteros* 'the older', *presbys* 'old person') is, moreover, formed and developed within a Christian tradition, the present author has suggested that it is better to use more neutral terms in Scandinavian contexts in order to avoid serious mis-interpretations (see e.g. Sundqvist 2007; cf. Rüpke 1996).[3] This type of criticism has indeed its limitation, since the concept of a 'priest' could be used as an etic construction and an operational concept, completely defined by the analyst (cf. Sinding Jensen 2014: 7) and thus more or less freed from its ordinary emic use and associations in, for instance, Christian contexts. Anyhow, in the present study, the description 'cult leader' is proposed. It refers here to a person who has temporary responsibility for certain religious functions in society at different types of cult sites, as the organiser of public cult and occasionally also as the performer of (sacrificial) rites. The cult leader has other (societal) duties beside his or her religious tasks. He or she also functions as a general (political) leader in different contexts and on various social levels. The term 'religious specialist' designates an exclusive religious office in the present study, that is, it describes that a more intensified and permanent specialisation has taken place and that the religious leader has become well-trained and professional (cf. Bell 1992: 130–141; Rüpke 1996; Turner 2010). One advantage with these terms is that they could be used for both male and female leaders. In what follows, I will thus use them when returning to the argument of this chapter, that is, that Friðgerðr was a housewife and a cult leader, who was in charge of a local sanctuary in a settlement of western Iceland, with her husband and son.

## The sources

Chapter 1 of *Kristni saga* narrates that the Icelander Þorvaldr víðfǫrli Koðránsson undertook a mission in Iceland with a Saxon bishop called Friðrekr in the 980s. It is stated that they were not badly received when they started their activities:

> ... the bishop and Þorvaldr travelled around the Northern Quarter, and Þorvaldr preached the faith to people because the bishop did not at the time understand Norse. And Þorvaldr preached God's message boldly, but most people made little response to their words. (Old Norse text in Sigurgeir Steingrímsson *et al.* 2003; trans. Grønlie 2006b)

It seems thus as if the pagans in the northern parts of Iceland were quite tolerant, since they could stay there for such long period with their mission work (Jón Hnefill Aðalsteinsson 1999: 75). When Þorvaldr and the bishop started to preach the faith at the old assemblies and cult sites the confrontation with the pagans became harsh. In chapter 2 of *Kristni saga* it is stated thus:

> Þorvaldr and the bishop went to the Western Quarter to preach the faith. They came to Hvammr during the Althing, to the home of Þórarinn fylsenni, and he was then at the assembly, but his wife Friðgerðr was at home with their son Skeggi. Þorvaldr preached the faith to people there, but meanwhile Friðgerðr was in the temple and sacrificed and each of them heard the other's words, and the boy Skeggi laughed at them. Then Þorvaldr uttered this verse:

| | |
|---|---|
| *Fór ek með dóm inn dýra,* | I preached the precious faith, |
| *drengr hlýddi mér engi;* | no man paid heed to me; |
| *gátum háð at hreyti* | we got scorn from the sprinkler |
| *hlautteins, goða sveini* | – priest's son – of blood-dipped branch. |
| *En við enga svinnu* | And without any sense, |
| *aldin rýgr við skaldi,* | old troll-wife against poet |
| þá kreppi *Guð gyðju,* | – may God crush the priestess – |
| *gall um heiðnum stalla.* | shrilled at the heathen altar. |

> No one had themselves baptised as a result of their words in the Western Quarter, as far as is known, but in the Northern Quarter many people left off sacrifices and broke up their idols, and some refused to pay the temple tax. (Old Norse text in *Kristni saga*: Sigurgeir Steingrímsson *et al.* 2003: 9–10)

We can note that two textual time-lines appear in the composition of this passage, one is related to the scribe who writes the tale in the middle or second half of the 13th century, and another one, which is connected to Þorvaldr's contemporary *lausavísa*, that we can date to the end of the 10th century. This *vísa* is thus an eye witness description of the old customs.

Similar versions of the saga text appear in the so called *Kristni þættir*, that is, short Christian stories on the conversion of Iceland, which appears in the manuscripts of *Óláfs saga Tryggvasonar en mesta*. It was compiled soon after 1300. *Þorvaldr þáttr Víðfǫrla* I (Sigurgeir Steingrímsson *et al.* 2003: 73–75) presents Friðgerðr with some details not mentioned in *Kristni saga*. It is stated that she is Þórarinn bóndi's *húsfreyja* and the daughter of Þórðr Bjarnarson from Hǫfði. Þórarinn was son of the powerful man Þorðr gellir, who is well-attested in reliable sources (*Kristni saga*: Sigurgeir Steingrímsson *et al.* 2003: 9–10; *Íslendingabók*, Jakob Benediktsson 1986: 11–13; *Landnámabók* ch. S116, Jakob Benediktsson 1986: 158). The *þáttr* reports that Friðgerðr first received Þorvaldr and the bishop well at Hvammr. However when Þorvaldr started to preach to the people there, Friðgerðr sacrificed while she was indoors. It is also mentioned that no one had themselves baptised as a result of their words in the Western Quarter, but in the Northern Quarter many people abandoned the worshipping of idols, pagan customs, and some refused to pay the temple tax. This *þáttr* also quote Þorvaldr's *lausavísa* with a few minor variations compared to the version quoted in *Kristni saga*. Friðgerðr is also called *húsfreyja* in *Þorvaldr þáttr Víðfǫrla* II (Sigurgeir Steingrímsson *et al.* 2003: 95), which renders a text closely to *Þorvaldr þáttr Víðfǫrla* I, including Þorvaldr's *lausavísa*.

## The gyðja and the cultic context

Þorvaldr's *lausavísa* informs us about two or perhaps even three pagan cult leaders at the local sanctuary of Hvammr, one female and perhaps two male cultic actors. In Þorvaldr's *lausavísa* the concept *gyðja* appears, however, it does not tell whether this title refers to Friðgerðr or not. Indeed, the prose context indicates that she is the woman designated *gyðja* in this *lausavísa*. This stanza also states that Friðgerðr was shouting from the heathen 'altars' or 'platforms' (*gall um heiðnum stalla*). Even if the ritual context is not fully clear in the stanza, it seems as if the *gyðja* was performing sacrifices or some other type of religious ceremony at a ritual structure (*stallr/stalli*) of a sanctuary (see further below). This is also attested in the contextual prose: 'Friðgerðr was in the *hof*-sanctuary and sacrificed (*blótaði*)'.

The Sagas of Icelanders report about several female cult leaders or religious specialists, designated *gyðjur* or *hofgyðjur*, who could be in charge of *hof*-buildings in Iceland (see Sundqvist 2020b). *Vápnfirðinga saga* chapter 5 (Jón Jóhannesson 1950: 32–35), for instance, describes the *hofgyðja* called Steinvǫr. She was in charge of a major *hof*-building (*varðveitti hǫfuðhofit*) at the farm called Hof in Vápnfjǫrðr, in eastern Iceland. All the local farmers must pay sanctuary tributes to her. We cannot rule out that Steinvǫr also had some kind of political position in Vápnfjǫrðr since she according to the text took care of the sanctuary tributes. In order to carry out this task, she was however supported by the chieftain Brodd-Helgi, which indicates that she herself did not control any military or physical power. Other *gyðjur* and *hofgyðjur* also occur in the medieval texts. In *Landnámabók* (chs S180, H147; Jakob Benediktsson 1986: 223) and *Vatnsdæla saga* chapter 35, for instance (Einar Ól Sveinsson 1939: 71–72, 95), Þuríðr gyðja Sǫlmundardottir is mentioned. She was connected to the farm *Hof* in Vatnsdalr, where a *hof*-building had been erected by Ingimundr inn gamli. Þorlaug gyðja Hrólfsdóttir was, according to *Landnámabók*, associated with the *hof*-sanctuary at Reykjardalr in southwestern Iceland (*Landnámabók,* chs S41, H29; Jakob Benediktsson 1986: 79–80, 168–169), while Þuríðr hofgyðja Véþórmsdóttir and her brother Þórðr Freysgoði Ǫzurarson were linked to sanctuaries situated in Bakkárholt in south Iceland (*Landnámabók*, ch. H276; Jakob Benediktsson 1986: 321).

Magnus Olsen (1926) argued that the *gyðjur* were exclusively associated with the fertility cult directed towards Freyr and that these female cult leaders were regarded as this deity's wives (Norwegian *ektefelle*). In *Ǫgmundar þáttr dytts*, for instance, there is a female cultic leader, perhaps a *gyðja*, who is called *Freys kona*, 'Freyr's wife' (Jónas Kristjánsson 2001: 109–115). Folke Ström (1985) claimed that these women had only a function in the private cult. They sacrificed on the farm at simpler sanctuaries called *hǫrgr*. Sometimes, they could also sacrifice at a public sanctuary to the fertility gods, Freyr and Freyja. They were then called *hofgyðjur* but lacked political power and greater influence in public life. The weak evidence can neither deny nor corroborate this. But perhaps we can connect at least Þuríðr hofgyðja to Freyr, since she was the sister of Þórðr Freysgoði, whose family was called *Freysgyðlingar* 'the descendants of a Freyr cult leader (*Freysgoði*)'. In the region of their home there is, moreover, a place called *Freysnes* 'Freyr's headland'. Friðgerðr connection with a *hof*-sanctuary and sacrifice rituals (*blót*) harmonises thus well with information about *gyðjur* in other Old Norse sources. She probably had a function in the household cult, or perhaps in the local public cult at a *hof*-sanctuary in the settlements around Breiðafjǫrður.

### *The two male cult leaders* (goðar) *and their ritual functions*

In order to find out more about the cultic context of the gyðja Friðgerðr at Hvammr we must turn to the other cult performers probably mentioned in Þorvaldr's *lausavísa*. According to the prose text, Friðgerðr was in company with her son Skeggi, while her husband Þórarinn was at the General Assembly. Most likely the verse also refers to the son Skeggi with the two kennings *hlautteins hreytir* and *goða sveinn*. Grønlie interprets the former as 'the sprinkler of blood-dipped branch', but I prefer to interpreted it as 'the one who cast lottery twig(s)', which indicates that he sometimes appeared in divination contexts (see e.g. de Vries 1956–1957 I: 417; Düwel 1985: 31). The second element of *hlautteinn* is unproblematic; *teinn* means 'twig', 'sprout'. Evidence indicates that the first element in the compound, *hlaut*, in divination contexts refers to a 'lot' and not to 'sacrificial blood' (see Düwel 1985: 21–38).[4] Equivalent terms to *hlaut* in the Germanic languages have that or a similar meaning; for example Old English *hlōt* and Old High German *hlōz* have both the meaning 'lot, property' (*Los, Eigentum*) (de Vries 1961). In the eddic poem *Hymiskviða* stanza one, further, the word *hlaut* appears most likely with the meaning 'lot'. It says thus: *hristo teina/ oc á hlaut sá* '[the gods] shook the twigs and looked at the augury/lot(s) [that is, the outcome of it/them]' (Neckel and Kuhn 1983; Larrington 2014). In *Vǫluspá* stanza 63 it is stated: 'Then Hœnir will chose a wooden slip for prophecy' (*Þá kná Hœnir/hlautvið kiósa*) (Neckel and Kuhn 1983; Larrington 2014). Such a divination ritual is reminiscent of Tacitus's description of the Germanic casting of lots in *Germania* chapter 10 (*c.* AD 97 (Warmington and Hutton 1970 [1925]: 144–147):

> To divination and the lot they pay as much attention as anyone; the method of drawing lots is uniform. A branch is cut from a nut-bearing tree and divided into slips: these are distinguished by certain marks and spread casually and at random over white cloth:

> afterwards, should the inquiry be for the people the priest of the state, if private the father of the family in person, after prayers to the gods and with eyes turned to heaven, takes up one slip at a time till he has done this on three separate occasions, and after taking the three interprets them according to the marks which have been already stamped on each.

This account may be influenced by Roman augury or ethnographical clichés used when describing foreign customs. But some aspects convey an authentic impression; the method of using slips or twigs (*surculi*) seems to be similar to the Scandinavian usage of *blótspánn* 'chip used in divination' (Zoëga 2004 [1910]), or *hlautteinn* 'lottery twig'. According to Tacitus, these slips are distinguished with certain marks (*notae*). It is naturally tempting to imagine these marks as runes. But there is no evidence of runes in Tacitus's time. Hence, the kenning *hlautteins hreytir* should be interpreted as 'the one who cast lottery twig(s)'.

The latter kenning in Þorvaldr's *lausavísa* referring to the young man, *goða sveinn,* is interpreted by Grønlie as 'the priest's son', where the term *goða* is read as a genitive singular of *goði* (m.). If this interpretation is correct Þórarinn was designated *goði* 'chieftain, cult leader' in this stanza (see Murphy 2018). However, *goða sveinn* could also be interpreted 'the servant of the gods', where *goða* is read as a genitive plural of *goð* (n.pl.) 'gods'. The prose context indicates that Þórarinn was the *goði* at the sanctuary of Hvammr (see below). During the Viking Age and Early Middle Ages leadership functions in Iceland appeared in an office related to local chieftains called *goðar* (pl.). As noted above, the etymology of this term indicates an original cultic office. The *goði*'s authority or dignity was called *goðorð* 'god-dignity', 'dignity of a *goði*'. There are several instances in the Old Norse prose describing the close relationship between chieftains (*goðar*), cultic actions and the *hof*-sanctuaries in Viking Age Iceland. They could therefore sometimes be described as *hofgoðar*. It seems as if the *goði* usually performed the sacrificial rituals during public cult. For example, in the *Hauksbók* redaction of *Landnámabók* chapter 268 (Jakob Benediktsson 1986: 313), it is the *goði* himself who performs the sacrifices.

> A ring weighing two ounces or more should lie on the *stalli* in every chief *hof*-building, and every *goði* should have this ring upon his arm at all public law-assemblies at which he should be at the head of affairs, having first reddened it in the blood of a neat which he himself had sacrificed there. (author's translation)

This paragraph claims to originate from the very old and orally transmitted Úlfljótslǫg which is mentioned in *Íslendingabók* chapter 2 (Jakob Benediktsson 1986: 6–7).

The Sagas of the Icelanders report that local chieftains designated *goðar* also performed other societal functions beside their religious assignments. A *goði* exercised power in society and had authority over men or territory. Individual men of sufficient means entered sometimes into a personal contact with a single *goði* 'for protection and support for themselves and their households, a contract that either side could change if he wished' (Clunies Ross 2010: 9). The *goði* was accompanied by *þingmenn*, who followed him to assemblies and gave him support there, or when having private feuds. In the same time the *goði* was supposed to represent the interests of his *þingmenn*, at local assemblies (*þing*) and at the annual general assembly of the whole country (*Alþingi*). Most likely Þórarinn was occupied with this assignment when Þorvaldr víðfǫrli visited his farm at Hvammr.

We may thus assume that Þórarinn was a local chieftain at Hvammr designated *goði*, who was temporarily responsible for certain religious functions at the sanctuary situated at his farm. As a cult leader he also had other societal duties beside his religious tasks. He took part in the political and judicial meeting at Alþingi (see above). Friðgerðr and her son Skeggi acted as his deputies when he was at Alþingi. Most likely also Skeggi was a *goði*, or perhaps rather a candidate for the *goðorð* at Hvammr, as he would inherit this from his father. He was probably involved with divination rituals at the sanctuary there. It is possible that Þórarinn and Friðgerðr could have had a joint religious leadership function in the public cult there, since they were designated *goði* and *gyðja*.

### *The sanctuary at Hvammr*

The place at Hvammr in *Kristni saga* where Friðgerðr performed sacrifices is called Old Norse *hof* 'place of residence, residence', 'house of worship, court, temple' (*ONP*). Theophoric place-names in Norway testify that *hof* sometimes had a sacred meaning, as for instance in *Frøyshov* ('the sanctuary of the god Freyr') and *Torshov* 'the sanctuary of the god Þórr' (Sandnes and Stemshaug 2007). A support for a cultic interpretation of names including *hof* is an archaeological investigation of a place called *Hofstaðir*, at Mývatnssveit, in northern Iceland, where a Viking Age hall building was detected as early as 1908. Recent analyses of bone material from Hofstaðir have generated some sensational results. Bovine skulls have been found in two clusters outside the walls of the hall building. These skulls show clear signs that a very special type of slaughter took place at the site and that the skulls were exposed for a long time on the outside of the building. According to the excavators, Gavin Lucas and Thomas McGovern (2008), this should be interpreted as parts of bloody sacrifices. Whether it was the hall building or the farm where the sacrifices took place that generated the designation *Hofstaðir* is not completely clear.

Most likely the term *hof* in *Kristni saga* denoted a cult building, since the text states that Friðgerðr was 'in the sanctuary and sacrificed' (*í hofinu ok blótaði*). The scribe of *Kristni saga* was certainly inspired by the information from the Þorvaldr's *lausavísa* – that the *gyðja* was shouting from the heathen altars/platforms (*gall um heiðnum stalla*) – when stating this (on the concept *heiðinn*, see below). The Old Norse concept *stallr* (or *stalli*) appears clearly in connection to pagan buildings and sacrificial contexts in other reliable sources as well. In the medieval *Older Eidsivaþing Law*, which was used in south-eastern Norway, it says thus:

> No man shall keep in his house staff or podiums (*hafa i husi sinu staf eða stalla*), a sorcerer's tool or sacrifice, or things connected to pagan customs or anything else belonging to the pagan customs. But if he does, and is found guilty of this, he is [to be] outlawed and

> excommunicated, and will also [lose] every coin of [that is, all of] his property. (Keyser and Munch 1846: 383; Brink 2020: 472)

The Old Norse word *stafr* (m.) 'staff' is translated by Johan Fritzner (1954) as 'something used in the worship of pagan gods' (*noget som benyttedes ved afgudernes dyrkelse*), and *stallr* or *stalli* (m.) as 'stand on which the images of the gods are set up, altar' (*Stillads hvorpaa Afgudbilleder ere oppstillede, Alter*). The staff (*stafr*) and the podium (*stallr/stalli*) may thus very well refer to the pagan custom of having a cult image of the god placed on a sacrificial altar/platform in a cult building or in a ritual area of the hall or residence. This information actually harmonises well with Snorri Sturluson's description of the interior of the *hof*-sanctuary in Mære, Trøndelag, which says that Þórr sat on a podium (*stallr/stalli*):

> King Óláfr now goes into the temple and a small number of men with him and some farmers. And when the king came to where the gods were, there sat Þórr, and was most dignified of all the gods, adorned with gold and silver. King Óláfr raised up a gold-adorned ceremonial halberd that he had in his hand and struck Þórr, so that he fell off his pedestal (*fell af stallinum*). Then the king's men leaped forward and shoved down all the gods from their pedestals (*skýfðu ofan ǫllum goðum af stǫllunum*). (*Óláfs saga Tryggvasonar*, in *Heimskringla* 1, Bjarni Aðalbjarnarson 1941: 317; trans. Finlay and Faulkes 2017 [2011]: 198)

The basic meaning of the word *stallr/stalli* must be 'a stand upon which something could be placed' (Heggstad *et al.* 2012). Since we have the compound *véstallr* 'sacred stand/alter' in the early poetic language (Whaley 2012 1: 26), we may assume that some type of altars or ritual platforms really existed inside cult buildings during the Viking Age. The kenning referring to Óðinn, *fúrr stalla vinr* 'the friend of the fire of the altars/podiums' in Egill Skalla-Grímsson's *Berudrápa* (*c.* 970) indicates also the same (see Clunies Ross *et al.* 2022: 380–383). That the term was associated early on with some kind of altar may be supported by *Fjǫlsvinnsmál* stanza 40, where we have the expression 'to sacrifice at the altar-holy place' (*blóta ... á stallhelgum stað*). In this case the word **stallheilagr* is an adjective with the meaning 'altar-holy' or 'hallowed by an altar' (La Farge and Tucker 1992).

With no doubt the *gyðja* Friðgerðr was in some kind of a sanctuary at Hvammr when she was shouting from the *stalli/stallr*, either in a separate part of the main building of the farm or in a specific cult building located there. It is a bit enigmatic why she was screaming from this ritual construction. Perhaps also this should be interpreted in the context of the sacrificial rituals. Comparative material from other ancient religions testifies that the moment when the violence was carried out against the sacrificial animal and the blood was shed, constituted a dramatic element and an emotional climax. In the ancient Greek sacrificial ritual, the female participants would scream with a shrill voice just as the sacrificer plunged the axe into the animal and stained the altar red with blood (Burkert 1985: 56). Homer reports in the *Odyssey* (Murray and Dimock 1995 [1919]: 112–115) that when Nestor's son Trasymedes sacrificed to

Athena, he stabbed an axe with force in the neck of the heifer straight through the sinews, at the same time as the women cried out:

> Now when they had prayed, and had strewn the barley grains, at once the son of Nestor, Thrasymedes, height of heart, came near and dealt the blow; and the axe cut through the sines of the neck, and loosened the strength of the heifer, and the women raised the sacred cry (... ὀλόλυξαν), ... (Murray and Dimock 1995 [1919]: 112–113)

The 'sacred cry' of the women formed a climax during the ceremony. Then the animal was drained of blood and a burnt offering was performed. Could Friðgerðr's scream have played a similar role in the sacrifices at Hvammr? The 'sacred scream' attested in ancient Greek sacrificial customs may arguably have had a parallel in Old Norse sacrificial customs.

## The cultic role of the *húsfreyja/húsfrú*

According to *Þorvaldr þáttr Víðfǫrla* I (Sigurgeir Steingrímsson *et al.* 2003: 73–74), and *Þorvaldr þáttr Víðfǫrla* II (Sigurgeir Steingrímsson *et al.* 2003: 95), Þórarinn bóndi's wife Friðgerðr is described as a *húsfreyja* (cf. *húsfrú*). That ladies designated with this term could be related to sacrificial cult and the old gods, in a similar manner as Friðgerðr, is attested in other texts too. In *Ynglinga saga* chapter 10, Snorri makes a connection between the goddess Freyja, sacrifices and housewives (*húsfreyjur*):

> Freyja kept up the sacrifices, for she was the only one of the gods left alive, and she became the best known, so that all noble women came to be called by her name, just as now the name *frúvur* ('ladies') is used. Similarly everyone was called *freyja* ('mistress') of what she possessed, and *húsfreyja* ('mistress of a household') if she is in charge of a dwelling. (Text Bjarni Aðalbjarnarson 1941: 24–25; transl. Finlay and Faulkes 2017 [2011]: 14)

This quote indicates that the terms *freyja* and *húsfreyja* according to Snorri's vocabulary refer to high-ranked ladies, who could be in charge of the dwelling place, and via Freyja they were also indirectly related to sacrifices. Some sources, produced by people from an inside perspective, report on noble housewives (*húsfreyjur/húsfrúr*), who seem to be in charge of farms. In the runic inscription, dated to the 11th century, from Hassmyra, in Västmanland (Jansson 1964), Sweden, a house-wife (RSw *hīfrøyja*) is praised by her husband, Holmgautr:

> *Boandi goðr Holmgautr let ræisa æftiʀ Oðindisu, kunu sina. Kumbʀ hifrøya til Hasvimyra æigi bætri, þan byi raðr. Rauð-Balliʀ risti runiʀ þessaʀ. Sigmundaʀ vaʀ [Ōðindīsa] systiʀ goð.*
>
> The good farmer Holmgautr had this [stone] raised in memory of his wife Ōðindīsa. A better housewife will never come to Hassmyra to run the farm. Rauð-Balliʀ carved these runes. She was a good sister to Sigmundr. (Jansson 1964)

The information that the housewife 'runs' or 'rules over' the farm (*byi raðr*) is important. The term *byʀ* could be interpreted as 'farm, village', while the verb *raða* means 'advise, rule, care' (*Sw råda, härska, ombesörja*) (Peterson 1994: 43; Sundqvist

2016: 368–369). It indicates that she had a leading position, perhaps also outside the walls of the building. It is also mentioned that this housewife is called Ōðindīsa. This compound name, which is only evidenced here, is important for the interpretation. In the inscription, we meet the expression *æftiʀ Ōðindīsu*. Formally, the *iō*-stem *dīs* (Old Norse *dís*) should not appear with weak inflection in this case (*-u*) (Peterson 1981: 149). The accusative form of *dīs* is *-i*. This suggests that the woman's name was probably originally *Dīsa*, that is, a name which has a weak inflection. According to the onomastic specialists, this may have a simple explanation. The name of the god *Ōðin-* has been added to her secondarily, as a byname prefix (Otterbjörk 1983; Andersson 1993; Peterson 2007; Vikstrand 2009; cf. Sundqvist 2016: 368–369; 2020b). The name Ōðindīsa indicates that she had a specific relation to the god Óðinn and perhaps that she was faithful to him also after the conversion.

There are other contemporary sources that mention housewives in religious contexts. In the *Austrfararvísur* (Whaley 2012: 578–614), dating back to the early 11th century and preserved in *Óláfs saga Helga* chapter 91 (Bjarni Aðalbjarnarson 1945; Finlay and Faulkes 2014), a housewife is described as being involved in a sacrifice (*alfablót*) devoted to the mythical beings called álfar. This poem describes how the Christian skald Sigvatr Þorðarson, with some companions, made a journey to Svetjud *c.* 1018. One evening, they came to a farm called Hof (st. 4). Whether Hof in this case refers to a place name is uncertain. It is possible that it should be interpreted as an appellation *hof*, that is, a building where cultic activities took place. The poem says: 'the door was barred'. It also says that Sigvatr and his fellows were sent away, since the people there declared that it was 'holy' (*heilagr*). One could here follow Snorri's interpretation of the expression, that is, that the place was 'holy', but one could also understand this that this was a holy day (Murphy 2018; Wellendorf 2022).

Snorri's text mentions that they went to another farm. There was a housewife (*húsfreyja*) in the doorway, who told him not to enter there. In stanza five, we read thus:

*Gakkat inn,'kvað ekkja,*
*'armi drengr, en lengra;*
*hræðumk ek við Óðins*
*– erum heiðin vér – reiði.'*
*Rýgr kvazk inni eiga óþekk,*
*sús mér hnekkði, alfablót,*
*sem ulfi ótvín, í bœ sínum.*

'Do not come any farther in, wretched fellow,' said the woman; 'I fear the wrath of Óðinn; we are heathen.' The disagreeable female, who drove me away like a wolf without hesitation, said they were holding a sacrifice to the elves inside her farmhouse. (Old Norse text and trans. Fulk; Whaley 2012: 590–591)

When the Christian skald comes to the farm, this female stands in the doorway and tells him he cannot enter. Rather than seeing the rejection of the skald as caused by the private nature of the *álfablót* (Murphy 2018), it should probably be seen in the context of the encounter and clash between pagans and Christians (Wellendorf 2022).

The female also states that she fears the wrath of Óðinn and that the people of the farm were heathen. The concept *heiðinn*, 'heathen', can be perceived as somewhat odd in this context. But it also appears in the skaldic poem *Hákonarmál* stanza 21 (dating to *c.* 960; Whaley 2012): *með heiðin goð*, 'with the heathen gods'. This poem is usually accepted as a pre-Christian lay, describing the native gods. Thus, the adjective *heiðinn* could be used as an attribute to oneself in designations, such as *heiðnir menn* 'heathens' and often as a contrast to Christian men.

Whether Óðinn, in stanza 5, in some way was related to the *álfar* is uncertain. At any rate, this woman seems to be involved in the pagan cult of the *álfar*, or at least she protected the sacred space where this cult took place in a way, which can be compared to the *hofgyðja* called Steinvọr, who took care of and protected the major *hof*-building (*varðveitti họfuðhofit*) at the farm called Hof in Vápnfjọrðr (*Vápnfirðinga saga* chap. 5; Jón Jóhannesson 1950: 33). The Old Norse verb *varðveit(t)a* means 'to keep, to preserve', 'to observe' (Zoëga 2004 [1910]). Viking Age poems mention that male cult leaders and rulers were called *vọrðr véstalls*, 'the protector of the sacred stand', or *vés valdr*, 'the ruler of the sacred place' (Sundqvist 2016: 188–189, 290–315). We also come across this in medieval prose texts about Norwegian chieftains and Icelandic *goðar* who took care of (inf. *varðveita*) sanctuaries and probably also protected them from sacrilege (see e.g. *Landnámabók* ch. S368: 368; Jakob Benediktsson 1986: 368; *Eyrbyggja saga*, Einar Ól Sveinsson and Matthías Þórðarson 1985: 27; Sundqvist 2016: 163–198, 290–315). Most likely the stanza in *Austrfararvísur* indicates that the mistress in the door protected the sacred spacc. The skald burst out that she 'drove me away like a wolf', which may allude to the sacrilege called *vargr í véum* 'a wolf in sanctuaries'. According to Oddr's *Óláfs saga Tryggvasonar* (Ólafur Halldórsson 2006: 174), this expression refers to a person 'who has desecrated the property of a god by breaking it down and carrying away its valuables' (Wellendorf 2022: 479).

When quoting Sigvatr's stanza 5 in Óláfs saga Helga, Snorri uses the word *húsfreyja*, 'housewife' as a designation of the female mentioned there (Bjarni Aðalbjarnarson 1945: 137). In the stanza she is called *rýgr*, perhaps indicating that she was wealthy and powerful woman. In *Skáldskaparmál* chapter 67 (Faulkes 1998) it is stated: 'A woman who is very rich is called *rýgr*'. Sigvatr also uses the term *ekkja*, actually meaning 'widow', but in poetic context it also refers to 'woman'.

*Austrfararvísur* and the Hassmyra inscription indicate that when Friðgerðr at Hvammr is described as a *húsfreyja,* this term may have raised associations to ladies who were in charge of pagan worship of gods. It has recently been argued that such mistresses (*húsfreyjur/húsfrúr*) are visible in graves from the Late Roman Iron Age until the Viking Age, in Sweden, where females have been buried with lynx skins and phalanges. According to Torun Zachrisson (2022: 63), these 'lynx ladies' 'have been cult leaders at local farms, and some of them could have had ritual roles at larger gatherings and public sanctuaries'. Other, quite reliable sources, indicate that females designated *húsfreyja* and *húsfrú*, had such functions. These ladies probably also had other assignments at their farms. The runic inscription from Hassmyra, for instance, states that the housewife Ōðindīsa 'rules over' the farm, while Snorri states that those females who were designated *húsfreyja* were in charge of a dwelling place. Friðgerðr had probably similar leading functions at the farm of Hvammr.

## Is Friðgerðr a vǫlva like Þorbjǫrg?

It is highly likely that this pagan woman Friðgerðr mistreated the missionaries in some way and that she perhaps demonstratively performed the traditional rituals at the 'platform', while the two Christian men preached about God to the pagans at Hvammr. The poet's expression 'may God crush the priestess' (*þá kreppi Guð gyðju*) indicates this. She is also described as a *gýgr*. This term *gýgr* means 'giantess, ogress, hag, sorceress' or '(large) female troll, grotesque female person from the underworld' (see e.g. *ONP*; Zoëga 2004 [1910]) and it has probably a pejorative connotation and a polemic discourse, when referring to Friðgerðr in the verse. Could the word *gýgr* refer to a pagan sorceress, who performed the ritual called *seiðr*? Could it indicate that Friðgerðr was a *vǫlva*?

The *vǫlur* are well documented in the Icelandic sources, for example in the Sagas of the Icelanders. The most detailed description appears in chapter 4 of *Eiríks saga rauða* (Sveinsson and Þórðarson 1985), where we meet a *vǫlva* named Þorbjǫrg in the Norse settlement in Greenland. She is also designated *spákona* 'prophetess' in the text. The householder of a farm, Þorkell, called on Þorbjǫrg, since he needed to find out how long the famine would last. When Þorbjǫrg arrived at the farm together with the man who had escorted her, she was wearing a blue cloak with straps which was set with stones right down to the hem. She had glass beads about her neck, and on her head a black lambskin hood lined inside with white catskin. She had a staff in her hand (*hon hafði staf í hendi*), with a knob on it. It was ornamented with brass and set around with stones just below the knob. Round her middle she wore a belt made of touchwood, and on it was a big skin pouch in which she kept those charms of hers which she needed for her ritual. On her feet she had hairy calf-skin shoes with long thongs, and on the thong-ends big knobs of lateen. She had on her hands cat-skin gloves which were white inside and hairy.

Towards the end of the day, Þorbjǫrg was fitted out with the apparatus she needed for her ritual (that is, the *seiðr*). She asked too to procure her such women as knew the lore which was necessary for the spell (*til seiðsins*) and bore the name *Varðlokur* in the manuscript titled *Skálholtsbók*, AM557, 4to, while the manuscript called *Hauksbók*, AM 544, 4to has *Varðlokkur* (on these variants, see Dillmann 2006: 290–299). But no such women were to be found. Then Guðríðr said that her foster mother taught her the chant which is called *Varðlok(k)ur* but she said that she did not want to have a part in this ritual, since she now was a Christian. Now the householder Þorkell pressed Guðríðr hard and finally she said that she would do what he wished. The women now formed a circle round the platform (*hring um hjallinn*) on which Þorbjǫrg was seated. Guðríðr recited the chant so beautifully and well. After that the seeress thanked her for that and added that many spirits had been drawn there. She said that many things now were apparent for her which earlier were hidden. She said to Þorkell that the famine will not last longer than this winter (*Eiríks saga rauða*, Einar Ól Sveinsson and Matthías Þórðarson 1985: 206–209; on this paraphrase, see Jones's [1961] translation. The problems and credibility of this description are discussed by e.g. Strömbäck 1935; Dillmann 2006: 269–308).

The *vǫlur* ambulated often with an entourage from farm to farm, and according to some texts they were paid for their performances, above the bed and board they received (Dillmann 2006: 367–369; Price 2019: 72–75). In the sagas, the *vǫlur* are wise and often engaged in divinations and magic. They gain knowledge by performing the ceremony called *seiðr* (sorcery or divination), which could be of benefit to individuals or society. *Seiðr* is also mentioned in mythical traditions, often in the context of Óðinn. In the texts, the *seiðr* seems to be gender specific and linked to women. According to *Ynglinga saga* chapter four, Freyja was the first 'to teach the Æsir *seiðr*, which was customary among the Vanir'. The relation of *seiðr* to Óðinn is therefore ambiguous. In *Lokasenna* stanza 24, Loki addresses Óðinn thus:

*Enn þic síða kóðo Sámseyo í;*
*oc draptu á vétt sem vǫlor;*
*vitca líki fórtu verþjóð yfir,*
*oc hugða ec þat args aðal.*

But you, they say, practiced *seiðr* on Samsey,
and you beat on the drum as seeresses do,
in the likeness of a wizard you journeyed over mankind,
and that I thought the hallmark of a pervert.

(Larrington 2014 based on Neckel and Kuhn 1983)

In this poem, Óðinn is accused of behaving in an unmanly fashion when performing *seiðr* and beating on the drum as a *vǫlva*. The men who pursued *seiðr* were considered to be affiliated with *ergi*, that is, according to previous scholars 'sexual aberration', 'inordinate sexual desire' or 'lasciviousness' (cf. the adjective *argr*) (cf. Strömbäck 1935; Meulengracht Sørensen 1983; Dillmann 2006). In chapter 7 of *Ynglinga saga*, Snorri says the following about *seiðr*: 'But this magic, when it is practiced, is accompanied by such great perversion (*svá mikil ergi*) that it was not considered without shame for a man to perform it, and the skill was taught to the goddesses' (Bjarni Aðalbjarnarson 1941: 19; Finlay and Faulkes 2017 [2011]: 11). The context of *Lokasenna* and *Ynglinga saga* testifies that it is the cross-gender feature of Óðinn that is questioned. At any rate, Óðinn is the master of *seiðr*, and some have related this aspect of him to Nordic shamanism (cf. Strömbäck 1935; Price 2019; critically considered by Dillmann 2006). It has been suggested in previous research that descriptions of *vǫlur* and *seiðr* contain some anomalies (Raudvere 2003). On the one hand, the *vǫlur* are important to society. On the other hand, they are odd and different in terms of age, sex, and ethnicity. Not least, the last aspect has the function of marking deviations in the texts. One could interpret this as suggesting the *vǫlur* were predominantly found in marginal environments. Their activities would then have taken place in a kind of social periphery, far from the activities in the aristocratic halls. According to Folke Ström (1985: 224), *seiðr* was, on the whole, a feared and abhorred activity (*fruktad och avskydd hantering*). The French philologist Francois-Xavier Dillmann (2006) has a different view. He believes that the magicians in Iceland represented the 'norm' and that they were well integrated and respected in society. If we investigate other types of sources, in addition to the Icelandic texts, we may actually get a picture that resembles that interpretation. Archaeological finds from the Late Iron Age in Sweden and Norway indicate that *vǫlur* and *seiðr* appeared in aristocratic environments. In a rich double grave (a male and a female), from Klinta, on Öland, a powerful staff was found crowned with a small house. It has been interpreted as a *vǫlva*-staff (e.g. Gardeła 2016: 135–170; Price 2019: 139–141). In three chamber graves from Birka, objects have been detected that can be interpreted in a similar way. As the Klinta staff, they also testify to the highest social level. It has also been argued that the wooden staff found in the rich ship grave of Oseberg, in Norway, was a *vǫlr*. This burial is dated to AD 800 and considered to belong to a queen and her servant (Ingstad 1992; Myhre 1992). According to Neil Price (2019: 161), the cane in this grave was 'a symbol of sorcery', that is, a staff of a *vǫlva*. Early Latin texts suggest that certain females played a central role in Germanic societies (see, e.g., Tacitus, *Germania* chap. 8; Warmington and Hutton 1970 [1925]; Caesar, *De Bello Gallico* 1, 50; Page 1962). Tacitus mentions that Germanic people conceived that in woman is a certain uncanny and prophetic sense, and so they neither scorn to consult them nor slight their answers. During the reign of Vespasian, there was a famous seeress of the people who were called Veleda. She was treated as a deity by many. During bitter uprisings, she performed rites in an important role. From a high tower on the River Lippe, she gave oracles and political advice to the people (Tacitus, *Histories* 4, 61–65; Jackson 1962 [1931]). Also, other sources report that the seeresses had this public ritual role in Germanic society (Enright 1996).

It is not impossible that divinations rituals were performed in the context of the rites accomplished by Friðgerðr at the *stalli/stallr*. According to Þorvaldr's contemporary stanza, however, it is the male cult leader who is called *hlautteins hreytir* 'the one who cast lottery twig(s)', which indicates that he was performing divination rituals, while his mother (Friðgerðr), the *gyðja* at Hvammr, was shouting from the heathen altars/platforms (*gall um heiðnum stalla*). If we can rely on the 13th century prose context, she 'was in the *hof*-sanctuary and sacrificed'. As far as I know, no *vǫlva* is designated *gyðja* and no *vǫlur* perform sacrifices at a *stalli/stallr* in a *hof*-sanctuary. Indeed, *Ynglinga saga* chapter 7 states that Óðinn knew, and practised himself, the art which is accompanied by greatest power, called *seiðr*, ... But this 'skill was taught to the goddesses' (*ok var gyðjunum kennd sú íþrótt*) (Bjarni Aðalbjarnarson 1941: 19). The term *gyðjur* refers to the euhemerised goddesses and Freyja in this context, and not to earthly ritual performers.

It is quite unlikely that Friðgerðr included the functions of a *vǫlva* at Hvammr. In general, the *vǫlur* were ambulating between farms, where they performed the ritual called *seiðr* at a temporary ritual construction referred to as *seiðhjallr* (Sundqvist 2012). Friðgerðr, on the other hand, performed sacrifices (*blót*) at a stationary shrine (*hof*) located at her farm, perhaps both privately and publicly. The *gyðja* Friðgerðr, further, fits to the description of a female 'cult leader'. She was only temporarily responsible for certain religious functions in the local society of Hvammr. As a *húsfreyja*, she had also other functions, beside her cultic assignments, for instance, she ruled the farm, when her husband was at the General Assembly. The *vǫlva* Þorbjǫrg, on the other hand, fits the description of a female 'religious specialist'. She had an exclusive religious office, which included a more permanent and intensified specialisation. Þorbjǫrg was well-trained in the rituals she performed, and appeared as a professional religious specialist, who earned her income and lived by the *seiðr* performances she accomplished.

## Conclusion

There are strong reasons to assume that the *gyðja* Friðgerðr was a female cult leader at the shrine in Hvammr during the late 10th century. Whether this shrine belonged to the household religion or had a more public character is difficult to determine. Þorvaldr's *lausavísa* testifies that she performed rituals at a *stalli*/*stallr*, that is, a ritual platform or altar, which usually is located in a *hof*-sanctuary or a pagan house building in Old Norse prose texts. Her son, had probably some kind of ritual functions on the farm as well, since he is designated 'the one who cast lottery twig(s)'. The oral tradition surrounding the transmitted Viking Age verse about Þorvaldr's visit at Hvammr seems to have contained the information that Friðgerðr was in a *hof*-shrine and performed a sacrifice while the two missionaries were preaching. This tradition is reproduced in the manuscripts of *Kristni saga* and the *Þorvaldr þáttr Víðfǫrla* I and II. However, there is nothing to suggest that Friðgerðr was a *vǫlva* or a religious specialist who devoted herself exclusively to religious duties and the ritual called *seiðr*. Such religious and professional specialists are on the other hand well-attested in the Old Norse sources. Friðgerðr probably had other leading duties at the farm, in addition to her cultic assignments, in her capacity as a *húsfreyja*. In accordance with the classification system used in the present study, she should be described as a cult leader. Friðgerðr, Þórarinn and their son Skeggi probably had a leading position in the settlements around Breiðafjǫrðr. Þórarinn was probably a chieftain designated *goði*, who took care of the common cult for the people there. At the same time he was a chieftain, who represented his subjects at the Alþingi and protected them in various ways. When he was occupied with other duties, outside the farm, his wife and son, the *gyðja* Friðgerðr and Skeggi, the upcoming *goði*, appeared as cultic deputies at the local sanctuary situated at Hvammr. However, nothing excludes that Friðgerðr and Þórarinn could have had a joint religious leadership function, also when he was present, for example when annual sacrificial feasts were celebrated in the settlements there.

### *Notes*

1 This essay synthesises, builds on, and extends several previously published works in Swedish and English, including Sundqvist 2005, 2007, 2016, 2020a and 2020b.

2 At the time of writing this article, I was not aware of the important and comprehensive anthology *The Norse Sorceress: Mind and Materiality in the Viking World* (Gardeła *et al.* 2023). Many of the chapters in that book would have been relevant to the present work, but unfortunately, they have been impossible to incorporate into this study.

3 In the ancient Church, the religious leader was most often entitled *episkopos* 'overseer', while later the priest was designated *hiereus* in Greek tradition and *sacerdos* in the Roman-Latin tradition, while the priesthood was referred to as *sacerdotes*.

4 There are certainly descriptions in the Norse prose literature where *hlaut* is a designation for sacrificial blood. The present author has previously argued that *hlaut* in these descriptions should be interpreted as the sacrificial blood and the gift that was intended for the deity at a communion meal (i.e. 'the divine part') (Sundqvist 2017). In Þorvaldr's *vísa*, it is more likely that it should be understood simply as 'lot'.

## Bibliography


Andersson, T., 1993. Sakrala personnamn, eller profana: Klassifikations- och gränsdragningsproblem i det gamla nordiska personnamnsförrådet. In *Personnamn i nordiska och andra germanska fornspråk*, ed. L. Peterson. Uppsala universitet, Uppsala: 39–60.

Arwill-Nordbladh, E., 1998. *Genuskonstruktioner i nordisk vikingatid: Förr och nu*. Institutionen för arkeologi, Göteborg.

Back Danielsson, I.-M., Fahlander, F. and Sjöstrand, Y., 2012. *Encountering Imagery: Materilities, perceptions, relations*. Stockholms Universitet, Stockholm.

Bell, C., 1992. *Ritual Theory, Ritual Practice*. Oxford University Press, Oxford/New York.

Benediktsson, J. (ed.), 1986. *Íslendingabók. Landnámabók*. Íslenzk Fornrit 1, Reykjavík.

Bjarni Aðalbjarnarson (ed.), 1941. *Heimskringla* 1. Íslenzk Fornrit 26, Reykjavík.

Bjarni Aðalbjarnarson (ed.), 1945. *Heimskringla* 2. Íslenzk Fornrit 27, Reykjavík.

Brink, S., 2020. Laws and assemblies. In *The Pre-Christian Religions of the North. History and Structures. Volume II: Social, geographical, and historical contexts, and communication between worlds*, eds J.P. Schjødt, J. Lindow and A. Andrén. Brepols, Turhout: 445–477.

Burkert, W., 1985. *Greek Religion* (trans. J. Raffan). Harvard University Press, Cambridge MA.

Clunies Ross, M., 2010. *The Old Norse-Icelandic Saga*. Cambridge University Press, Cambridge.

Clunies Ross, M., Gade, K.E. and Wills, T. (eds), 2022. *Skaldic Poetry of the Scandinavian Middle Ages V. Poetry in Sagas of Icelanders*. Brepols, Turnhout.

Dillmann, F.-X., 2006. *Les magiciens dans l'Islande ancienne: Études sur la représentation de la magie islandaise et de ses agents dans les sources littéraires norroises*. Acta Academiae regiae Gustavi Adolphi 92, Uppsala.

Düwel, K., 1985. *Das Opferfest von Lade: Quellenkritische Untersuchungen zur germanischen Religionsgeschichte*. Wiener Arbeiten zur germanischen Altertumskunde und Philologie 27, Vienna.

Einar Ól Sveinsson (ed.), 1939. *Vatnsdæla saga*. Íslenzk Fornrit 8, Reykjavík.

Einar Ól Sveinsson and Matthías Þórðarson (eds), 1985. *Eiríks saga rauða*. Íslenzk Fornrit 4, Reykjavík.

Enright, M.J., 1996. *Lady with a Mead Cup: Ritual, prophecy and lordship in the European warband from La Tène to the Viking Age*. Four Courts Press, Dublin.

Faulkes, A. (ed.), 1998. *Edda. Skáldskaparmál* Vols 1–2. Viking Society for Northern Research. University College London, London.

Finlay, A. and Faulkes, A. (trans.), 2014. *Heimskringla* 2. Viking Society for Northern Research, University College London, London.

Finlay, A. and Faulkes, A. (trans.), 2017 [2011]. *Heimskringla* 1. Viking Society for Northern Research, University College London, London.

Fritzner, J., 1954 [1883–1896]. *Ordbog over det gamle norske sprog.* Vols 1–3 (reprint). Tryggve Juul Møller Forlag, Oslo.

Frog, E. and Roper, J., 2011. Verses *versus* the 'Vanir': Response to Simek's 'Vanir Obituary'. *RMN Newsletter* 2: 29–37.

Gardeła, L., 2016. *(Magic) Staffs in the Viking Age.* Studia Medievalia Septentrionalia 27, Vienna.

Gardeła, L., Bønding, S. and Pentz, P. (eds), 2023. *The Norse Sorceress: Mind and materiality in the Viking world.* Oxbow Books, Oxford.

Gräslund, A.-S., 2001. *Ideologi och mentalitet: Om religionsskiftet i Skandinavien från en arkeologisk horisont.* Uppsala universitet, Uppsala.

Gräslund, A.-S., 2011. Female elites in Viking Age Scandinavia during Christianization. In *Weibliche Eliten in der Frühgeschichte international Tagung vom 13. Bis zum 14. Juni 2008 im RGZM im Rahmen des Forschungsschwerpunktes 'Eliten'*, ed. D. Quast. Verlag des Römisch-Germanischen Zentralmuseums, Mainz: 267–278.

Grønlie, S.S., 2006a. No longer male and female: Redeeming women in the Icelandic conversion narratives. *Medium Aevum* 75: 293–318.

Grønlie, S.S. (trans.), 2006b. *Íslendingabók/Kristni Saga. The Book of the Icelanders/The Story of the Conversion.* Viking Society of Northern Research. University of London, London.

Guðbrandur Vigfússon and Unger, C.R. (eds), 1860–1868. *Flateyjarbók: En samling af norske konge-sagaer med inskudte mindre fortællinger* 1–3. Malling, Christiania.

Hedenstierna-Jonson, C., Kjellström, A., Zachrisson, T., Krzewińska, M., Sobrado, V., Price, N., Günther, T., Jakobsson, M., Götherström, A. and Storå, J. 2017. A female Viking warrior confirmed by genomics. *American Journal of Physical Anthropology* 164.4: 853–860. DOI:10.1002/ajpa.23308.

Heggstad, L., Simensen, E. And Hødnebø, F. (eds), 2012. *Norrøn Ordbok.* Samlaget, Oslo.

Heide, E., 2006. Gand, seid og åndevind. Unpublished PhD. University of Bergen.

Hållans Stenholm, A.-M., 2019. Minnesvärda kvinnor. In *Tidens Landskap. En vänbok till Anders Andrén*, eds Cecilia Ljung, A.A. Sjögren, I, Berg, E. Engström, A.-M. Hållans Sttenholm *et al.* Nordic Academic Press, Lund: 131–133.

Ingstad, A.S., 1992. Oseberg-dronningen – hvem var hun? In *Osebergdronningens grav: Vår arkeologiske nasjonalskatt i nytt lys*, eds A.E. Christensen, A. Stine and B. Myhre. Schibsted, Oslo: 224–256.

Jackson, J. (trans.), 1962 [1931]. Tacitus: *The Histories./The Annals.* Harvard University Press, London/ Cambridge MA.

Jansson, S.B.F. (ed. and trans.), 1964. *Västmanlands Runinskrifter.* Sveriges Runinskrifter 13, Stockholm.

Jesch, J., 1991. *Women in the Viking Age.* Boydell, Woodbridge.

Jón Hnefill Aðalsteinsson, 1999. *Under the Cloak. A Pagan Ritual Turning Point in the Conversion of Iceland* (2nd edn). Háskólaútgáfan Félagsvísindastofnun, Reykjavík.

Jón Jóhannesson (ed.), 1950. *Vápnfirðinga Saga.* Íslenzk Fornrit 11, Reykjavík.

Jónas Kristjánsson (ed.), 2001. *Ǫgmundar þáttr dytts* in *Eyfirðinga sögur.* Íslenzk fornrit 9, Reykjavík.

Keyser, R. and Munch, P.A. (eds), 1846. Norges Gamle Love indtil 1387. Vol. 1. Christiania.

La Farge, B. and Tucker, J., 1992. *Glossary to the Edda.* Winter, Heidelberg.

Larrington, C. (trans.), 2014. *The Poetic Edda* (2nd edn). Oxford University Press, Oxford.

Lindow, J., 2020. Vanir and Æsir. In *The Pre-Christian Religions of the North. History and Structures. Volume III: Conceptual frameworks: The cosmos and collective supernatural beings*, eds J.P. Schjødt, J. Lindow and A. Andrén. Brepols, Turnhout: 1033–1050.

Lucas, G. and McGovern, T., 2008. Bloody slaughter: Ritual decapitation and display at the Viking settlement of Hofstaðir, Iceland. *European Journal of Archaeology* 10.1: 7–30.

Meulengracht Sørensen, P., 1983. *The Unmanly Man: Concepts of sexual defamation in early Northern society* (trans. J. Turville-Petre). Odense Universitetsforlag, Odense.

Murphy, L.J., 2018. Paganism at home: Pre-Christian private praxis and household religion in the Iron-Age North. *Scripta Islandica* 69: 49–97.
Murray, A.T. (trans.) and Dimock, G.E. (rev.), 1995. *Homer: The Odyssey*. Harvard University Press, London/Cambridge MA.
Myhre, B., 1992. Kronologispørsmålet. In *Osebergdronningens grav: Vår arkeologiske nasjonalskatt i nytt lys*, eds A.E. Christensen, A. Stine and B. Myhre. Schibsted, Oslo: 267–271.
Neckel, G. (ed.) and Kuhn, H. (rev.), 1983 [1914]. *Edda: Die Lieder des Codex Regius nebst verwandten Denkmälern*. Carl Winter Universitätsverlag, Heidelberg.
Nordberg, A., 2004. *Krigarna i Odins sal: Dödsföreställningar och krigarkult i fornnordisk religion*. Stockholms Universitet, Stockholm.
Olsen, M., 1926. *Ættegård og helligdom: Norske stednavn sosialt og religionshistorisk belyst*. Bonnier, Stockholm.
*ONP = Ordbog over det norrøne prosasprog*. https://onp.ku.dk/onp/onp.php
Otterbjörk, R., 1983. Starka och svaga kvinnonamn i fornsvenskan. *Namn och bygd* 71: 101–114.
Page, T.E. (ed.) and Edwards, H.J. (trans.), 1966. *Julius Caesar: De Bello Gallico*. Harvard University Press, London/Cambridge MA.
Peterson, L., 1981. *Kvinnonamnens böjning i fornsvenskan: De ursprungligen starkt böjda namnen*. Uppsala Universitet, Uppsala.
Peterson, L., 1994. *Svenskt runordsregister* (2nd edn). Uppsala universitet, Uppsala.
Peterson, L., 2007. *Nordiskt runnamnslexikon*. Institutet för språk och folkminnen, Uppsala.
Price, N.S., 2019. *The Viking Way: Magic and Mind in Late Iron Age Scandinavia*(2nd edn). Oxbow Books, Oxford.
Raudvere, C., 2003. *Kunskap och insikt i norrön tradition: Mytologi, ritualer och Trolldomsanklagelser*. Nordic Academic Press, Lund.
Rüpke, J., 1996. Controllers and professionals: Analyzing religious specialists. *Numen* 43.3: 241–262.
Sandnes, J. and Stemshaug, O., 2007. *Norsk stadnamnleksikon*. Samlaget, Oslo.
Sawyer, B., 2000. *Kvinnor och familj i det forn- och medeltida Skandinavien* (2nd edn). Viktoria Bokförlag, Göteborg.
Sigurgeir Steingrímsson, Ólafur Halldórsson and Foote, P. (eds), 2003. *Biskupa sögur* I, vol. 2. Íslenzk fornrit 15, 2, Reykjavík.
Simek, R., 2010. The Vanir: An obituary. *RMN Newsletter* 1: 10–19.
Sinding Jensen, J., 2014. *What is Religion?* Acumen, Durham.
Steinsland, G. and Vogt, K., 1981. 'Aukinn ertu Uolse og vpp vm tekinn': En religionshistorisk analyse av Völsaþáttr i Flateyjarbók. *Arkiv för nordisk filologi* 96: 87–106.
Ström, F., 1985. *Nordisk hedendom: Tro och sed i förkristen tid* (3rd edn). Akademiförlaget-Gumpert, Göteborg.
Strömbäck, D., 1935. *Sejd. Textstudier i nordisk religionshistoria*. Geber, Stockholm.
Sundqvist, O., 1998. Kultledare och kultfunktionärer i det forntid Skandinavien. *Svensk Religionshistorisk tidskrift* 7: 76–104.
Sundqvist, O., 2005. Kvinnliga kultledares religiösa och sociala position i forntida Skandinavien. *Chaos. Dansk-Norsk tidsskrift for religionshistoriske studier* 43: 9–29.
Sundqvist, O., 2007. *Kultledare i fornskandinavisk religion*. OPIA 41, Uppsala.
Sundqvist, O., 2012. Var sejdhjällen (fvn. *seiðhjallr, hjallr*) en permanent konstruktion vid kultplatser och i kultbyggnader? *Fornvännen* 107: 280–285.
Sundqvist, O., 2016. *An Arena for Higher Powers: Ceremonial Buildings and religious strategies for rulership in Late Iron Age Scandinavia*. Brill, Leiden.
Sundqvist, O., 2017. Blod och blót. Blodets betydelse och funktion vid fornskandinaviska offerriter. *Scripta Islandica* 68/2017: 275–308.
Sundqvist, O., 2020a. Female cultic leaders and religious (ritual) specialists in Germanic and ancient Scandinavian sources. In Re-imagining Periphery: *Archaeology and text in Northern Europe from Iron Age to Viking and early medieval periods*, eds C. Hillerdal and K. Ilves. Oxbow Books, Oxford: 145–156.

Sundqvist, O., 2020b. Cultic leaders and religious specialists. In *The Pre-Christian Religions of the North. History and Structures. Volume II: Social, geographical, and historical contexts, and communication between worlds*, eds J.P. Schjødt, J. Lindow and A. Andrén. Brepols, Turhout: 739–779.

Tolley, C., 2009. *Shamanism in Norse Myth and Magic*. Suomalainen Tiedeakatemia, Helsinki.

Turner, V.W., 2010. Religious Specialists. In *Ritual and Belief: Readings in anthropology of religions* (3rd edn), ed. D. Hick. Alta Mira Press, Walnut Creek CA: 138–149.

Þorleifur Hauksson and Marteinn Helgi Sigurðsson (eds), 2018. *Vǫlsa þáttr* in *Jómsvíkinga saga*. Íslenzk fornrit 33, Reykjavík.

Vikstrand, P., 2009. Förkristna sakrala personnamn i Skandinavien. *Studia anthroponymica Scandinavica* 27: 5–31.

Vries, J. de., 1956–1957. *Altgermanische Religionsgeschichte*. Grundriss der germanischen Philologie 12.1–2. de Gruyter, Berlin.

Vries, J. de., 1961. *Altnordisches etymologisches Wörterbuch*. Brill, Leiden.

Warmington, E.H. (rev.) and Hutton, M. (trans.), 1970 [1925]. *Tacitus: Agricola, Germania, Dialogus*. Harvard University Press, London/Cambridge MA.

Wellendorf, J., 2022. *Austfararvísur* and interreligious contacts in conversion age Scandinavia. In *The Wild Hunt for Numinous Knowledge*, eds K. Bek-Pedersen, S. Bønding, L.J. Murphy, S. Nygaard and M. Warmid. *Religionsvidenskabeligt Tidsskrift* 74, Special issue: 469–489.

Whaley, D. (ed.), 2012. *Skaldic Poetry of the Scandinavian Middle Ages*. Brepols, Turnhout.

Zachrisson, T., 2022. Lodjursdamerna från folkvandrings- och vendeltid: husfruar med speciella kultfunktioner? In *Kultledare i fornnordisk religion: ett symposium*, eds S.K. Björk and O. Sundqvist. Acta Academiae regiae Gustavi Adolphi 164, Uppsala: 111–124.

Zoëga, G.T. 2004 [1910]. *A Concise Dictionary of Old Icelandic* (reprint). Dover Books, Mineola NY.

# Chapter 8

# The *Vǫlva*'s toolkit: Viking Age ritual specialists and the tools of their trade

*Leszek Gardeła*

## Introducing the *vǫlur* and their kind

The rich corpus of Old Norse literature abounds with stories of human and non-human figures who interact with the supernatural world, cast spells, and foretell the future. Eddic poetry and various saga genres dating from the 13th and later centuries reveal that these individuals were known under many different names, which today can provide valuable hints about the nature of their craft.[1] One of the most frequently occurring terms, usually attributed to women, is *vǫlva* (pl. *vǫlur*). Conventionally translated as 'staff bearer', it is believed to stem from the word *vǫlr* which literally means 'staff' (e.g. Price 2002; but see alternative views in Motz 1980 and discussion in Gardeła 2016: 154–156).[2] As will be demonstrated further below, staffs used by Norse ritual specialists were nothing like ordinary 'walking sticks', and instead served as important, powerful, and potentially dangerous elements of their attire (Gardeła 2016; 2023a). It is worthy of note that such attribute-derived terminology is not wholly unique to Scandinavia and Iceland. In the early medieval Baltic/Prussian area, for instance, pagan priests were known as *krive*, a term referring to the main tool of their trade – a crooked staff known as *krivula* (e.g. Mierzyński 1885; Tomicki 2000; Szczepański 2013).

The Eddic poem *Völuspá* is the most iconic text that centres the *vǫlva* and her craft. In a series of gnomic verses, a female sorceress reveals before her audience the mythic origins and construction of the universe. She also describes the various beings that inhabit it and prognosticates an impending catastrophe – known as Ragnarökr – that will befall the Norse world at some point in the future (on *Völuspá*, see Dronke 1997: 7–153; McKinnell 2005; Gunnell and Lassen 2013).

The *vǫlva* of *Völuspá*, as well as similar female ritual specialists from other Eddic poems, are clearly figures of myth and imagination; in some instances, it is evident that they are not even human (Dronke 1997; McKinnell 2005). Magic-working individuals are not exclusive to the Eddic corpus, however, and appear in a range of saga genres such as *Íslendingasögur*, *fornaldarsögur*, and *konungasögur*. In these non-poetic texts, rather than being supernatural or semi-supernatural entities, the *vǫlur* are portrayed as actual people of flesh and bone who form an integral part of Norse society, even though they sometimes function on its margins and have a somewhat ambivalent status (e.g. Dillmann 2006 with references therein; see also Gardeła *et al.* 2023). 'Ordinary' people interact with the *vǫlur* and other ritual specialists whenever they need (supernatural) advice, guidance, or protection. They visit the sorceresses and sorcerers in their homes (which are sometimes located in isolated places) or attend special ceremonies or 'seances' where public prophecies are offered. The sagas demonstrate that the sphere of magic was mainly, although not exclusively, a domain of women. When magic was performed by men this could lead to severe accusations of 'effeminacy' or 'obscenity' (for further details, see Ström 1973).

The most detailed non-Eddic textual account that may arguably provide a glimpse into the life of a Viking Age *vǫlva* is preserved in *Eiríks saga rauða*, a 13th century source which survives in two different versions in two manuscripts known as *Hauksbók* and *Skálholtsbók* (Einar Ól. Sveinsson and Matthias Þórðarson, 1935; for various translations into English, see Tolley 2009b: 138–141; Price 2019: 39–42). The event involving the *vǫlva* takes place at a Norse farm at Herjolfsnes in Greenland where the local community is suffering from famine. The situation becomes hopeless which is why, seeing no other alternative, the farm owner Þorkell decides to invite a sorceress named Þorbjörg *lítil-vǫlva* to perform a public ritual. It is expected of her that through her magic she will be able to reveal if there is brighter future ahead. The account of the woman's visit and her performance is remarkably rich in detail (for extensive analyses, see Tolley 2009a; Gardeła 2016; Price 2019: 39–42, 72) and too lengthy to discuss in full here, which is why in the following attention will be focused on her costume and accoutrements. As is said in *Eiríks saga rauða* (chap. 4):

> *En er hon kom um kveldit ok sá maðr er í móti henni var sendr, þá var hon svá búin, at hon hafði yfir sér tyglamǫttul blán ok var settr steinum allt í skaut ofan; hon hafði á hálsi sér glertǫlur; hon hafði á hǫfði lambskinnskofra svartan ok við innan kattskinn hvítt. Staf hafði hon í hendi, ok var á knappr; hann var búinn messingu ok settr steinum ofan um knappinn. Hon hafði um sik hnjóskulinda, ok var þar á skjóðupungr mikill; varðveitti hon þar í taufr þau er hon þurfti til fróðleiks at hafa. Hon hafði kálfskinnsskúa loðna á fótum ok í þvengi langa ok sterkliga <ok> látúnsknappar miklir á endunum. Hon hafði á hǫndum sér kattskinnsglófa ok váru hvítir innan ok loðnir.* (Text after Tolley 2009b: 138–139)

> When she arrived in the evening, along with the man who had been sent to meet her, she was fitted out in such a way that she was wearing a dark mantle with fastening straps, which was adorned with stones down to the hem. She had about her neck a string of glass beads. She had on her head a hood of black lambskin lined with white catskin. She carried in her hand a staff [*stafr*] with a knob at the top; it was adorned with brass and set with stones at the top around the knob. About her waist she had a touchwood belt, and on it there was a large purse; in it she kept the charms [*taufr*] which she needed for her craft. She wore shaggy calfskin boots on her feet, with long, strong laces and large brass knobs

> on the ends. On her hands she wore gloves of catskin, white on the inside and furry. (Trans. after Tolley 2009b: 140)

The precision with which the saga describes the *vǫlva*'s costume and toolkit is remarkable. No other Old Norse text pertaining to ritual specialists provides this much information about their attire, and it is generally very rare to see such detailed descriptions of costumes even when sagas portray people belonging to royalty and other elevated social classes (e.g. Sauckel 2013). For this reason, scholarly approaches to this unusual passage from *Eiríks saga rauða* have been polarised – while some researchers hold the opinion that it provides a fairly accurate portrayal of what an actual Viking Age *vǫlva* may have looked like (e.g. Price 2002; Gardeła 2016), others claim that it is largely fictitious. Clive Tolley (2009a: 491), for instance, has argued that the costume of Þorbjörg *lítil-vǫlva* mimics bishop's robes, whereas her staff (ON *stafr*) is an equivalent of a crozier. Tolley's arguments, although interesting, are difficult to sustain, especially in view of the fact that the details of the *vǫlva*'s costume, as well as her various accoutrements, correspond very closely to the furnishings of opulently furnished female graves from Denmark, Norway, and Sweden. These Viking Age graves not only contain iron staffs (some of which have copper alloy knobs, just like the *stafr* from the saga), but also glass beads and other small paraphernalia of likely amuletic significance – the latter could potentially echo the enigmatic *taufr* or charms that Þorbjörg *lítil-vǫlva* carried at her waist.

Over the course of the last 20 years, so-called '*vǫlva* graves' have been the subject of several detailed investigations (e.g. Price 2002; Gardeła 2008; 2016; 2020; Pentz *et al.* 2009; Ulriksen 2018; Westlye 2019; see also the various contributions in Gardeła *et al.* 2023). Although much has already been achieved within this field of research, there are still many aspects that remain untapped and deserve further study. This chapter shall therefore revisit, reflect on, and revise some of the formerly proposed views on Viking Age magic and its practitioners and will attempt to chart new trajectories for interdisciplinary research.

## A concise history of the archaeology of Viking Age magic

Although Viking Age objects which probably played a role in the sphere of magic and religion had been known to scholars as early as the 19th century, serious interest in them arose many years later, mainly as a result of significant theoretical and methodological developments associated with the advent of post-processualism (e.g. Trigger 2009). In the last two decades of the 20th century, international academia witnessed a surge of publications concerning small Viking Age miniature objects that resembled weapons, everyday tools, as well as zoo- and anthropomorphic figurines (e.g. Arwidsson 1989; Fuglesang 1989; Zeiten 1997). At this point in research history, these curious artefacts were conventionally regarded as amulets and were linked with supernatural beings, deities, and various religious concepts and practices known from Old Norse textual sources. Those who dealt with this material were certainly the precursors of interdisciplinary research on pre-Christian religions of the North, but today some of their pioneering interpretations may appear associative or superficial. For instance, in most publications released in the 20th century, Viking Age anthropomorphic figurines tended to be uncritically described as '*valkyries*', whereas small-size weapons such as swords and spears were associated with Óðinn on account of his competences within the sphere of war (e.g. Petersen 1992; Zeiten 1997). Regardless of the fact that these early studies had some obvious shortcomings, in the 1980s and 1990s interdisciplinary approaches to Viking Age archaeology – actively incorporating literary sources pertaining to religion and related phenomena – were both very novel and 'brave' endeavours. Few scholars had previously dared to tread this path, perhaps out of concern that delving into a sphere of prehistoric and early medieval magic would be regarded by their peers as controversial or even unscientific (for broader discussions of these concerns and extensive references, see Gilchrist 2008: 119; Gardeła 2016: 42–90; Price 2019).

Miriam Koktvedgaard Zeiten, who in 1997 published a thorough analysis of Viking Age amulets from Denmark, was one of the first scholars to associate two categories of miniature artefacts – namely those resembling chairs and staffs – with the practice and practitioners of *seiðr*, i.e. exactly the kind of magic that was performed by the aforementioned *vǫlva* Þorbjörg during her visit to Herjolfsnes. In her study, Zeiten drew particular attention to a well-known grave (no. 4) from a Viking Age cemetery adjacent to the fortress of Fyrkat in Jylland, Denmark where a (presumed) woman was buried in the body of a wagon in the company of opulent and exotic goods (cf. Roesdahl 1977; 2023; Price 2002; 2019: 105–113; Pentz *et al.* 2009; Mannering and Rimstad 2023; Pentz 2023). As Zeiten (1997: 44) argued:

> The woman in Fyrkat grave 4 thus represents the only potential substantiation of the hypothesis that certain women wearing amulets were themselves active in magic, perhaps as practitioners of seidhr (...) If some (upper class?) women wore amulets as signs of their seidhr knowledge, they must be assumed to have been representatives of the private cult. Generally, however, one may conclude that the vast majority of amulets from Denmark's Viking Age cannot substantiate any association between the active practice of magic and the women and maybe men who used them.

Five years after the publication of Zeiten's work, the Fyrkat grave became one of the core case studies in Neil Price's monograph *The Viking Way: Religion and war in late Iron Age Scandinavia* (2002; see also the second edition from 2019), which provided the first truly interdisciplinary approach to Viking Age magic. In this ground-breaking work, Price convincingly argued that Fyrkat 4 was not an isolated case of a Viking Age ritual specialist's grave and he identified over 30 other examples in Denmark, Iceland, Norway, and Sweden. The main premise that guided his interpretations was the presence of large iron staffs or rods in the funerary assemblages. Old Norse texts such as *Eiríks saga rauða* and *Laxdœla saga* (which mention staffs as important accoutrements of the *vǫlur* in both life and death respectively – Einar Ól. Sveinsson and Matthias Þórðarson 1935; Einar Ól. Sveinsson 1943), as well as the fact that, in addition to staffs, the graves identified by Price (2002) contained objects with probable amuletic significance, provided additional solid arguments to support these claims.

Overall, Price's work transformed scholarly approaches to medieval pre-Christian beliefs in an unprecedented way. Shortly after the publication of *The Viking Way* and its very positive reception in international scholarly circles, discussions of pre-Christian magic started to be treated more seriously, laying the foundations for what is now known as 'the archaeology of the Viking mind'.

## Magic staffs re-interpreted

Around the time when Price published his book, textual scholar and folklorist Eldar Heide investigated the phenomenon of Old Norse magic (or *seiðr* and *gandr* specifically) from a linguistic, anthropological, and folkloristic perspective (Heide 2006a; 2006b; 2006c). In a series of thought-provoking articles culminating in a doctoral thesis published in 2006, Heide put forward convincing arguments suggesting that *seiðr* magic was intimately linked with the practice of spinning, imitating it in both conceptual and performative sense. He noted that this link is clear in the very name of *seiðr*, which can be straightforwardly translated to mean 'snare, cord, string, halter' (Heide 2006b: 164). The spinning connection can also be seen in what *seiðr* was actually intended for – extant medieval and folkloristic sources imply that the ritual performers would send forth a 'mind emissary' in the form of a thread or rope in order to attract things or to conduct various other deeds at a distance (Heide 2006b: 166). In a recent online podcast, Heide has observed that in a conceptual sense Viking Age *seiðr* would have resembled modern 'drone warfare', a very illustrative and remarkably suitable comparison (see the Brute Norse Podcast 2021; accessed 16.12.2021).

*Seiðr*'s associations with spinning extend much further, however, and can be witnessed also in the paraphernalia used by its practitioners (e.g. Hayeur Smith 2020), in particular in the designs of their most significant attributes – i.e. the aforementioned staffs. When Price (2002) published the first edition of *The Viking Way*, he noted that the iron staffs known from archaeological contexts often possessed an openwork basket-like feature at one end. He was aware of the fact that other Viking Age items, such as lamps, keys, and chains, had similar designs but could not fully explain their symbolic significance (Fig. 8.1). The explanation of this puzzle was provided by Heide (2006a; 2006b; 2006c), who observed that exactly the same kind of 'basket-like' features were integral elements of wooden distaffs, essential tools used in the practice of spinning. The purpose of the 'basket-like' features or 'cages' (as they are more appropriately called) was to hold the raw fibres together in the process of spinning and allowed one to draw them from the cage so that they could be formed into a thread with the use of a drop spindle. As Heide concluded, in the course of *seiðr* practices ritual specialists would send forth their mind-thread in order to achieve their goal, and when the task was complete they would attract it back to themselves and their (di)staff (Fig. 8.2a). Interestingly, the use of distaffs (and other seemingly mundane objects) in magic is also attested in other non-Norse cultural milieus and can be seen very clearly in high medieval and Renaissance art. A particularly striking example is an engraving by Albrecht Dürer (1471–1528) which portrays a witch flying on a ram and holding a distaff between her thighs (Fig. 8.2b). Another noteworthy case is an illustration by Hans Holbein (1497/1498–1543) depicting a witch who uses a distaff to raise a storm. Apparently, distaffs could sometimes also be used as weapons, too, as shown in an illustration by Israhel van Meckenem (1440/1445–1503) (Fig. 8.2c).

Inspired by new international research on the *seiðr* phenomenon, since 2007 I have also been actively involved in exploring various aspects of Viking Age magic and its practitioners (e.g. Gardeła 2008; 2009; 2011; 2013a; 2014; 2016; 2019; Gardeła *et al.* 2023). The culmination of these studies is a monograph published in 2016 entitled *(Magic) Staffs in the Viking Age*, an interdisciplinary work critically combining archaeological, textual, and ethnographic material. Careful analyses of Eddic poems and saga accounts have helped to elucidate the rich terminology used by Icelandic medieval writers to refer to staffs, revealing as many as 13 different names attributed to these objects (Gardeła 2016: 135–170). In alphabetical order these are: *gambanteinn*, *Griðavölr*, *hlautviðr*, *iárnlurkr*, *járnstafr*, *krókrstafr*, *lævateinn*, *reyrsproti*, *seiðstafr*, *skógarvöndr*, *stafr*, *stafsprota*, and *tamsvöndr*. One particularly remarkable aspect of the staffs known from Old Norse texts is that they generally fall within two distinct categories based on the material used for their production. Wooden staffs, as implied by the elements *-teinn* 'twig' and *-vöndr* 'wand' in their names, seem to have been used for magic acts intended to tame or manipulate weaker minds. Other types of staffs, sometimes evidently made of iron and carrying compound names containing elements like *-vǫlr*, *-lurkr*, and *-stafr*, appear to have been employed mainly as emblems of status and profession (as in the case of the *stafr* held by the *lítil-vǫlva* from *Eiríks saga rauða*) and/or as items facilitating travel to the Otherworld (as in the case of the crooked staff, or *krókstafr*, from *Þorsteins þáttr bæjarmagns*: Herman Pálsson and Edwards 1985: 259).

It is noteworthy that the occurrence of both wooden and iron staffs in the Old Norse literary corpus has striking parallels in antiquity, especially in Greek and Roman traditions. In a seminal study published in 1927 entitled *The Magic Staff or Rod in Graeco-Italian Antiquity*, historian and archaeologist Ferdinand Joseph Maria de Waele observed that in the Greek world also two types of staffs were in use: *skeptron* and *rhabdos*. The term *skeptron* referred to a rigid staff of office (in fact, the modern English word 'sceptre' is derived from it), whereas the term *rhabdos* was used to denote staffs or wands that were flexible and thus probably made of wood (de Waele 1927: 29).

According to surviving sources, in the traditions of ancient Greece and Rome staffs were carried by gods (e.g. Hermes-Mercurius), rulers, judges, minstrels, and poets as well as by various kinds of ritual specialists (e.g. Kirke and Medeia) who would employ them in the practice of *rhabdomanteia* (divination with a staff), *hydromanteia* (divination which involves the use of water), and *necromanteia* (necromancy) (de Waele

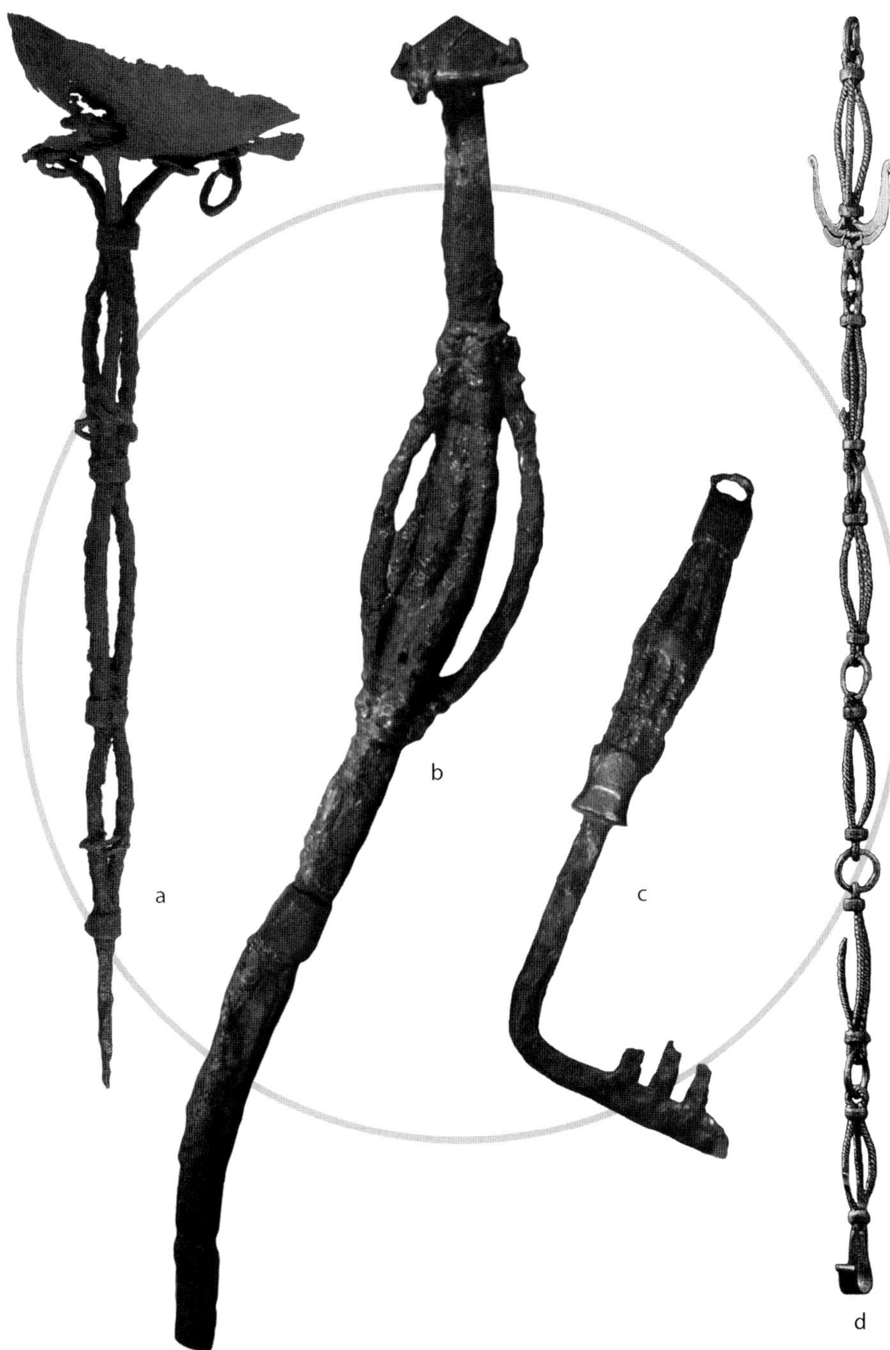


*Figure 8.1. Selection of Viking Age objects with 'basket features': a. lamp from Hurum, Buskerud, Norway (photo by Kirsten Helgeland, CC BY-SA 4.0); b. staff from Klinta, Öland (photo by Leszek Gardeła); c. key from Buttle, Ange, Gotland (photo by Leszek Gardeła); d. chain from Oseberg, Vestfold, Norway (photo by Eirik Irgens Johnsen, CC BY-SA 4.0) (image design by Leszek Gardeła).*

*Figure 8.2. a. Modern artistic impression of a* seiðr *ritual where the sorceress sits on a chair and holds a (di)staff between the legs (drawing by Melissa Hocking-Lorenz, used by kind permission); b. witch flying on a ram and holding a distaff between her legs (woodcut by Albrecht Dürer, 1500–1501); c. a woman using a distaff to beat a man (illustration by Israhel van Meckenem, 1495–1503).*

1927: 109–132, 144–168, 181–183). Careful exploration of the different applications of staffs in the ancient world reveals that they had much in common with their early medieval counterparts. The main takeaway from such comparative analyses – which form an important part of *(Magic) Staffs in the Viking Age* (Gardeła 2016) – is the idea that staffs in past societies were often regarded as 'multivalent objects' possessing a range of ostensibly different yet semiotically interrelated layers of meaning. It is likely that the staffs known from the Scandinavian Viking Age archaeological record carried profound symbolism and corresponded in a literal and/or figurative sense with the idea of the *axis mundi* (the world axis), distaffs, weapons, phalluses, weighing implements, whip-shanks, roasting spits, keys, and lamps. Some of the staffs may have also been used, perhaps in the context of ritual performances, as musical instruments – the rings attached to their 'basket handles' would have produced a loud jingling sound (Gardeła 2016: 206–207).

In conclusion, similar to several other categories of Viking Age 'magic' objects that have been recently subject to academic scrutiny (e.g. Gardeła 2020; 2022), the staffs can thus be seen as things enmeshed in what Howard Williams calls 'a web of citational relationships'. The concept of citation, first introduced by Williams in 2016, is a very useful tool in our modern attempts to decode the Viking mind and has been defined as:

> (...) practices of selection and deployment of artefacts, substances, images, architectures, monuments, and spaces that, separately and in combination, created mnemonic material references to other things, places, peoples, and times. (Williams 2016: 407)

For the purposes of the present study, a visual representation of the web of citational relationships in which the Viking Age staffs were likely enmeshed has been created (Fig. 8.3). This illustration demonstrates their material links with other things and people as well as with symbolically charged concepts that may have existed in the minds of Viking Age individuals and their 'prolonged echoes' that survive in Old Norse literature.

Research on the materiality and burial contexts of magic staffs that I conducted in 2007–2016 led to the hypothesis (which is now shared by other researchers, e.g. Knutson 2020) that the staffs were believed to possess their own agency and a kind of personhood. As Chris Fowler (2004: 7) notes, personhood is 'attained and maintained through relationships not only with other human beings but with things, places, animals and the spiritual features of the cosmos'. Like persons, magic staffs from the Viking world were 'constituted, de-constituted, maintained and altered in social practices through life and after death' (Fowler 2004: 7). In several funerary contexts iron staffs were found intentionally bent, broken, or even held under large stones (e.g. the staffs from Aska, Fuldby, Gutdalen, and Klinta: Arne 1932; Petersson 1958; Westlye *et al.* 2023). These deliberate and symbolically charged ways of depositing the staffs in graves across Scandinavia, as well as the fact that some of the staffs from Old Norse texts were given personal names (e.g. *Griðavölr*, *Högnuðr*) strongly align with

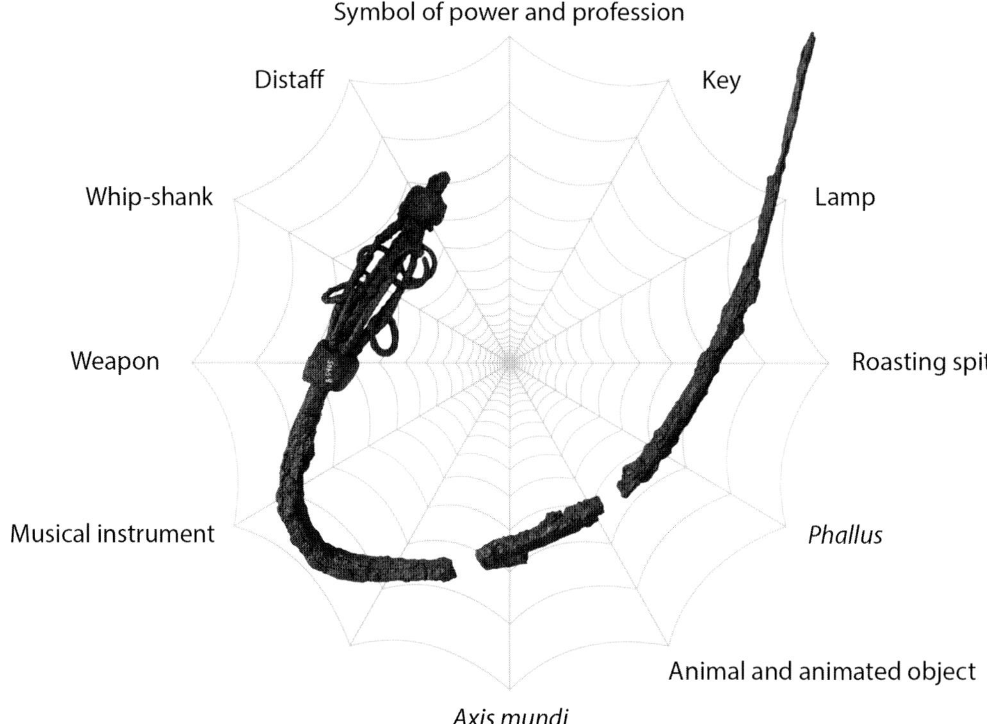


*Figure 8.3. Visual representation of the web of citational relationships between magic staffs and other objects and concepts. The photo in the centre (taken by Klaudia Karpińska and used by kind permission) shows a staff from Gutdalen, Sogn og Fjordane, Norway (image design by Leszek Gardeła).*

Fowler's (2004) idea that objects *can* indeed have their own distinct identity and/or personhood. On the one hand, these customs imply that the mourners deliberately destroyed the staffs to neutralise their power and perhaps the power of their owners, too (as in the case of a memorable passage from *Eyrbyggja saga* where the breaking of a sorceress's (di)staff also 'breaks' or neutralises her spell; see Dillmann 1983). On the other hand, they clearly reflect the ways some magic workers would be treated in death: intentional damage inflicted to the archaeologically discovered staffs, which involved burning, bending, breaking, and pressing them with stones, mimics the most popular ways of dealing with malevolent sorcerers in Old Norse literature. *Laxdæla saga*, *Eyrbyggja saga*, and other texts contain vivid and detailed accounts of people (often women) who were burnt, drowned, and stoned to death for performing harmful magic (Ström 1942). In light of the above, one can argue that in the Viking mind the magic staff was an animated object, sometimes actually inseparable from its owner and likewise requiring special treatment in death (on related concepts, especially with regard to 'living swords', see Brunning 2019 with further references).

## Stones and atypical burials

Towards the end of the first decade of the 2000s, the realisation that some iron staffs from Viking Age graves were intentionally 'crushed' or pressed to the ground with stones (e.g. Gardeła 2008; 2009) and that stoning was one of the most common ways of executing people accused of performing malevolent sorcery spurred an interest in so-called 'atypical burials', thus charting a new trajectory of research pertaining to the material remains of Viking Age magic and its practitioners.

Atypical burials are a global phenomenon and can be encountered in many cultures across space and time. In Anglo-Saxon archaeology they are known by the somewhat controversial and negatively charged term 'deviant burials' (e.g. Reynolds 2009), whereas in German scholarship they tend to be labelled in a more neutral manner as *Sonderbestattungen* or 'special burials'. According to Edeltraud Aspöck, the most basic definition of such burials, which can be applied across cultures and historical periods, is that they are:

> (...) burials different from the normative burial ritual of the respective period, region and/or cemetery. These differences may occur in body position or treatment, location or construction of the grave or types of grave goods. (Aspöck 2008: 17)

In the case of Scandinavian archaeology, it is not always immediately straightforward to isolate 'non-normative/atypical' from 'normative/typical' graves within a given site. This is due to the fact that funerary practices in 8th–11th century Northern Europe, including the areas of Denmark, Sweden, Norway, and Iceland, were very diverse (e.g. Brøndsted 1936; Svanberg 2003; Nordeide 2011). Regardless of the fact that 'no two burial tableaux are exactly the same' (Price 2012: 82), however, it is possible to determine some features of 'normative' funerary behaviour and some patterns and 'rules' that would be observed by the mourners and burial specialists across space and time. Most scholars agree, that on the most basic taxonomical level, Scandinavian Viking Age graves can be divided into two categories: cremations and inhumations.

The identification of 'atypical' or 'deviant' characteristics within the corpus of cremation burials is challenging due to the often fragmentary and ambiguous nature of what survives of them in the archaeological record. Some graves, however, display clear traces of acts that may be interpreted as atypical, preventive, or apotropaic measures intended to literally and/or metaphorically 'bind' the dead to their resting place. The most vivid examples are those where sharp objects, especially weapons, are purposefully driven into the cremation layer (e.g. Nordberg 2002). One such grave, labelled as A24 and discovered on the shore of lake Dalstorp in Västergötland, contained as many as ten bent spearheads intentionally thrust into the ground (Artelius 2005). Based on the funerary assemblage, the overall composition of the grave, and its landscape setting, it has been argued that it belonged to a woman whom the local society feared would rise from the dead to harm the living; this is apparently what necessitated the undertaking of special preventive measures during her funeral.

When one situates this unusual burial in the context of medieval written sources, early modern folklore, and apotropaic practices known from other areas of Europe (e.g. Gardeła 2017; Kozak 2021), there are good reasons to believe that the deceased person from Dalstorp had indeed dealt with magic. Several Old Norse sagas and other medieval texts preserve descriptions of violent executions of variously gendered magic workers who contravened social norms and who were burned to death for their malevolent deeds (e.g. *Haralds saga ins hárfagra* chap. 34; *Ólafs saga Tryggvasonar* chap. 62; *Historia de Antiquitate Regum Norwagiensium* chap. 11; for more details, see Ström 1942: 189–198; Gardeła 2016: 42–90). Admittedly, none of these accounts mentions burning people and pinning their cremains with weapons – as seen in Dalstorp – but they do illustrate the existence of extreme modes of behaviour that were deemed appropriate to punish wrongdoers and, in this way, restore order.

Although external and internal compositions of inhumation burials appear more complex and more ambiguous to interpret than cremation burials, it is possible to distinguish among them concrete physical traits that clearly communicated 'difference' of the deceased. Eva Thäte's pioneering monograph (2007) entitled *Monuments and Minds: Monument re-use in Scandinavia in the second half of the first millennium AD* defined the basic criteria for isolating such instances in the Scandinavian Viking-Age archaeological record. According to Thäte, these include unusual body position (prone burials) as well as evidence of *peri-* or *post-mortem* violence (decapitation and/or stoning). Two evocative cases that display such 'divergent' traits include the now well-known Danish graves discovered in the 1980s at Gerdrup on Sjælland (a double inhumation grave of a man and a woman, with the latter individual covered with boulders) and Bogøvej on Langeland (a man buried prone and covered with stones). These had often been linked with apotropaic acts but, until 2008, nobody had seriously investigated them in the context of *seiðr* and its practitioners.

Inspired by the work of Thäte and international cross-disciplinary studies of revenants, between 2008 and 2017 I conducted extensive research into the practice of decapitation, stoning, prone burial, and related mortuary phenomena among Viking Age Scandinavians and Slavs (Gardeła 2011; 2013a; 2013b). The results of this research were summarised in a monograph entitled *Bad Death in the Early Middle Ages: Atypical burials from Poland in a comparative perspective*, which – notwithstanding its major focus on the Western Slavic world – included extensive discussions of atypical burial customs in Northern and Western Europe (Gardeła 2017). The main takeaway from this study is that across 8th–13th century Europe atypical burials had a plethora of meanings, not all of them negative. Therefore, their material remains should be approached on a case by case basis and by taking into regard the results of osteological analyses, the internal and external composition of the graves, as well as their wider context and socio-political setting (Gardeła 2017: 230–235). A substantial proportion of atypical burials, especially from the period around the 10th and 11th centuries, appear to reflect profound social changes associated with the process of state formation and the introduction of new judicial systems. Against this socio-political background, all around Europe decapitations and prone burials in particular can be plausibly interpreted as ways of dealing with criminals, social 'others', and individuals who failed to conform to the (newly introduced) norms.

Regardless of the multiplicity of meanings attributed to broadly understood atypical burial practices, there are very good reasons to believe that both in Scandinavia and the Western Slavic world the practice of stoning (involving the casting of stones with the intention to kill an individual and/or the placing of stones on the cadaver) was the most common form of *peri-* and *post-mortem* punishment for people accused of performing malevolent magic (Gardeła 2017: 160–204). A few Viking Age graves from Denmark which contain stones or large boulders lying directly on the deceased as well as other 'atypical traits' can thus be convincingly interpreted as the graves of ritual specialists.

It is noteworthy that in addition to stones, the above-mentioned Gerdrup grave contained a spearhead placed along the woman's side. The point of this weapon was directed 'downwards' towards the foot end of the grave, a custom rarely observed in Viking Age graves and thus arguably indicating 'difference' both of the item itself and the individual(s) buried with it. Since in Old Norse literature weapons such as spears occasionally alternate with reeds or staffs, the specimen from Gerdrup may be perceived not as a weapon *per se*, but as a symbol of office or even a kind of magic staff (Gardeła 2016: 185–187; Kastholm and Margaryan 2021; Kastholm Hansen *et al.* 2023). A parallel situation is observed in the Trekroner-Grydehøj grave, also from Sjælland (Ulriksen 2018; Kastholm Hansen *et al.* 2023). Here, too, a spear or arrowhead-like object had been placed by the side of a woman whose body was later covered with large stones and pebbles. The object's copper alloy blade with an inserted iron tip has no direct parallels in the archaeological record, but the fact that – just like the Gerdrup spearhead – it was buried pointing towards the foot end of the grave permits the careful interpretation that it had once served as a kind of magic staff. All this adds yet another dimension to the ambiguity of the material culture we encounter in the graves of presumed ritual specialists.

Overall, the examples presented here demonstrate that iron staffs with 'basket handles' should not be seen as the only plausible designators of magic workers' burials. Other 'atypical' features that occur in mortuary contexts – such as stones lying directly on the bodies and 'unusual' grave goods – should also be taken into consideration when searching for the *vǫlur* and their kind in the archaeological record. It is to the unusual small size paraphernalia that we will now turn our attention.

## Miniatures, myths, and magic

Many graves of presumed female ritual specialists contain small size artefacts made of metal or organic material. The overall form and decoration of these items, as well as their deliberate placement in burial contexts, collectively imply that they were regarded by their users as more than just body adornments and may have had very particular roles to play, for instance as mnemonic and sentimental objects, protective amulets, symbols of devotion to particular deities or supernatural beings, or even special accoutrements that were deemed necessary for the successful conduct of ritual performances. Based on available data, it is possible to isolate four broad categories of miniature paraphernalia from these admittedly special mortuary contexts, each of which has a couple of sub-groups: 1. metal pendants (including Thor's hammers, crosses, round pendants, and miniatures resembling masks/faces, helmets/heads, snakes, chairs, and other things); 2. organic pendants; 3. tools; and 4. beads (e.g. Zeiten 1997; Price 2002; 2019; Jensen 2010; Gardeła 2020; Jessen and Ramsøe Majland 2021). Due to constraints of space, in this chapter attention will be focused only on the metal finds and their different sub-groups (Fig. 8.4).

Thor's hammers are broadly distributed across the Viking world. They appear in all kinds archaeological contexts, including cremation and inhumation graves, settlements, and hoards, which collectively implies that they were used by people representing different age, gender, and social groups (e.g. Staecker 1999; Jensen 2010). In light of this evidence, it does not seem valid to consider them as distinct markers of ritual specialists, although it is highly probable that they were, at least occasionally, worn and used by such individuals as well as buried with them. One illustrative case is a grave from Hilde in Sogn og Fjordane, Norway which held a small ring with as many as nine Thor's hammers (Fig. 8.4h; Price 2002: 192; Gardeła 2016: 298–299). The same can be said about crosses which – just like Thor's hammers – appear in a plethora of contexts and thus cannot be regarded as distinct markers of ritual specialists' graves. Bj 660 from Birka in Uppland, Sweden (Price 2019: 85–88) is actually the only example of a grave of a presumed female magic worker which contains a silver crucifix (Fig. 8.4e). In this unusual case, it appears that the pendant was not an indicator of the deceased person's Christian identity but simply 'an object of spiritual power, and the fact of its symbolism in a different faith would not contradict its use in a non-Christian ritual context – indeed, this might have been the very point' (Price 2019: 88).

Only one grave of a presumed ritual specialist, discovered at Gutdalen in Sogn og Fjordane, Norway (Westlye *et al.* 2023), has yielded mask- or face-shaped pendants (Fig. 8.4b). Analogous artefacts are very unusual in this part of Scandinavia but are well known from the archaeological record in Denmark and Iceland (Lemm 2007) where they are usually found stray. They have been interpreted in a variety of ways, for instance as representing the gods Óðinn or Loki (Lemm 2007; Schaadt and Grundvad 2016; Pentz 2018: 24–25). While the latter reading may perhaps be substantiated when the mouth of the mask/face is shown sewn tight (presumably in reference to the myth where the gods silence Loki to punish him for his foul behaviour), it does not hold water in the case of specimens lacking this particular iconographic feature. The stylistic details of mask/face pendants correspond closely to the 10th century Mammen style imagery of runestones from Denmark (e.g. Aarhus; DR 66 and Skjern; DR 81) and southern Sweden (e.g. Hunnestad; DR 286 and Lund; DR 314), which is believed to have served apotropaic roles. Even though no casting moulds have been noted in the archaeological record so far, the relatively large number of mask/face

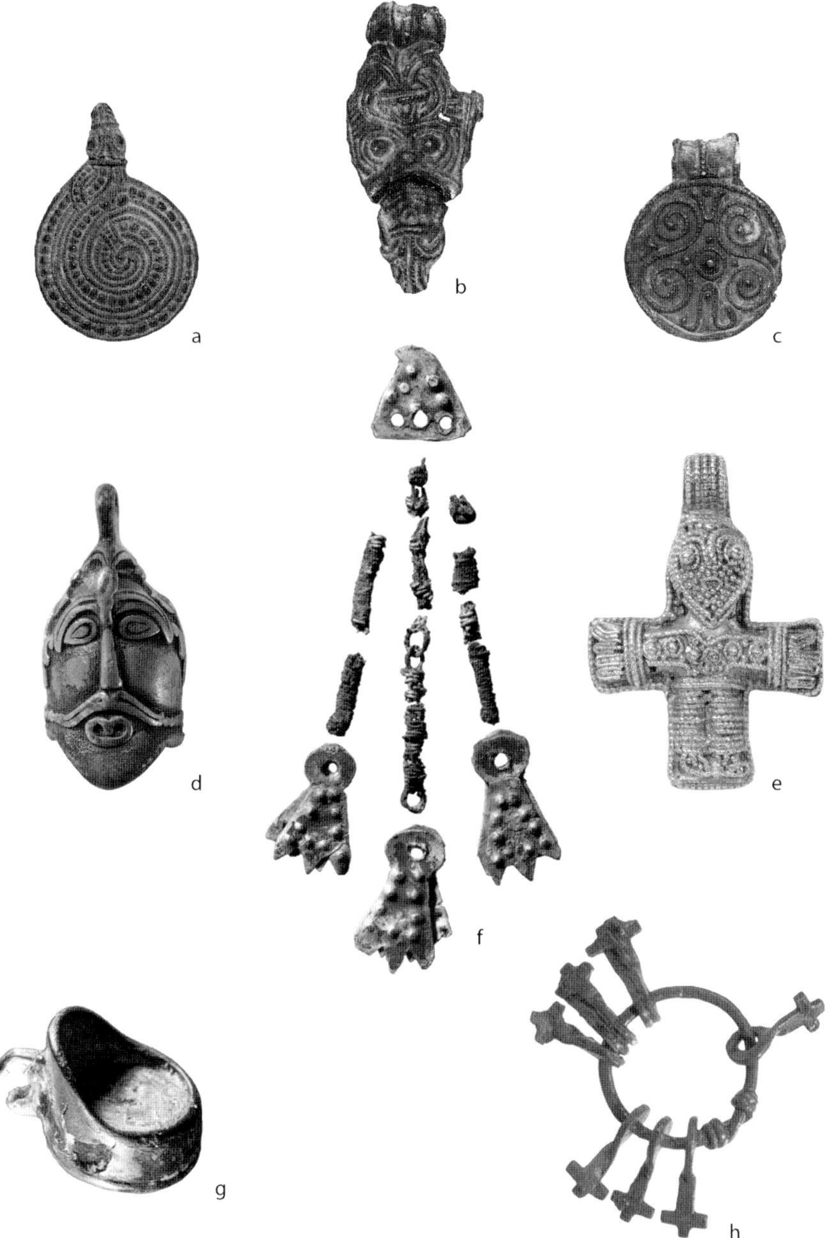


*Figure 8.4. Selection of miniature metal paraphernalia found in the graves of presumed ritual specialists: a–c. miniature snake, mask/face, and round pendant from Gutdalen, Sogn og Fjordane, Norway (photos by Leszek Gardeła); d. miniature helmet/head from Aska, Hagebyhöga, Sweden (photo by Gabriel Hildebrand, CC BY 2.5 SE); e. silver crucifix from grave Bj 660 at Birka, Uppland, Sweden (photo by Gabriel Hildebrand, CC BY 2.5 SE); f–g. bird-feet pendants and chair pendant from grave 4 at Fyrkat, Jylland, Denmark (photos by the National Museum of Denmark; h. ring with nine Thor's hammers from Hilde, Sogn og Fjordane, Norway (photo by Ann-Mari Olsen, CC BY-SA 40) (image design by Leszek Gardeła).*

pendants in Denmark – discovered mostly via metal detecting – implies that this is where they were originally produced. Keeping in mind also the fact that runestones with similar imagery originate from south Scandinavia, it is permissible to speculate that the miniature masks/faces from Gutdalen were brought to Norway from Denmark. They may have formed a set together with six round pendants found in the same grave (Fig. 8.4c), all of which represent a very rare jewellery-type that – statistically speaking – likewise appears to be of 'Danish' manufacture. Regrettably, due to poor bone preservation, it is impossible to determine whether or not the deceased person from Gutdalen was a local or a foreigner, but the above-mentioned 'artefactual hints' strongly point to the latter alternative. Interestingly, a grave from Arnestad in Sogn og Fjordane, Norway, which contains round pendants of exactly the same type as those from Gutdalen, also held a large iron staff, implying that the deceased was versed in magic (Westlye 2019: 39–40).

Apart from the discoveries of miniature masks or faces, recent amateur metal detecting endeavours carried out in Denmark have revealed a number of pendants resembling three-dimensional helmeted heads or helmets with full facial guards (Gardeła 2023b). So far, only one item of this type is known from a well recorded grave. The grave in question, discovered at Aska in Hagebyhöga in Sweden (Arne 1932), also happens to contain an iron staff and is commonly regarded as belonging to a magic worker (Fig. 8.4d). Regrettably, as in the isolated case of the miniature masks/faces from Gutdalen, it is impossible to determine if the miniature helmet from Aska formed part of the ritual toolkit of the deceased individual or if it had another purpose. Neil Price (2002: 158), for instance, has suggested that it may have symbolised the cut-off head of the Giant Mímir.

Admittedly, it is challenging to say anything certain about the significance of the miniature paraphernalia from these special mortuary contexts. While it is clear that they all served *some* purpose – either for the dead or for the mourners – we usually have too little comparative and contextual data to determine whether their role was always fixed or fluid and resting on individual preferences of the owner. In seeking for patterns that can enhance and guide our understanding of Viking Age mentalities as well as the functional and symbolic significance of miniscule items encountered in graves of presumed ritual specialists, it is much more promising to take a more inquisitive look at miniature snakes and chairs.

Although only one miniature chair has so far been noted in a grave together with an iron staff found at Fyrkat in Jylland, Denmark (Fig. 8.4f), there are very good reasons to believe that artefacts of this particular kind were closely associated with people who dealt with magic and thus had a more fixed frame of reference (Pentz 2023). This assertion results from a number of premises derived from careful studies of textual as well as archaeological sources, which have recently been conducted by Mads Dengsø Jessen and Kamilla Ramsøe Majland (2021; see also Jessen 2023). As their studies show, in Old Norse literature chairs, thrones, and platforms are often used by deities and humans versed in magic to acquire insight into another world. The best examples are Óðinn and his throne Hliðskjálf as well as the afore-mentioned *vǫlva* Þorbjörg who conducts her ritual from a special seat or platform interchangeably referred to as *hásæti* and *seiðhjallr*. Sitting in a chair or throne can be conceptualised as an act of literal and symbolic 'elevation' and a way to manifest both secular and sacral power. All this evidence combined, together with the fact that miniature chairs tend to co-occur in silver hoards as well as in graves with miniature snake pendants (to which we shall turn below) (Gardeła 2020; Jessen and Ramsøe Majland 2021), gives very good reasons to believe that these items were indeed important elements of the ritual toolkit and perhaps even markers of people versed in magic. One can thus hazard a guess that in funerary contexts they designate burials of ritual specialists, regardless of whether these burials contain staffs or other evocative traits (e.g. stones on the deceased).

Finally, let us turn our attention to silver and copper alloy pendants shaped like coiled snakes (Fig. 8.4a). Interdisciplinary investigations of their complete find corpus (Gardeła 2020) have demonstrated that the cremation and inhumation graves in which these items have been encountered also contain iron staffs and/or objects evidently charged with religious meanings and/or associated with the practice of magic. In particular, the discoveries from the graves at Birka, Gutdalen, and Trå strongly imply that the people they were buried with (presumably women) held very high positions in their society, a claim emphasised by the fact that the same graves contain other rare and expensive goods (Kaland 2006; Price 2019; Westlye *et al.* 2023). Considering the 'concept of citation' discussed above, it has also been argued recently (Gardeła 2020) that coiled snake pendants symbolised the potency of reptiles known to Viking Age people from real life as well as from heroic and mythic traditions (such as, for instance, the Miðgarðr serpent or Niðhöggr: Simek 2006: 215, 231). Furthermore, in a visual as well as conceptual sense, coiled snake pendants may also have echoed other elements of Viking Age material culture, such as 'dragon ships' with coiled prows (e.g. the Oseberg ship), keys and staffs with coiled metal motifs, and even the widespread custom of bending/coiling weapons conducted on funerary occasions.

In summation, all these immaterial and material citations appear to have predestined miniature chairs and snake pendants to become markers of people who dealt with the supernatural. The question that still remains open, however, is how exactly were they used?

In trying to explain the purpose of miniature objects from all kinds of places and cultural milieus, Douglass Bailey (2005) has argued that rather than concentrating on their potential relation to deities and supernatural beings, we ought to focus more attention on their material aspects and consider how they could have made their wielders and observers feel. One inherent aspect of *all* miniatures is that they enlarge the individual viewing or holding them, which can make them feel empowered or, as Bailey (2005: 33) says, allow them to 'indulge in flights of fantasy'.

Viking Age individuals who presumably used miniatures in the performance of their magic may have benefitted from these objects' miniscule size. The artefacts were very easy to 'manipulate' and could be thrown, scratched, bent, subjected to fire or ice, and treated in a plethora of other ways. As custodians of objects intricately woven into a web of material and immaterial citations – ranging from deities and supernatural entities to various mythical and real world concepts – the *vǫlur* and their kind held the power to influence and transform this 'miniature environment,' simultaneously affecting the lives of those who witnessed their rituals.

To the people of the Viking Age, 'miniature magic' and the effects it was expected to evoke was probably very real and worked by the power of suggestion and mental manipulation, a skill the ritual specialists must have mastered to perfection.

## Conclusions and future research trajectories

This chapter has critically chartered the latest advancements in interdisciplinary studies of Viking Age magic and its practitioners. As demonstrated above, the last 30 years of research have re-invigorated the field, bringing to light previously unknown material and offering new perspectives on formerly obscure themes. It is now more clear than ever that variously gendered Viking Age ritual specialists were not only figures that existed solely in the vivid imagination of medieval poets, story-tellers, and writers, as some scholars in the 1980–1990 were keen to believe. Tangible traces of the material culture used in magic rituals, as well as the physical remains of the people who conducted them, can be convincingly tracked down in the archaeological record. Aside from the iron staffs and stones placed directly on the deceased, it appears that also certain types of miniscule items (found singly or in assemblages) can be regarded as material markers of these individuals' presence in a particular area or funerary context. While our chances to read and interpret these 'silent' archaeological sources are bound to remain limited, new avenues may open up if we more closely investigate their materiality and the psychological reactions they may have evoked in people.

Although in mortuary archaeology there appears to be a tendency to shy away from typo-chronological analyses of the artefactual material, these endeavours still hold great potential and may contribute to revealing previously unacknowledged ideas, motifs, as well as cross-cultural connections of the presumed ritual specialists and the people who buried them. Meticulous overviews or various artefact types (supplemented by high quality images, drawings, and measurements) *can* and certainly *will* push our research forward.

Future explorations of Viking Age magic should also take place in the cross-disciplinary spirit that has become the hallmark of 'the archaeology of the Viking mind' (e.g. Pentz *et al.* 2009; Kastholm and Margaryan 2021). There are many tantalising details that can be revealed about the toolkits of the *vǫlur* and their kind by conducting specialist physico-chemical analyses of organic materials from their graves. Some new insights into these and other themes have been gained as a result of the *Tanken bag Tingene* ('Thoughts behind Things') project conducted at the National Museum of Denmark in 2020–2023 (Gardeła *et al.* 2023) as well as in the course of other research endeavours led by international scholars all around Europe, the Americas, and beyond. As long as we conduct our research in a methodologically and ethically sound manner, there is room for everyone and a promising future for our discipline.

## Acknowledgements

This study was written as part of the *Tanken bag Tingene* project which was conducted at the National Museum of Denmark in 2020–2023 and generously funded by Krogagerfonden. Many thanks are also due to Melissa Hocking-Lorenz and Klaudia Karpińska for kindly sharing their illustrations.

### *Notes*

1 Old Norse written sources provide a remarkably wide terminology for ritual specialists which cannot be elaborated here due to constraints of space. Male magic workers can be called, for instance, *galdramaðr* ('*galdr*-man'), *seiðberendr* ('*seiðr*-carrier'), *seiðmaðr* ('*seiðr*-man'), or *spámaðr* ('prophecy-man'). In addition to the commonly used term *vǫlva*, female magic workers can also be called, *seiðkona* ('*seiðr*-woman'), *spákona* ('prophecy-woman'), or *kveldriða* ('evening-rider'). For further details and a full list of names, see Price (2019: 83). In this chapter, the term *vǫlva* (pl. *vǫlur*) is used as an umbrella term for all female individuals who practised magic and especially its one very particular form known as *seiðr*.

2 In her study, Lotte Motz (1980: 200) suggested that the word *vǫlr* ought to be derived from the root *uel (referring to the performance of circular motion) and/or that it may have been employed to describe 'a closed or secret place'. Although these views are interesting, they have not been accepted by other specialists dealing with Viking Age magic.

## Bibliography

Arne, T.A.J., 1932. Ein Bemerkenswerter Fund in Ostergötland. *Acta Archaeologica* 3: 67–112.

Artelius, T., 2005. The revenant by the lake. Spear symbolism in Scandinavian Late Viking Age burial ritual. In *Dealing with the Dead. Archaeological Perspectives on Prehistoric Scandinavian Burial Ritual*, eds T. Artelius and F. Svanberg. National Heritage Board, Stockholm: 261–276.

Arwidsson, G., 1989. Veschiedene Gegenstände/Amulette in Form von Menschenfiguren, Reitern, Pferden, Vierfüßlern, Vögeln und Schlangen. In *Birka II: 3. Systematische Analysen der Gräberfunde*, ed. G. Arwidsson. Kungl. Vitterhets Historie och Antikvitets Akademien, Stockholm: 55–62.

Aspöck, E., 2008. What actually is a deviant burial? Comparing German-language and Anglophone research on 'deviant burials. In *Deviant Burial in the Archaeological Record*, ed. E.M. Murphy. Oxbow Books, Oxford, 17–34.

Bailey, D.W., 2005. *Prehistoric Figurines: Representation and corporeality in the Neolithic*. Routledge, London and New York.

Brøndsted, J., 1936. Danish Inhumation Graves of the Viking Age. A Survey, *Acta Archaeologica* 7: 81–228.

Brunning, S., 2019. *The Sword in Early Medieval Northern Europe: Experience, identity, representation.* Boydell, Woodbridge.

Brute Norse Podcast 2021. Episode 34: Viking Drone Warfare Spinning, seiðr & gandr with Eldar Heide. https://soundcloud.com/brutenorse/34-viking-drone-warfare-spinning-seir-gandr-with-eldar-heide, 1 May 2021.

de Waele, F.J.M., 1927. *The Magic Staff or Rod in Graeco-Italian Antiquity*. Erasmus, The Hague.

Dillmann, F.-X., 1983. Katla and her distaff. An episode of the tri-functional magic in *Eyrbyggja saga?* In *Homage to Georges Dumézil*, ed. E.C. Polomé. *Journal of Indo-European Studies* Monograph Series 3, Washington DC: 113–124.

Dillmann, F.-X., 2006. *Les magiciens dans l'Islande ancienne: Études sur la représentation de la magie islandaise et de ses agents dans les sources littéraires norroises.* Kungl. Gustav Adolfs Akademien för svensk folkkultur, Uppsala.

Dronke, U. (ed.), 1997. *The Poetic Edda. Volume II. Mythological Poems.* Oxford University Press, Oxford.

Einar Ólafur Sveinnson. (ed.), 1943 *Laxdœla saga. Halldórs þættir Snorrasonar. Stúfs þáttr.* Hið íslenzka fornritafélag, Reykjavík.

Einar Ól. Sveinsson and Matthias Þórðarson. (eds), 1935. *Eyrbyggja saga. Brands þáttr örva. Eiríks saga rauða. Grœnlendinga saga. Grœnlendinga þáttr.* Hið íslenzka fornritafélag, Reykjavík.

Fowler, C., 2004. *The Archaeology of Personhood. An Anthropological Approach.* Routledge, London and New York.

Fuglesang, S.H., 1989. Viking and medieval amulets in Scandinavia. *Fornvännen* 84: 15–25.

Gardeła, L., 2008. Into Viking minds. Reinterpreting the staffs of sorcery and unravelling seiðr. *Viking and Medieval Scandinavia* 4: 45–84.

Gardeła, L., 2009. A biography of the seiðr-staffs. Towards an archaeology of emotions. In *Between Paganism and Christianity in the North*, eds L.P. Słupecki and J. Morawiec. Wydawnictwo Uniwersytetu Rzeszowskiego, Rzeszów: 188–217.

Gardeła, L., 2011. Buried with honour and stoned to death? The ambivalence of Viking Age magic in the light of archaeology. *Analecta Archaeologica Ressoviensia* 4: 339–375.

Gardeła, L., 2013a. The dangerous dead? Rethinking Viking-Age deviant burials. In *Conversions: Looking for ideological change in the early Middle Ages*, eds R. Simek and L.P. Słupecki, Fassbaender, Vienna: 96–136.

Gardeła, L., 2013b. The headless Norsemen. Decapitation in Viking Age Scandinavia. In *The Head Motif in Past Societies in a Comparative Perspective/Motyw głowy w dawnych kulturach w perspektywie porównawczej*, eds L. Gardeła and K. Kajkowski. Muzeum Zachodniokaszubskie w Bytowie, Bytów: 88–155.

Gardeła, L., 2014. *Scandinavian Amulets in Viking Age Poland.* Fundacja Rzeszowskiego Ośrodka Archeologicznego, Instytut Archeologii Uniwersytetu Rzeszowskiego, Rzeszów.

Gardeła, L., 2016. *(Magic) Staffs in the Viking Age.* Fassbaender, Vienna.

Gardeła, L., 2017. *Bad Death in the Early Middle Ages: Atypical Burials from Poland in a Comparative Perspective.* Fundacja Rzeszowskiego Ośrodka Archeologicznego, Instytut Archeologii Uniwersytetu Rzeszowskiego, Rzeszów.

Gardeła, L., 2019. *Magia, kobiety i śmierć w świecie wikingów.* Wydawnictwo Triglav, Szczecin.

Gardeła, L., 2020. Uncoiling the serpent: Snake figurines in the Viking Age. *Viking and Medieval Scandinavia* 16: 27–61.

Gardeła, L., 2022. Miniatures with nine studs: Interdisciplinary explorations of a new type of Viking Age artefact. *Fornvännen* 117: 15–36.

Gardeła, L. 2023a. Magic Staffs in the Viking World. In Gardela *et al.* (eds): 419–434.

Gardeła, L., 2023b. Miniature weapons in the Viking world: Small things with great meaning. In Gardela *et al.* (eds): 479–496.

Gardeła, L., Bønding S. and Pentz, P. (eds), 2023. *The Norse Sorceress: Mind and Materiality in the Viking World.* Oxbow Books, Oxford.

Gilchrist, R., 2008. Magic for the dead? The archaeology of magic in later medieval burials. *Medieval Archaeology* 52: 119–159.

Gunnell, T. and Lassen A. (eds), 2013. *The Nordic Apocalypse: Approaches to Völuspá and Nordic Days of judgement.* Brepols, Turnhout.

Hayeur Smith, M., 2020 *The Valkyries' Loom: The Archaeology of Cloth Production and Female Power in the North Atlantic.* University Press of Florida, Gainesville.

Heide, E., 2006a. *Gand, seid og åndevind.* Universitetet i Bergen, Bergen.

Heide, E., 2006b. Spinning seiðr. In *Old Norse Religion in Long-Term Perspectives. Origins, Changes and Interactions*. eds A. Andrén, K. Jennbert and C. Raudvere. Nordic Academic Press, Lund: 164–170.

Heide, E., 2006c. Spirits through respiratory passages. In *The Fantastic in Old Norse/Icelandic Literature. Sagas and the British Isles*, eds D. Ashurst, D. Kick, and J. McKinnell. Preprint Papers of the 13th International Saga Conference, 2006, Durham: 350–358.

Hermann Pálsson and Edwards, P. (transl.), 1985. *Seven Viking Romances*. Penguin Books, London.

Jensen, B., 2010. *Viking Age Amulets in Scandinavia and Western Europe*. British Archaeological Report S2169, Oxford.

Jessen, M.D., 2023. Miniature chairs: On seeresses, the future, and conflict. In Gardeła *et al.* (eds): 451–462.

Jessen, M.D. and Ramsøe Majland K., 2021. The sovereign seeress – on the use and meaning of a Viking Age chair pendant from Gudme, Denmark. *Danish Journal of Archaeology* 10: 1–23.

Kaland, S.H.H., 2006. Kvinnegraven fra Trå i Granvin – en gydjes grav? In *Samfunn, symboler og identitet. Festskrift til Gro Mandt på 70-årsdagen*, eds R. Barndon, S. Innselset, K. Klæboe Kristoffersen and T. Lødøen. Arkeologisk Institut, Universitetet i Bergen, Bergen: 351–362.

Kastholm, O.T. and Ulriksen J., 2023. Burials of ritual specialists? Case studies of the graves from Trekroner-Grydehøj and Gerdrup, Sjælland. In Gardeła *et al.* (eds): 381–400.

Kastholm, O.T. and Margaryan A., 2021. Reconstructing the Gerdrup Grave – the story of an unusual Viking Age double grave in context and in the light of new analysis. *Danish Journal of Archaeology* 10: 1–20.

Knutson, S.A., 2020. When objects misbehave: Materials & assemblages in the ancient Scandinavian myths. *Fabula* 61.3–4: 257–277.

Kozak, L., 2021. *Upiór. Historia naturalna*. Fundacja 'Evviva L'arte', Warszawa.

Lemm, T., 2007. Maskendarstellungen der Wikingerzeit. *Offa* 61–62 (2004–2005): 309–352.

Mannering, U. and Rimstad C., 2023. The textiles from the Fyrkat 4 grave. In Gardeła *et al.* (eds): 329–338.

McKinnell, J., 2005. *Meeting the Other in Norse Myth and Legend*. Brewer, Cambridge.

Mierzyński, A., 1885. Nuncius cum baculo. Studjum archeologiczne o krzywuli. *Wisła* 9: 361–397.

Motz, L., 1980. Old Icelandic völva: A new derivation. *Indogermanische Forschungen. Zeitschrift für Indogermanistik und Allgemeine Sprachwissenschaft* 85: 196–206.

Nordberg, A., 2002. Vertikalt placerade vapen i vikingatida graver, *Fornvännen* 97: 15–24.

Nordeide, S.W., 2011. *The Viking Age as a Period of Religious Transformation: The Christianisation of Norway from AD 560–1150/1200*. Brepols, Turnhout.

Pentz, P., 2018. Viking art, Snorri Sturluson and recent metal detector finds. *Fornvännen* 113.1: 17–33.

Pentz, P., 2023. *The Fyrkat 4 grave*. In Gardeła *et al.* (eds): 301–328.

Pentz, P., Panum B.M., Karg S. and Mannering, U., 2009. Kong Haralds vølve. *Nationalmuseets Arbeidsmark 2009*: 215–232.

Petersen, P.V., 1992. Valkyrier i Ribe. *By, Marsk og Geest* 1992: 41–46.

Petersson, K.G., 1958. Et gravfynd från Klinta, Köpings sn., Öland. *Tor* 4: 134–150.

Price, N., 2002. *The Viking Way. Religion and War in Late Iron Age Scandinavia*. Uppsala University, Uppsala.

Price, N., 2012. Wooden worlds. Individual and collective in the chamber graves of Birka. In *Birka nu. Pågående forskning om världsarvet Birka och Hovgården*, ed. C. Hedenstierna-Jonson. Historiska Museet, Stockholm: 81–93.

Price, N., 2019. *The Viking Way: Magic and Mind in Late Iron Age Scandinavia* (2nd edn). Oxbow Books, Oxford.

Reynolds, A., 2009. *Anglo-Saxon Deviant Burial Customs*. Oxford University Press, Oxford.

Roesdahl, E., 1977. *Fyrkat. En jysk vikingeborg. II. Oldsagerne og gravpladsen*. Det kgl. nordiske Oldskriftselskab, København.

Roesdahl, E., 2023. The Fyrkat völva revisited. In Gardeła *et al.* (eds): 293–300.
Sauckel, A., 2013. *Die literarische Funktion von Kleidung in den Íslendingasǫgur und Íslendingaþættir.* de Gruyter, Berlin-Boston MA.
Schaadt, N. and Grundvad, L., 2016. Lokemasken. Var Loke en beskytter? *Chaos* 66: 91–110.
Simek, R., 2006. *Dictionary of Northern Mythology.* Brewer, Cambridge.
Staecker, J., 1999. *Rex regum et dominus dominorum. Die wikingerzeitlichen Kreuz- und Kruzifixanhänger als Ausdruck der Mission in Altdänemark und Schweden.* Almqvist & Wiksell, Stockholm.
Ström, F., 1942. *On the Sacral Origin of the Germanic Death Penalties.* H. Ohlssons boktryckeri, Lund.
Ström, F., 1973. Nid och ergi. *Saga och sed* 1973: 27–47.
Svanberg, F., 2003. *Death Rituals in South-East Scandinavia AD 800-1000. Decolonizing the Viking Age Vol. 2.* Almqvist & Wiksell International, Lund.
Szczepański, S., 2013. 'Eikim kruwom!' Czyli 'chodźmy na zebranie!' Uwagi o kolekcji kriwul ze zbiorów etnograficznych Altertumsgesellschaft Insterburg i trwałości staropruskiej tradycji. *Pruthenia* 8: 181–193.
Thäte, E.S., 2007. *Monuments and Minds. Monument Re-use in Scandinavia in the Second Half of the First Millennium AD.* Wallin & Dalholm, Lund.
Tolley, C., 2009a. *Shamanism in Norse Myth and Magic. Volume 1.* Suomalainen Tiedeakatemia/Academia Scientiarum Fennica, Helsinki.
Tolley, C. 2009b. *Shamanism in Norse Myth and Magic. Volume 2: Reference materials.* Suomalainen Tiedeakatemia/Academia Scientiarum Fennica, Helsinki.
Tomicki, R., 2000. Czy Krive krzywał? Kilka uwag o pożytkach z przeżytków. In *Archeologia w teorii i praktyce*, eds A. Buko and P. Urbańczyk. Instytut Archeologii i Etnologii Polskiej Akademii Nauk, Warszawa: 459–462.
Trigger, B., 2009. *A History of Archaeological Thought.* Cambridge University Press, Cambridge.
Ulriksen, J., 2018. A völva's grave at Roskilde, Denmark? *Offa* 71–72 (2014–2015): 229–240.
Westlye, J.B., 2019. 'Den Sterke Kvinnen': Fra husfrue til volve – En kritisk studie av kjønn, status og magi med utgangspunkt i graver med stav fra yngre jernalder på Vestlandet. Unpublished MA Thesis, University of Bergen.
Westlye, J.B., Gardeła L. and Karpińska, K., 2023. The völva from Gutdalen: Identity, belief and the performance of power in Viking Age western Norway. In Gardeła *et al.* (eds): 355–380.
Williams, H., 2016. Viking mortuary citations. *European Journal of Archaeology* 19(3): 400–414.
Zeiten, M.K., 1997. Amulets and amulet use in Viking Age Denmark. *Acta Archaeologica* 68: 1–74.

# Chapter 9

## Women's textile magic in Viking Age Iceland

*Michèle Hayeur Smith*

> She soon fell asleep and she had a dream which she related to Pálnir on awakening. 'I dreamed', she said, 'that I was staying here on this estate, and I thought that I had a grey colored cloth in the loom. It seems as though the weights were attached to the cloth, and I was weaving. When one of the weights fell down behind from the middle of the cloth, I noticed that the weights were the heads of men. I took up that head and recognised it'. When Pálnir asked whose head it was, she said that it was King Haraldr Gormsson's. (*Jómsvikinga Saga*: Blake 1962: 10)

### Introduction

The depictions of Viking women in both popular culture and academia are confusing and often contradictory. Viking women have been perceived as subservient, traditional, and quiet within a male centered world, engaged in a litany of domestic chores while passing through 'stages of life' without 'being allowed' to excel or fulfil themselves as individuals. As presented in the introduction to this volume scholars have catered to age-old stereotypes of women as caregivers, with women's positions in society focused on their roles as natural mothers and guardians of the within-doors and domestic realms. Until recently this approach has dominated interpretations of women in Viking studies. Alongside these academic interpretations, the media actively depicted sexualised Viking women in comic books and paperback covers from the 1970s onwards with current representations of female warriors popularised by the burial find from Birka (Bj 581) (Price *et al.* 2019).

The concept of the 'strong woman' emerged from the Icelandic sagas. However, the Viking 'strong woman' has been challenged by both Auður Magnúsdóttir (2008: 41) and Helgi Þórlaksson (1981), who suggested the authors of these narratives were powerful 13th century men and that those they described as strong Viking Age women more often than not presided over social disaster rather than success. These 'strong women' could therefore amount to literary conventions meant to convince Christian women that such behaviour came to no good end. Further, Þórlaksson (1981) convincingly demonstrated that women were considered anything but strong; in looking at wages, workloads, salaries, etc. in medieval legal sources, he concluded that compared to men, conditions were unfavourable for women, and that their work was not highly regarded, their status being not much higher than that of an ordinary maid. The Viking 'strong woman' was also challenged by Raffield *et al.* (2017: 167) who argued that, while the trope was not without validity, it probably applied to a small proportion of women.

In this chapter I will address one facet of female power and social control: textile work. My own research has demonstrated that Viking Age societies were in essence patriarchal with the term 'patriarchy' evoking and over-riding monolithic concepts of male dominance (Kandyoti 1988: 274–275). However, the forms that patriarchy took during the Viking Age are somewhat distinct from the more extreme aspects of patriarchy encountered in other parts of Europe during the same period. Within traditional patriarchal societies, women frequently strategised and negotiated within the system to acquire power that they would otherwise lack. I will use the concept of Deniz Kandyoti known as the *patriarchal bargain*, published in *Gender and Society* in September 1988 and discussed at some length in the introductory chapter of this volume. Textile work and its association with the supernatural realm comprised one such mechanism of bargaining with the patriarchy. It is not textile work *per se* that was the mechanism but what it symbolised, and I will argue that a mixture of interconnected elements is at the basis of this belief.

*Seiðr* was one form of female magic that was believed to have come to humans under the tutelage of the goddess Freyja. *Seiðr* had its own specialised practitioners known as *vǫlur* (regarding other female magical practitioners, see Sundqvist's chapter in this volume), whose symbolic iron distaffs (see Heide 2007 and Gardeła, this volume) were appropriate symbols of female power since textile work was potentially connected to either the goddess Frigg or Freyja, though this is not clear (Hayeur Smith 2020). Along with symbolic distaffs,[1] of the many names given to the goddess Freyja, *Hörn* stands out as particularly revealing of the goddess's connection with textile work, signifying the term 'flax' (Ellis Davidson 1990: 116; 1998). Through textile work we can trace not only connections with this female magic, but also with life, death, and the control of fate, as immortalised through images of the *nornir* spinning the fates of men under Yggdrasil, the world tree (Norrman 2008: 390; Bek Pedersen 2013: 123). From the official magic of *seiðr* female magic may have trickled down to the domestic realm in a form of 'household magic', expressed through the tools and practice of textile production itself, and this fusion of concepts helped provide a formidable strategy that women could deploy when negotiating with the patriarchal system around them. Further, female magic connected to textile production brought the bargaining and negotiations of power down to the household level by instilling a level of trepidation (and at the same time respect for women's relationship with the divine) in male householders (see Hayeur Smith 2020).

## Female magic and textile production: Evidence from the sagas

For millennia, within and well beyond the Norse world, women have woven textiles, made and repaired clothing, created the very items that have protected humans from the elements, and through doing so take active part in visually crafting and projecting cultural identities and affiliations. This is particularly true in Europe and the Northern Hemisphere, including the areas of interest in the present study (Hayeur Smith 2000; 2004; 2020; Tranberg Hansen 2004). But why is this the case? Not all cultures delegate textile production to women. In some societies (for example, in much of Africa), men are the weavers (Schneider and Weiner 1989: 21) and in other cultures textile production has shifted through time from women's to men's work.

Burial data from the Iron Age and medieval periods, literary descriptions in medieval documents and sagas, folk songs and folk tales from the post-medieval period, and ethnographic accounts and lived experience from the past centuries allow us to infer that in Northern Europe, from the Iron Age through the Middle Ages, women sat together spinning and weaving for hours, at the same time, talking, singing, and coordinating their individual efforts to create cloth. In fact, women were responsible for all textile production, from the preparation of the wool to its final product as textiles. This activity was so gender specific that one might ponder why men avoided it altogether. In Iceland, from the end of the Viking Age to the end of the medieval period, cloth production had reached such importance as a form of currency (see Hayeur Smith 2014; 2020; Hayeur Smith *et al.* 2019) that it seems odd that men were not trying to control all aspects of the textiles that became fundamental to the economic, political, and domestic life of the country. Women wove money, which men seem to have distributed locally or internationally (Hayeur Smith 2020).

Mythological sources and vignettes contained in the sagas suggest that the work of producing cloth consisted of somewhat spiritual, even magical, activities, wrapped in mythological beliefs that were frowned upon or feared by men. Almost every incident of magic performed by women in the saga literature has an element of cloth production, whether involving the cloth itself, the wool, or the tools used to transform one into the other (see examples below, *Vatnsdœla Saga*, *Erbryggja Saga*, *Landnámabók*, *Njál's Saga*, etc.). In parts of Europe, the production of cloth on a day tom day basis, was linked to female deities or other supernatural beings with whom women negotiated: from Athena and Arachne in ancient Greece to Rumpelstiltskin in Northern Europe (Schneider 1989; Ellis Davidson 1990; Norrman 2008).

Archaeological excavations, for example, have documented women's burials from the Viking Age equipped with implements that were associated with textile production and use, such as spindle whorls, wool combs, weaving swords, loom weights, needle cases, and needles, distaffs, weaving tablets, and glass linen smoothers. Literary sources, on the other hand, suggest that in the Scandinavian Viking Age powerful female deities (Frigg or Freyja) oversaw textile work, while spinning itself may have been linked to the female practice of *seiðr*, whose forms of ecstatic magic and divination were practised mostly by women (Price 2002; Heide 2007; for a list of male practitioners, see introductory chapter to this volume).

According to *Ynglinga Saga* the goddess Freyja was well versed in *seiðr* and taught it to Oðinn. It is unclear if she was the goddess of weaving and textile work, as mentioned above, *Hörn* was one of her names, and is thought to refer to the term *horr* = flax (Ellis Davidson 1990: 117). However, Frigg was also associated with spinning and according to Ellis Davidson, the *Lokasenna* mentions that Frigg was to preside over spinning and also had knowledge of destiny (Ellis Davidson 1998: 121). It is very possible that much of our knowledge of these two goddesses is lacking and that the two are one and the same, or intricately interconnected (Ellis Davidson 1998). Based on the role that Freya appears to hold regarding *seiðr*, fate, and the use of a distaff as a magical tool, along with her associations with flax, I believe her role to be more significant in textile production than assumed. Ingunn Ásdísardóttir (2007: 158, 266), on Freyja's name Hörn, reflects on her specific qualities connected to that name such as weaving and prophecies, as well as her relationship to the *vǫlva* who 'weave people's fates', while at the same time referencing the land and vegetation but also the working of linen.

Some scholars have argued that the etymology of the word *seiðr* itself – meaning 'cord', 'snare', or 'halter' – is compatible with *seiðr* as an ecstatic form of sorcery because there is a notion of sending forth: in the case of sorcery, the sorcerer's mind is sent to the spirit world, often in the shape of a thread or rope and regarded as something spun or the result of spinning (Heide 2007). Men rarely (if ever) engaged in *seiðr* for fear it would lead to allegations of homosexuality, as it contained a lot of *ergi* (described in detail below), which Meulengracht Sørensen (1983) defined as something or someone perverse in sexual matters, cowardly, and effeminate, and – of relevance here – versed in witchcraft. Furthermore, *seiðr*, was a form of female witchcraft, itself linked to spinning, the production of thread, and therefore weaving, all of which were distinctly female domestic chores (Price 2002; Heide 2007).

As noted earlier, additional connections between the practice of *seiðr* and textile production are evident in the tools of its practitioners, specifically the *seiðr* staff itself. The nature of this staff has provoked much debate among scholars, though its connection with textile work was acknowledged by Gardeła (see this volume for a discussion of the *vǫlur*'s tools). To anyone involved in textile work, the visual connections of *seiðr* staffs with distaffs are obvious, especially those with little baskets on top which, on distaffs, are intended to hold flax – the basket is particularly useful to tie down the long strands of fibre. These symbolic staffs may have implied that they held the threads connecting worlds, people, or spirits and the seers' tools were clearly not functional distaffs as some were made of iron and too heavy to use; in contrast, the functional ones (and modern ones) are of wood (Marianne Gukelsberger pers. comm.). These symbolic iron distaffs emphasise their connections to female magic, to textile work, and, I would argue, to the control of life, death, and fate, all elements deeply entrenched in the goddess's attributes.

Norse mythology linked the concept of fate with spinning, a potent concept expressed through the Norse myth that the three *nornir* – elemental female beings – sat under the world tree, Yggdrasil, spinning the fates of gods and humans.[2] The *nornir* – Urðr, Verðandi, and Skuld – are generally interpreted as the present, past, and future, and are credited with creating the destinies of men before their birth (Norrman 2008). These three *nornir* were not alone, as Norse mythology describes additional ones, both good and bad (Ellis Davidson 1990: 26). According to Snorri Sturlusson's *Edda*, bad lives were attributable to the evil *nornir*, whereas good *nornir* shaped the lives of the lucky (Normann 2008). Barber (1994) suggested that the connections between thread, spinning, and fate, while not unique to the Norse world, stem from the action of women creating thread out of nowhere, just as babies are created from nowhere (Barber 1995; Norrman 2008). The uncanny visual similarities to the umbilical cord, joining child and mother, is most likely behind Barber's comment. The connection between the creation of life and of thread is clear in English, and Norrman argues that even the term 'lifespan' in English contains the word 'spin', initially meaning to draw out (Normann 2008), though no such equivalent was noted in Old Norse (wherein spinning is *spinna* and the term for span, as in length, is *spenna*. It is unclear if there is a connection between these two words).

Connections between spinning and fate occur frequently in Northern European folklore. According to Heide (2007), for instance, the Saami poem *The Son of the Sun* refers to a cord with three 'wind-knots' containing the soul of an unborn child. A central theme of the poem involves untying the three wind-knots while at sea, resulting in the conception and birth of a baby.

The same connection is seen in an early Christian context, in the apocryphal *Book of James* which, in describing the Annunciation, depicts Mary spinning when the Angel comes to her, implying that the making of thread was a symbol for the making of a child (Badalanova Geller 2006: 223–234; Bek Pedersen 2009: 180). A similar motif occurs in a Norse context: in *Orkneyinga Saga*, Earl Sigurðr of Orkney consults his mother – a sorceress – about the outcome of an impending battle; she responds negatively, adding:

> I would have kept you for a long time in my wool basket, if I knew that you would live forever, but it is fate which rules life and not where a man comes from; better to die with dignity than to live with shame. (trans. Bek Pedersen 2009: 179)

Hermann Pálsson and Edwards translation is not dissimilar:

> Had I thought you might live forever, she said, I'd have reared you in my wool basket. But lifetimes are shaped by what will be not by where you are. (Hermann Pálsson and Edwards 1981: 36)

Keeping someone inside the wool basket suggests ideas of enduring life and protection from death, and of the basket as a symbolic womb with its unspun wool that has not yet been transformed into textile, symbolising a person-to-be, or a person's fate (Ellis Davidson 1998: 118–119; Bek Pedersen 2009: 179–180). This resonates with Terence

Turner's labelling of textiles and dress as a 'second skin', a social and cultural skin that we wear over our naked 'biological bodies', where we can display and manipulate information about who we are and where we belong (Turner 1993).

Spinning associations with witchcraft during the Viking Age suggest that fate or the giving of life may come from a thread and also imply that a life itself can be manipulated through spinning. An example from the sagas pertains to a woman who harms others through the act of spinning (and practising sorcery). In *Laxdaela Saga*, Bolli, who is married to Guðrun, returns after killing Kjartan (the man Guðrún truly loves, though he has married another woman), at which point Guðrún remarks that 'morning tasks are often mixed: I have spun yarn for twelve ells of cloth and you have killed Kjartan' (Magnússon and Hermann Pálsson 1969: 176; Ellis Davidson 1998: 101; Heide 2007). While she has not killed her lover directly, many have argued (Ellis Davidson 1998; Bek Pedersen 2007; 2009; Heide 2007) that Guðrún's spinning is similar to the spinning of the *nornir*, and that it was a magical act intended to influence the outcome of a fight between these two men.

Probably the most telling association with wool and textile production and the control of life, death, and fate occurs in the poem *Darraðarljóð* in *Njál's Saga*. The saga sets a scene in Caithness, Scotland, before the battle of Clontarf, in which Dorruð, a young man, observes 12 female riders approaching a woman's hut and disappearing inside. He peers through the window and sees these 12 Valkyries weaving cloth on a warp-weighted loom made from the entrails of men fallen in battle. As they weave, they chant:

> ...Blood rains
> From the cloudy web
> On the broad loom
> Of Slaughter.
> The web of man
> Grey as armour
> Is being woven.
> The Valkyries
> Will cross it
> With a crimson weft.
>
> The warp is made
> Of human entrails.
>
> Human heads
> Are used as weights;
> The heddle rods
> Are blood-wet spears;
> The shafts are iron-bound,
> And arrows are the shuttles.
> With swords we will weave
> This web of battle... (*The Darraðarljóð, Njal's Saga*, trans. Magnus Magnusson and Hermann Palsson 1983: 349)

This gruesome poem describes warrior women using their weapons and human body parts as components of the warp-weighted loom: the loom weights are human heads, the heddle rods their spears, the shuttle their arrows, and their swords are the beaters. Some scholars feel that the *valkyries* worked in a capacity similar to that of their sisters the *nornir* in determining fate, since the *valkyries* appeared on battlefields to collect the dead and convey them to Valhalla (Bek Pedersen 2007; Else Guðjónsson 1989). The poem is presented in the context of a dream foretelling the death of several men in an upcoming battle (Norrman 2008; Bek Pedersen 2009). Here, in keeping with the spinning imagery, are depictions of weaving, textile work, and the weaving implements themselves, linked to the body and body parts, to fate, and the giving and taking of life. Each thread may symbolise the fate of a man about to die in battle and, interestingly, the heads suspended from loom weights are upside down, like those of infants in the womb.

Toward the end of the poem, the cloth woven by the *valkyries* is cut down and divided into 12 pieces, for each one to take with her. They leave the weaving hut the same way they arrived, after which terrible things befall various Christian and or Viking leaders and men across the North, not to mention the terrible outcome of the battle (Magnus Magnusson and Hermann Pálsson 1983). The poem also suggests that powerful magic and the control of fate could be realised in these weaving huts, through textile production.

While the present examples recount only a few connections between female magic and textile production, there are many more in the saga literature. In fact, this theme is so prevalent that it clearly stems from a deep rooted mythological mindset that was present in Late Iron Age Scandinavia.

Additional examples can be found, for example, in *Eyrbyggja Saga*, in scenes where the witch Katla tries to conceal her son Odd and in one instance turns him into a distaff. Following repeated visits by men looking to kill him, she transforms him into a goat (and combs his wool and beard). It requires the power of another witch to break through Katla's spells (Hermann Pálsson and Edwards 1989: 61).

Also in *Eyrbyggja Saga* is the tale of Þórgunna and her bedsheets. Þórgunna was a weaver possibly involved with the magical arts; her enchanted bedsheets caused all manner of curses and hauntings after her death because people did not do as she instructed and kept them, rather than burning them after she died (Hermann Pálsson and Edwards 1989: 132–133). The sheets themselves may have been magical, or more likely imbued with her life essence and thus could not be shared by others, in a theme of associations between textiles and individuals that is echoed in *Njál's Saga*'s account of Höskuld's cloak (see below).

*Vatnsdaela Saga* (Wawn 2001) contains additional examples of links between magic and clothing, where it is evident the textiles themselves had the ability to be used in the context of witchcraft. In the tale of Ljót the witch and her loathsome son Hrolleif, Ljót bewitches his clothes on more than one occasion, making him invincible to attacks. Possibly the most fantastic description of textile magic can be seen in the last passage of this narrative, where both wrongdoers end up dead at the hands of the sons of Ingimund, who was killed by Hrolleif. Before reaching that point, Ljót performs magic involving her clothes, in this case playing on opposites and reversed order to turn the world upside down:

> She had cast her clothes up over her head and was walking backwards and had thrust her head back between her legs; the look in her eyes was ugly as hell as she glared at them like the witch she was. (Jones 1944: 74)

Later on, Ljót admits her intention to turn the whole land topsy turvy with her magic.

In the same saga, Þórdís, both a wise woman versed in the law and a practitioner of magic, became involved at the Alþing with the Þórkell, a man who was on trial for murder. To help him win his case and avoid outlawry, she lent him her black hooded cloak and staff called Hognund, to take with him in order to win his case against Guðmund, his opponent. Wearing the cloak and apparently invisible to his opponent, he tapped Guðmund's left cheek three times making him delay his prosecution, so that Þórkell could not be prosecuted. Eventually, still under Þórkell's spell, Guðmund agreed to a settlement from Þórkell, after which Þórkell returned with the cloak and tapped Guðmund's right cheek to undo the spell (Jones 1944: 119–120). In *Vatnsdaela Saga*, the witch Gróa performs a magic spell by walking around a house backwards waving a kerchief or piece of cloth (McCreesh 2010: 82).

In *Landnámabók*, chapter 75 (Hermann Pálsson and Edwards 1972) Hildigunn, the wife of Sigmund Ketil Thistle's son, was summoned for sorcery by Lón Einar, her neighbour, and his six companions. When her own son Einar returns she recounts what happened to her with Lón Einar and gives her son a new tunic. Her son, wearing the new tunic mounts a 'cart-horse' (presumably because he is not a valiant warrior) with his sword and shield and chases Lón Einar and his companions. He kills four of Lón Einar's men, two escape. He eventually gives him his death blow after Lón Einar's trouser belt breaks and as he tries to pull up his trousers. One might wonder if the 'newly made tunic' was in some way endowed with magic? (Hermann Pálsson and Edwards 1972: 40).

In each of these examples, textiles, cloth, spinning, looms, parts of looms, weaving tools such as spindles and distaffs, or clothing all figure prominently in female magic. In fact, Gilchrist argued that spindle whorls were buried so regularly in early medieval graves across the UK that she interpreted them as protective amulets, adding: '... they are also significant for their link with spinning and weaving activities that sometimes carried undercurrents of magic' (Gilchrist 2008: 133). Further, Burchard, Bishop of the Imperial City of Worms, who wrote a Canon Law, consisting of 20 books and included in its 19th book a penitential titled the *Corrector* or *Medicus*, *c.* AD 1010, also suggests this connection between magic, spells, and weaving cloth:

> Have you been present at or consented to the vanities which women practice in their woollen work, in their weaving, who when they begin their weaving, hope to be able to bring it about that with incantations and with their own actions that the threads of the warp and woof

> become so intertwined that unless [someone] makes use of these other diabolical counter incantations he will perish totally? If you have ever been present or consented you must do penance for thirty days on bread and water. (In Gilchrist 2008: 133; cf. McNeill and Gamer 1965: 330; Meaney 1981: 185)

## The archaeology of textile magic in Iceland

In the poem *Darraðarljoð* the *valkyries* wove on a warp-weighted loom inside a *dyngja* or small room separated from the central farm building. Archaeological evidence in both Scandinavia and Iceland has revealed the existence of such huts – generally semi-subterranean pit houses – which have been the subject of varying interpretations regarding their use and function. Some believe these huts were used for weaving, while others argue they were for private ritual and religious activity or served different roles – as needed – on different sites (Mortensen 1997; Bjarni Einarsson 2008; Milek 2012; K. Smith, pers. comm.). The literature on weaving huts and pit houses is extensive, not only pertaining to Scandinavia but also the American north-west (see Gillman 1987; Smith 2003). Milek (2012) discusses at length the uses and purposes of these huts in Iceland. While not all pit houses have evidence of textile production, the presence of textiles, spindle whorls, and loom weights in the majority of these huts in Iceland and on the Scandinavian mainland indicates they many were used for weaving and textile activities (see also Mortensen 1997), which ties in with the imagery and action depicted in *Darraðarljóð*.

The pit houses Milek examined had an internal dimension of 5–16 $m^2$, suitable for a small number of people, and were generally rectangular or ovoid in shape, with wooden walls or an inner wooden structure (an unusual feature in Iceland, where wood large enough for architectural use is rare and the preferred construction material is turf). The absence of clear entryways in most of these structures suggests they may have been entered through doors cut in the roofs or in the upper walls of their above-ground superstructures (K. Smith, pers. comm.; Mortensen 1997: 187). Mortensen described a Norwegian pit house with a maximum depth of 0.5 m and Milek (2012: 102) identified possible furnishings in 62% of 24 Icelandic examples (2012: 93). She identified raised platforms at a maximum height of 0.3 m at Grelutóttir I, Stóraborg, Hvítárholt V and VII, Sveigakot MT2 and T1, and Vatnsfjörður 10. The interiors were equipped with small corner or side ovens, using a building technique not customary in longhouses. Others in Scandinavia contained four hearths, with one located in the south-west corner of the pit and made of three standing slabs (Mortensen 1997). Milek (2012) argues that this type of corner oven was suitable for keeping houses warm, while reducing the risk of sparks that could have inflicted serious damage on cloth being woven.

The most frequent category of artefacts in Icelandic pit houses relates to textile work: loom weights were found in 76% of the pit houses, that Milek recorded, and spindle whorls in 43% (Milek 2012). Additionally, these pit houses contained what Milek (2012: 105) called 'pinholes' or perforations in the floors, 1–3 cm in diameter and filled with charcoal-rich floor sediment. They are present in 72% of the floors of excavated Icelandic pit houses and have been tentatively associated by Guðmundur Ólafsson (1992) with distaffs – which seems correct particularly the longer distaffs used in spinning flax, though Milek thought the symbolic ones frequently found in burial contexts and associated with spinning, were associated with the magical practices of *seiðr* (Price 2011; Milek 2012). All these elements of Icelandic pit houses point toward longstanding cultural traditions from mainland Scandinavia, and toward the possible associations described above relating to textile work, magic, and *seiðr*. Pit houses associated with textile production have been found at GUS in Greenland (Olafsson, pers. comm.), Viklem in Norway (Sauvage and Mokkelbost 2017) on the large farms of Lejre and Tissø in Zealand, Denmark, where several pit houses were found, some used for textile production but others for other types of craft: Övra Wannborga on Öland and Järrestad in Scania according to Fallgren (2008: 70).

The Icelandic sagas are also informative about the function and use of the houses called *dyngja*. Bek Pedersen (2009) and Milek (2012) have argued that because the warp-weighted loom requires a more permanent installation, all weaving took place inside the *dyngja* where these looms were set up, and that this was a strictly female space from which men were excluded. Two scenes, one from *Njáls Saga* and the other from *Gisla Saga Súrsonnar*, recount incidents where men overhear conversations inside a *dyngja* and, in both cases, the men cannot help acting upon the information overheard, resulting in fatal consequences and implying the *dyngja*'s association with otherworldly happenings (Magnus Magnusson and Palsson 1963; Bek Pedersen 2009). Otherworldly events also occur in the poem *Darraðarljóð,* from *Njál's Saga* cited above, and in a passage from *Jómsvíkinga Saga*, where a woman called Ingibjörg dreams that while she is weaving linen inside the *dyngja*, a loom weight falls off the loom and turns out to be a man's head (Blake 1962: 10).

Bek Pedersen (2009) argued that examples in the sagas described here, indicate the connection of activities inside the *dyngja* to death and fate, and mark it as a place where decisions about life and death are made. By analogy, the production of textiles is almost akin to the making of a human being, with the *dyngja* constituting a type of womb-like space. This womb-like element is further supported by the lack of a clear doorway, making it completely enclosed.

As mentioned, spindle whorls are frequently found inside the *dyngja*. They are also recovered from burials, in fact the most common items recovered in women's burials from Viking Age Iceland are shears and spindle whorls (Hayeur Smith 2004). Textile tools occur predominantly in female burials in Scandinavia as well attesting to the gendered nature of this activity (Domnases 1982; Hedenstierna Jonson and Kjellström 2014: 187). Some spindle whorls in Iceland bear runic inscriptions that either point directly to magical practice or are declarations of ownership such as one from Stóraborg, inscribed with the words 'Anna owns me' (Mjöll Snæsdóttir, pers. comm.) or another from the Alþingisreitur in downtown Reykjavík that reads 'Þórunn owns me' (Garðarsdottir n.d.). Many inscriptions, however, are more cryptic, with a sequence of repeated runes suggesting magico-religious formulae (Flowers 2010). A spindle whorl from the site of Urriðakót, a shieling (or women's summer farm) in western Iceland, bore a runic inscription dated to the 12th century; however, because the spindle whorl was badly worn and the runes quite faded, it remains unclear whether the spindle's runes only spelled out the owner's name or included the runic alphabet as a magical formula (Ragnheiður Traustadóttir 2015: 322). Overall, artefacts decorated with runes are uncommon in Iceland; yet among these are 11 spindle whorls dating from the 11th–14th centuries. From Stóramörk in Rangárvallasýsla, a spindle whorl was found with the inscription *mariafuþorkhniastbmly* (*ibid.*). The runic alphabet itself (*fuþorkhniqstbmly*) was thought to constitute a magical formula (Flowers 2010).

Weaving implements with runic magical formulae are more common in Scandinavia, yet a whalebone weaving sword from Kornsá in Vestur-Húnavatnssýsla, Iceland, does have an X rune very faintly carved on its blade (Krisán Eldján and Adolf Friðriksson 2000: 400). From Lund, in Sweden, comes an example of a more deliberate runic formula from the Viking Age, specifically a curse, carved on a bone weaving tablet: 'Ingmar, Sigvor's son (or Sigvor's Ingmar), shall have my weeping (or my misfortune), *aallaati'* (Moltke and Foote 1985: 358). This straightforward example of a curse is clearly aided by the incomprehensible string of runes at the end: *aallaati* (Moltke and Foote 1985). These particular weaving items with carved magical runic formulae mirror some of the stories, myths, and beliefs discussed above. It is also interesting to note that most items of material culture that are carved with runic inscriptions related to textile work and it is not customary to find knives or other implements of daily life caved with runes.

By the 12th century, the weaving huts in Iceland were abandoned, though we can suspect that some of the tools may have retained their magical properties and continued to bear runic inscriptions (Milek 2012: 120). According to Milek, the weaving 'space' was moved into the central house, with little change in its overall layout. For Milek, this shift and the disuse of the pit houses reserved for textile work must represent some wider social and economic changes in Icelandic society, possibly the conversion to Christianity,[3] as the *dyngja* encoded pre-Christian beliefs. Milek also noted that several pit houses had been almost ritually sealed or transformed into middens and rubbish dumps. The relocation of textile production to a central space in the main dwelling may also correlate with an increase in the production and use of textiles as currency in medieval Iceland (see also Hayeur Smith 2014; 2015; 2018). Perhaps because textiles had become economically viable, men saw this as a way to oversee production and the creation of wealth. While this may have been the intent, they still avoided textile work until the 18th century, when the Danish colonial authorities established the first weaving workshops run by men, in Reykjavik (Róbertsdóttir 2008; Hayeur Smith 2015; 2018). The same thing occurred in the Faroe Islands and in both these island settings the adoption and transformation of textile production to a European model (including the adoption of the flat loom and spinning wheel) correspond to the renewed interest in North Atlantic wool by the Danish colonial authorities (see Hayeur Smith 2018; 2020: 143).

## Defining Late Iron Age patriarchy in the Viking world

The traditional roles of Viking Age women have been touched upon by many scholars (Sawyer 1991; 1992; 2004; Jochens 1995; Gräslund 2001; 2003; Jesch 2005; Gräslund and Quast 2011; Hedenstierna-Jonson and Kjellström 2014). Scholars consider the more extensive rights of women in Scandinavia to constitute a unique situation in which women enjoyed greater power, perhaps because extensive travelling on the part of men, forcing women to assume more central roles as farmers and traders (Hedenstierna-Jonson and Kjellström 2014: 184).

Overall, though, the common view of women's roles in the Viking Age was one of an agricultural society in which women's work was focused on indoor activities and male work on those performed outdoors, where women had little agency (Randsborg 1980; Dommasnes 1982; Roesdahl 1988; Jesch 1991). These views seem outdated and perpetuate gendered assumptions about passive women's roles in the past, ascribing domesticity to females and political and economic roles to males (Mortensen 2004: 103). They also shed little insight on the actual negotiations of gender in Viking societies. According to Marie-Louise Stig Sørensen (2000: 60), a central premise of gender archaeology is that gender is negotiated. Assumptions of female passivity only describe an outward appearance of the presumed *status quo*, while failing to acknowledge that within the system there was far more complexity, entailing slightly subtler gender roles. We know today that women's agency stretched well beyond the confines of the home to other activities, including trade (Stalsberg 1991, Pedersen, this volume; Sanmark and Athanasiou, this volume) and possibly warfare (MacLeod, this volume), establishing that powerful women did exist. It does not suffice to compartmentalise women in domestic caregiving roles without acknowledging how they negotiated those roles within that system, as women 'constructed and maintained them, thereby fundamentally anchoring power relations in social situations' (Mortensen 2004: 104).

From a purely anthropological perspective, the distinctly male character of Icelandic Viking culture is obvious. This is confirmed by information in *Grágás* (the Icelandic law code) and this patriarchy shared commonalities with other systems: men were heads of households; they held control over political and economic leadership anything a woman could do legally required her to have a 'legal administrator' particularly if unmarried and, when she married, her husband would take on this role (Dennis *et al.* 2000: 402). Women also did not have free movement if they tried to leave Iceland without the consent of kinsmen or administrators. Any man who knowingly assisted such a woman would face charges of lesser outlawry (Dennis *et al.* 2000: 72). Men also had the sole power to acknowledge children and offspring. Men of means were able to be polyamorous, and wives had to tolerate their husbands' mistresses or concubines, though this does appear to be more common among elites and royalty

(Karras 1990: 141) and in a society where slavery was widespread, slaveholders had easy sexual access to their slaves. While *Grágás* condemns such behaviour and claims that, if prosecuted of having intercourse with a slave woman, the man would be required to pay three marks (Dennis *et al.* 2000: 70) the reality seems to have been quite other. A common theme in the sagas is a man taking a concubine while on expedition as was the case in *Laxdæla Saga* when Hoskuld Dala Kollson purchased the Irish slave, Melkorka, from a Rús merchant and brought her back to Iceland, much to the dissatisfaction of his wife (Magnus Magnusson and Hermann Pálsson 1969: 67). There appears to be a disassociation in the sources between the law code and the sagas, which could be explained by the Christian overtones in *Grágás* who did not look upon slavery and promiscuity favourably. On the other hand, according to Óttar Guðmundsson (2016: 92), the laws were frequently broken by those who considered themselves in positions to do so, such as elites.

Icelandic Viking Age society was profoundly structured around issues of (male) honour, family, and the requirement to protect and avenge family honour, with an emphasis on ultra-masculinity and masculine behaviour (Kandioti 1988; see Miller 1990). Nothing is more telling when looking at the laws regulating sexual behaviour outside of wedlock. *Grágás* lists quite strict penalties to those who were adulterous, the avenging parties include (in the case of a woman committing adultery), the husband, then her father, then a son born a lawful heir who is at least 16 winters old, then the man who is married to her daughter, then her mother ... and the list goes on suggesting that the adultery was a significant offence to the family honour that it required compensation (Dennis *et al.* 2000: 70). But this does not mean that women were passive players lacking in agency.

Households and family were of prime importance, and a family could include not only blood relatives but also fictive kin resulting from fosterage or blood-brotherhoods (Miller 1990: 166). As a result, protecting and avenging family members were significant concerns, resulting in long-lasting feuds and fights between groups of people (see Miller 1990). On the other hand, men harboured considerable anxiety over allegations of homosexuality linked to their sense of honour, and accusations to that effect or even perceptions of effeminacy were problematic, since this connoted not only a lack of bravery but dishonour to the extended family. Women played on this fear abundantly.

Women 'goaded' male kinsmen by nagging, insulting, or 'performing witchcraft', in essence impugning one's masculinity (Meulengracht Sørensen 1983). All of these are common themes in the saga literature (Miller 1990: 181). From *Njáls Saga*, Hildigunn and Flosi provide an example of this type of female goading, and of women seeking revenge for a killing to restore family honour:

> She [Hildigunn] took out the cloak which Flosi had given Höskuld and which he was wearing when he had been killed. She had preserved all his blood in it. She returned to the hall with the cloak and quietly went up to Flosi. Flosi had eaten and the food had been cleared from the table. Hildigunn flung it over Flosi and the blood clots showered all over him. Then she said: 'You gave this cloak to Höskuld, Flosi, and now I am giving it back to

> you. He was killed in it. I call God and all good men to witness that I charge you by all the powers of your Christ and your manhood and bravery to avenge the wounds he had on his body when he was killed or else be called a niðing, and contemptible creature, by all men' (*Njals Saga* in Miller 1990: 181).

This passage exemplifies female goading and the questioning of male importance and family honour. Hildigunn incites her kinsman to avenge the death of her husband by pushing him to seek retribution. Goading should be perceived as a mechanism in the negotiation of power, as women played on this to obtain the outcomes they wanted, as well as to have a say in family dynamics. Of particular importance to this discussion is Hildigunn's threat that Flosi would be killed or called a *niðing* if Höskuld were not avenged.[4]

The term *niðing* (ON *níðingr*) calls for some explanation. *Niðing* is cognate with *níð*. The concept of *níð*, as a form of curse, is specific to the male Norse conceptual universe as it engages the antithesis of the masculine ideal described above. By accusing Flosi of being a *niðing*, Hildigunn is questioning his masculinity; to be cursed with a *níð* was in essence to be accused of homosexuality and of being unmanly (Meulengracht Sørensen 1983: 17). To be an accused homosexual was punishable by outlawry, and therefore by death without retribution, in the Icelandic and Norwegian law codes (Dennis *et al.* 1980; 2000; Larsson 2010). *Grágás*, without addressing the full impact of the word *nið* or concepts of homosexuality states: 'if a man makes a shaming slander [Ice: *nið*] about someone then the penalty is lesser outlawry. And it is shaming slander if a man carves or incises a "wood-shame" directed against him or raises a "shame-pole" against him. He is to prosecute with a panel of 12' (Dennis *et al.* 2000: 197). According to Price (2002), *níð* could be communicated in more than one way, either verbally, as described above, or with a *tréníð*, i.e., a wooden *níð* (what Dennis *et al.* translated as 'wood-shame') created by carving runes onto a wooden sculpture depicting men engaged in sexual acts (Price 2002: 211). Occasionally in the saga literature one will find descriptions of *níð* poles, where the head of a mare was placed on top of a pole and pointed in the direction of the accused. *Nið* poles occur in *Gisla Saga*, chap. 2, Egils Saga, chap. 57, *Vatnsdæla Saga*, chap. 33K34 (Dennis *et al.* 2000: 197). To accuse a man of *níðingr* was the most powerful insult in Viking Age warrior ideology (Price 2002: 212), and linked to it was the concept of *ergi*, which was even more closely connected with witchcraft.

The noun *ergi* is the basis for the adjective *argr* and the metathesis *regi/ragr* (Meulengracht Sørensen 1983: 18). *Ergi* is thought to have had many meanings in 13th and 14th century Iceland, and was rarely used in reference to women, except to describe uninhibited lust and sexuality. It was also used to refer to two men engaging in sexual relations with each other, which was thought to detract from their 'manhood', as well as to describe something that would lead men to become effeminate, and not something they could do without losing manliness. Additionally, *ergi* was used to connote a lack of courage, again believed to be the result of unmanliness, since cowardly men were thought to have switched genders. Lastly, it was used to describe something that was done or that had occurred during the performance of magic (Ármann Jacobssen 2008: 55).

According to Meulengracht Sørensen (1983: 19), the term relates more specifically to 'perversity in sexual matters', along with being 'versed in witchcraft'. Mary Douglas (1966), argued that the practice of witchcraft and sorcery involves sexual activities and taboo breaking and occasions when men appear as women and *vice versa*: basically, the disruption of social norms and desired social behaviours. In *Heimskringla* and *Ynglinga Saga*, when Óðinn practices sorcery he breaks all the rules in ways that only a god could, because it is said that 'when sorcery takes place it is accompanied by so much *ergi* that men could not be associated with it without disgrace and this is why this pertains to the goddesses' (Meulengracht Sørensen 1983: 19).

In *Egils saga* and *Gunnars saga Keldugnúpfífls*, *seiðr* was said to make a victim fidget. This was interpreted by Almqvist as making 'their bottoms itch', and that *seiðr* attacked the backside, in keeping with the homosexual associations of *ergi* and with potential penetration by another man (Almqvist 2000: 258; Heide 2007). In *Þórleifs saga Þáttrjarlsskálds*, verbal *níð* makes the earl's bottom itch so much that he has two men pull a coarse woollen cloth, with three knots, between his buttocks, again linking textiles and textile production with witchcraft and allegations of unmanliness (Heide 2007).

This homophobia or fear of perceived sexual deviance in Norse society was at odds with ideals of manhood. Successful manhood was a requisite proof of social success. To achieve it, men defined themselves in contradiction to the 'other' and by the exclusion of the 'other', in this case, women and women's work, such as textile production that was thought to contain *ergi*. The scrutiny of other men was important (Kimmel 2012: 87) and provided weight to allegations of *níð* or of having too much *ergi*, as men feared being perceived as inadequate, unmanly, or humiliated by other men. According to Mary Douglas (1966: 96), danger also lies in transitional states because transition is neither one state nor the next and is undefinable. Underlying the anxiety of appearing 'unmanly', not only is a man perceived as inadequate, but he is put into a transitional state, and thus a dangerous position at variance with, and marginal to, accepted norms of manliness. Additionally, Douglas (1966: 99) suggests that when people hold ambiguous roles, they become dangerous, and are associated with uncontrolled, dangerous, disapproved powers such as witchcraft.

## Women's bargaining for power and concluding remarks

The sagas' instances of women goading, playing on fears of masculinity, and questioning the honour of male kinsmen with allegations of *ergi* or of being a *níðingr* are to my mind power negotiations wielded by women over their male kinsmen, and a mechanism to exercise some degree of power in what was a male focused society.

Kandiyoti (1988: 275) argued that women will strategise within a set of constraints that she termed the 'patriarchal bargain'. While works on gender from the 1980s might generally seem outdated, the concepts developed by Kandiyoti are *à propos* to the current analysis. She argues that the patriarchal bargain 'exerts a powerful influence on the shaping of women's gendered subjectivity'. In the Norse context, goading and textile work appear to have provided women some wiggle room, abilities to influence the outcomes of family events, and control over some of the narratives within the family unit and within society at large.

Until now I have discussed the existence of one type of official female magic, *seiðr*. I have also argued that it was linked to Freyja, who taught it to Oðinn. We know that men, according the to the Icelandic sources, in general did not engage in this magic, as it contained too much *ergi* and could lead them astray into a lifestyle of homosexuality which was in contradiction to an honourable masculine life. As a result, they remained fearful of any associations with this form of female magic. However, this magic was in turn associated with the control of fate as well as divination. This *female magical complex* as I would label it, included an amalgamation of concepts: Goddess (possibly the goddesses) Freyja)/*seiðr*/magic/women/*ergi*/fear of homosexuality for men, taboo/control of life and death, fate/textile work/textile tools, and possibly war, if we are to acknowledge the events of the *Darraðarljóð* and recall that Freyja was also a goddess of war.

Not all women in Iceland practised this magic, and clearly not all women were *vǫlur* or magical practitioners, although there is evidence both archaeologically and in the sagas that those who did dedicate their lives to this pursuit appear to have been wealthy and well-respected, as alluded to in *Eirik the Red's* saga with Þórbjorg the prophetess (Magnus Magnusson and Hermann Pálsson 1965: 81).

On a day to day basis there appears to have been many other forms of magic occurring simultaneously along with *seiðr* (see Sundqvist, this volume), there also appears to be a similarly a wide range of male sorcerers and magical practitioners (see chapter 1, this volume; Kevin Smith in prep.). Within the context of female magic it is possible that a form of 'textile magic' also existed, to which most women probably had access, and which they would have practised when together. We do not know all the categories of magic that existed in the Viking Age though undoubtedly there were many manifestations in use that provided direct intervention, communication and/or assistant of the gods for pressing matters. The bulk of archaeological material pointing to the existence of a type of textile magic is convincing, with runic magical formulae etched across weaving or spinning objects that reflect a long-lost practice where ordinary women may have engaged in a more secret form of magic within the practice of weaving on their farms. All the saga references discussed above are the tales of ordinary women, not professional *vǫlur*, and goading likely provided them with a mechanism of control and a tool for bargaining with the patriarchy. Whether they were official *vǫlur* or ordinary women, women's textile magic provided them with a mechanism of control – the control of fate that was pre-determined before birth. Women, through their connection to the goddess and to the *female magical complex*, had at their disposal the ultimate bargaining tool that gave them agency, power, and control over life and death, and that also allowed them to produce one of the most fundamental items of material culture needed in colder climates: cloth, into which fate was metaphorically woven through the actions of spinning and weaving. Cloth and its production became symbolically gendered and associated with a women's world and with female power. Schneider and Weiner's characterisation of associations between women and cloth ring true for Scandinavia:

> ... women not only make cloth but also preside over its allocation at major rituals of death and regeneration, marriage and the establishment of new families, investiture and the transmission of ancestral authority. (Schneider and Weiner 1989: 21)

Women's magic provided them with tools to bargain with the patriarchy, making women terrifying by fuelling men's fears. The words of the sociologist Goldwater ring true, that men's fear of women is ancient and stems from women's ability to bring new life, and from the male perception that women are able to control men's sexuality, whether for procreation or other purposes (Goldwater 1998: 211). This fear is unconscious, and Goldwater adds:

> Men's other great fear is very ancient. But it continues to crop up whenever men think about women... it is the fear of women as *witch*. What women lack in might, they sometimes make up for in magic. (Goldwater 1998: 216)

And yet one may ask, if she who can control life and death, and who can foresee the future, whether as an official practitioner with her iron distaff, or in a more domestic sphere through the things she makes, the textiles she weaves, the tools she uses, the thread she spins; if she who controls thread and fate does not hold the ultimate power over all, as the control of destiny goes well beyond the powers of mortal men, then who does?

### Notes

1 Distaffs come in many shapes and forms and tend to be used with a drop spindle. Some are straight, others are paddle shaped, while others contain a small basket at the end and are called 'caged distaffs'. When drafting wool, one can hold the carded wool in one's hand (some wrap it around their wrist) while others prefer the use of the distaff which can rest on one's hip or with a shorter staff, held higher up. It has the advantage to hold a larger quantity of wool to be spun, particularly the caged distaffs, but the choice to use or not use a distaff is simply a matter of preference. It would seem that the *vǫlur*'s staff, like regular distaffs, came in these same shapes as well, and as argued by Gardela this volume, other implements were used as staffs, the distaff being one of them (see Fig. 8.1, above).

2 Bek Pedersen (2007; 2013) has argued, to the contrary, that the association of the *nornir* with textile production is simply absent in the historic texts, and while they may not have been spinning under the World Tree, the *nornir* and related supernatural female beings are associated with textile work, as illustrated in the *Darraðarljóð*.

3 Iceland converted to Christianity in AD 1000, roughly the same time as the Faroe Islands, while Greenland was settled by Christians; thus no pre-Christian Viking settler burials have been found in Greenland.

4 The story of Höskuld's cloak and Hildigunn's goading also demonstrates the intimate relationships between women and textiles, as well as the power that textiles had as a symbol of being human possibly even of human 'skin' or of 'being'. It also reveals how women were perceived as having control over the destiny and fate of other humans, and the types of allegations that were incompatible with perceived male ideals of the time.

## Bibliography

Almqvist, B., 2000. I Margfinalen till Sejd. In *Sejd Och Andra Studier i Nordisk Själsuppfattning*, ed. G. Gidlund. Hedemora: Kungl. G.A. Akademien/Gidlungs Förlag, Uppsala: 237–271.

Ármann Jacobssen., 2008. The trollish acts of Þorgrímr the Witch: The meanings of *troll* and *ergi* in medieval Iceland. *Saga-Book* 32: 36–68.

Auður G. Magnúsdóttir., 2008. Women and sexual politics. In *The Viking World*, eds S. Brink and N. Price. Routledge, London and New York: 40–48.

Badalanova Geller, F., 2006. The Spinning Mary: Towards the iconology of the Annunciation in the Slavonic tradition. *Cosmos* 20: 211–260.

Barber, E.W., 1995. *Women's Work: The first 20 000 years; Women, cloth and society in early times*. Norton, New York.

Bek Pedersen, K., 2007. Are the spinning Nornir just a yarn. *Viking and Medieval Scandinavia* 3: 1–10.

Bek Pedersen, K., 2009. Weaving swords and rolling heads, a peculiar space in Old Norse tradition. *Viking and Medieval Scandinavia* 5: 23–39.

Bek-Pedersen, K., 2013. *The Norns in Old Norse Mythology*. Dunedin: Edinburgh.

Bjarni Einarsson, F., 2008. Blót houses in Viking Age farmstead cult practices. *Acta Archaeologica* 79.1: 145–184.

Blake, N.F., 1962. *The Saga of the Jomsvikings*. Thomas Nelson and Sons: London.

Dennis, A., Foote, P., and Perkins, R. (trans.), 1980. *Laws of Early Iceland, Grágás*. Vol. I. Winnepeg: University of Manitoba Press.

Dennis, A., Foote, P. and Perkins, R. (trans.), 2002. *Laws of Early Iceland, Grágás*. Vol. II. Winnepeg: University of Manitoba Press.

Dommasnes, L.H., 1982. Late Iron Age in western Norway. Female roles and ranks as deduced from an analysis of burial customs. *Norwegian Archaeological Review* 15: 70–84.

Douglas, M., 1966. *Purity and Danger, and Analysis of the Concepts of Pollution and Taboo*. Routledge & Kegan Paul, London.

Ellis Davidson, H.R., 1998. *Roles of the Northern Goddess*. Routledge, London.

Ellis Davidson, H.R., 1990. *Gods and Myths of Northern Europe*. Penguin, London.

Else Guðjónsson., 1989. Jarnvarðr Yllir. A fourth weapon of the Valkyries in Darraðarljóð? *Textile History* 20.2: 185–197.

Flowers, S.E., 2010. *Runes and Magic: Magical formulaic elements in the older Runic tradition* (rev and expand. 3rd edn). Runa-Raven Press, Smithville TX.

Gilchrist, R., 2008. Magic for the dead? The archaeology of magic in later medieval burials. *Medieval Archaeology* 52.1: 119–159. https://doi.org/10.1179/174581708x335468.

Gilman, P., 1987. Architecture as artifact: Pit structures and Pueblos in the American Southwest. *American Antiquity*52.3: 538–564.

Goldwater, E., 1998. What do Men Fear? *Modern Psychoanalysis* 23: 211–224.

Gräslund, A.S., 2001. The position of Iron Age Scandinavian women, evidence from graves and Rune stones. In *Gender and the Archaeology of Death*, eds B. Arnold and N.L. Wicker. Alta Mira Press, Walnut Creek CA: 81–102.

Gräslund, A.S., 2003. The role of Scandinavian Women in Christianisation: The neglected evidence. In *The Cross Goes North: Processes of conversion in northern Europe A.D. 300–1300*, ed. M. Carver. Boydell, Woodbridge: 483–496.

Gräslund, A.S. and Quast, D., 2011. Female elites in Viking Age Scandinavia during Christianisation. In *Weibliche Eliten in Der Frühgeschitchte, Female Elites in Protohistoric Europe*. Verlag des Römanisch Germanischen Zentralmuseums, Mainz: 267–278.

Guðmundur Ólafsson., 1992. Jarðhús að Hjálms- stöðum í Laugardal: rannsókn 1983–1985. *Árnesingur* 2: 39–56.

Hayeur Smith, M., 2004. *Draupnir's Sweat and Mardöll's Tears: An archaeology of jewellery, gender and identity in Viking Age Iceland*. British Archaeological Report S1276, Oxford.

Hayeur Smith, M., 2014. Thorir's Bargain: Gender, Vaðmal, and the law. *World Archaeology* 45.5, Special Issue: *The Archaeology of Legal Culture*, eds A. Reynolds and K.P. Smith: 730–746.

Hayeur Smith, M., 2015. Weaving wealth: Cloth and trade in Viking Age and medieval Iceland. In *Textiles and the Medieval Economy: Production, trade, and consumption of textiles, 8th–16th centuries*, eds A. Ling Huang and C. Jahnke Ancient Textile Series 16, Oxford: 23–40.

Hayeur Smith, M., 2018. Vadmal and cloth currency in Viking and medieval Iceland. In *Silver, Butter, Cloth Monetary and Social Economies in the Viking Age*, eds J. Kershaw and G. Williams. Oxford University Press: 251–277.

Hayeur Smith, M., 2020. *The Valkyries' Loom: The archaeology of cloth production and female power in the North Atlantic*. University Press of Florida, Gainesville FL.

Hayeur Smith, M., Smith, K.P. and Frei, K.M., 2019. 'Tangled up in blue': A case study of death, dress and identity for an early Viking Age female settler from Ketilstaðir, Iceland. *Medieval Archaeology* 67.1: 91–127.

Hedenstierna-Jonson, C. and Kjellström, A., 2014. The Urban woman, On the role and identity of women in Birka. In *Kvinner i Vikingtid*, eds N.L Colemand and N. Løkka. Scandinavian Academic Press, Oslo: 183–204.

Heide, E., 2007. Spinning Seiðr. In *Old Norse Religion in Long-Term Perspectives, Origins, Changes and Interactions*, eds. A. Andren, K. Jennbert and C. Raudvere. Nordic Academic Press, Lund: 164–170.

Helgi Þórlaksson, H., 1981. Arbeidskvinnens, särlig veverskens, ökonomiske stilling på Island i middelalderen. In *Kvinnans ekonomiska ställning under nordisk medeltid*, B. Strand, Gothenburg: 50–65.

Hermann Pálsson and Edwards, P., 1972. *The Book of Settlements: Landnámabók*. University of Manitoba Icelandic Studies 1, Winnipeg.

Hermann Pálsson and Edwards, P. (eds), 1981. *Orkneyinga Saga: The history of the Earls of Orkney*. Penguin Classics, Harmondsworth.

Hermann Pálsson and Edwards, P. (eds), 1989. *Eyrbyggja Saga*. Penguin Classics, Harmondsworth.

Hrepna Róbertsdóttir, H., 2008. *Wool and Society: Manufacturing policy, economic thought and local production in 18th-century Iceland*. Centrum För Danmarkstudier 2, Göteborg.

Ingunn Ásdísardóttir, I. 2007. *Frigg og Freyja: kvenleg goðmögn í heiðnum sið*. Íslensk menning. Hið Íslenska Bókmenntafélag [u.a.], Reykjavík.

Jesch, J., 2005. *Women in the Viking Age*. Boydell, Woodbridge.

Jochens, J., 1995. *Women in Old Norse Society*. Cornell University Press, Ithaca NY.

Jones, G. (trans.), 1944. *The Vatndler's Saga*. Princeton University Press, Princeton NJ.

Kandiyoti, D., 1988. Bargaining with patriarchy. *Gender and Society* 2.3, Special Issue: 274–290.

Karras, R.M., 1990. Concubinage and slavery in the Viking Age. *Scandinavian Studies* 62.2: 141–162.

Kimmel, M.S., 2012. Masculinity as homophobia: Fear, shame, and silence in the construction of gender identity. In *Theorising Masculinities*, eds H. Brod and M. Kaufman. Sage, London: 119–141.

Kristján Eldján and Adolf Friðriksson., 2000. *Kuml Og Haugfe Úr Heiðnum Sið á Íslandi*. Mál og Menning, Reykjavik.

Larsson, L. (trans.), 2010[1935]. *The Earliest Norwegian Laws: Being the Gulathing Law and the Forstathing Law*. Reprint, Lawbook Exchange Ltd, Clark NJ.

Magnus Magnusson. (ed.), 1965. *The Vinland Sagas: the Norse discovery of America*. Penguin Classics, Harmondsworth.

Magnus Magnusson and Hermann Pálsson. (trans.), 1969. *Laxdaela Saga*. Penguin Classics. Harmondsworth.

Magnus Magnusson and Hermann Pálsson. (eds), 1993. *Njal's Saga*. Penguin Classics, Harmondsworth.

McCreech, B., 2010. The Structure of Vatnsdæla Saga. *Saga Book of the Viking Society for Northern Research* 34: 75–86.

McNeill, J.T. and Gamer, H.M., 1965. Medieval Handbooks of Penance. Columbia University Press, New York.

Meaney, A.L., 1981. Anglo-Saxon Amulets and Curing Stones. British Archaeological Report 96, Oxford.
Meulengracht Sørensen, P., 1983. The Unmanly Man: Concepts of sexual defamation in early Northern society. Odense University Press, Odense.
Milek, K., 2012. Gendered space and the role of the pit house on Viking Age farmsteads in Iceland. *Medieval Archaeology* 56: 85–130.
Miller, W.I., 1990. Bloodtaking and Peacemaking – Feud, Law and Society in Saga Iceland. University of Chicago Press, Chicago IL.
Moltke, E. and Foote, P., 1985. *Runes and Their Origin: Denmark and elsewhere.* Nationalmuseets Forlag, Copenhagen.
Mortensen, L., 2004. The 'marauding pagan warrior woman'. In *Ungendering Civilisation*, ed. K.A. Pyburn. Routledge, New York: 94–116.
Mortensen, M. 1997. For women only? Reflections on a Viking Age settlement at Stedje, Sogndal in western Norway. *Studien zur Sachsenforschung* 10: 195–206.
Murphy, L.J., 2018. Ingår i. *Scripta Islandica: Isländska Sällskapets Årsbok* 69: 49–97.
Norrman, L.E., 2008. *Viking Women: The narrative voice in woven tapestries.* Cambria Press, Amherst NY.
Óttar Guðmundsson., 2016. Sex in the Sagas – Love and Lust in the Old Icelandic Literature. Skrudda, Reykjavík,
Price, N., 2002. *The Viking Way: Religion and war in Late Iron Age Scandinavia.* University of Uppsala, Uppsala.
Price, N.S., 2011. Sorcery and circumpolar traditions in Old Norse belief – popular religion in the Viking Age. In *The Viking World*, eds S. Brink and N. Price. Routledge, London: 244–248.
Price, N., Hedenstierna-Jonson, H., Zachrisson, T., Kjellström, A., Storå, J., Krzewińska, M., Günther, T., Sobrado, V., Jakobsson, M. and Götherström, A., 2019. Viking warrior women? Reassessing Birka chamber grave Bj.581. *Antiquity* 93 (367):181–198.
Ragnheiður Traustadóttir., 2015. Spindle whorls from Urriðakot. In *Nordic Middle Ages – Artefacts, Landscapes and Society*, eds I. Baug, J. Larsen and S.S. Mygland. University of Bergen Archaeological Series 8, Bergen: 317–329.
Raffield, B., Price, N. and Collard. M., 2017. Polygyny, concubinage, and the social lives of women in Viking-Age Scandinavia. *Viking and Medieval Scandinavia* 13: 165–209.
Randsborg, K., 1980. *The Viking Age in Denmark: The formation of a state.* Duckworth, London.
Roesdahl, E., 1998. *The Vikings.* Penguin, Harmondsworth.
Sauvage, R and Mokkelbost, M., 2016. Rural buildings from the Viking and early medieval period in central Norway. In *The Agrarian Life of the North, 2000 BC–AD 1000. Studies in Rural Settlement and Farming in Norway*, F. Iversen and H. Petersseon (eds), Portal Kristiansand, NTNU University Museum, Trondheim.
Sawyer, B., 1991. Women as bridge-builders; The roles of Women in Viking Age Scandinavia. In *People and Places in Northern Europe 500–1600*, eds I. Wood and N. Lund. Boydell, Woodbridge: 211–224.
Sawyer, B., 1992. *Kvinnor Och Familj Det Forn- Och Medeltida Skandinavien.* Occasional Papers on Medieval Topics 6, Berkeley CA.
Sawyer, B., 2004. Viking Age Women. *Viking Heritage* 2: 3–6.
Schneider, J., 1989. Rumpelstiltskin's bargain: Folklore and the merchant capitalist intensification of linen manufacture in early modern Europe. In *Cloth and the Human Experience*, eds A.B. Weiner and J.S. Schneider. Smithsonian Series in Ethnographic Inquiry, Washington DC: 177–207.
Schneider, J.S. and Wiener, A.B., 1989. *Cloth and the Human Experience.* Smithsonian Series in Ethnographic Inquiry, Washington DC.
Smith, C.S., 2003. Hunter-gatherer mobility, storage, and houses in a marginal environment: An example from the mid-Holocene of Wyoming. *Journal of Anthropological Archaeology* 22.2: 162–189.
Stalsberg, A., 1991. Women as actors in north European Viking Age trade. *Social Approaches to Viking Studies* 5: 75–83.

Sørensen, M.-L.S., 2000. *Gender Archaeology*. Polity Press, Cambridge.
Tranberg Hansen, K., 2004. The world in dress: Anthropological perspectives on clothing, fashion, and culture. *Annual Review of Anthropology* 33.1: 369–392.
Turner, T.S., 1993. The social skin. In *Reading the Body Social*, eds J.D. Ehrenreich and C.B. Burroughs. University of Iowa Press, Iowa city IA.
Vala Garðarsdóttir., nd. Alþingisreiturinn, Bindi 1 og 2. Unpublished excavation report.
Wawn, A. (trans), 2001. The Saga of the people of Vatnsdal. In *The Sagas of Icelanders: A selection*, eds J. Smiley and R.L. Kellogg. Penguin Books, New York.